Sentencing *Orlando*

Sentencing *Orlando*

Virginia Woolf and the Morphology of the Modernist Sentence

Edited by Elsa Högberg and
Amy Bromley

EDINBURGH
University Press

Edinburgh University Press is one of the leading university presses in the UK. We publish academic books and journals in our selected subject areas across the humanities and social sciences, combining cutting-edge scholarship with high editorial and production values to produce academic works of lasting importance. For more information visit our website: edinburghuniversitypress.com

© editorial matter and organisation Elsa Högberg and Amy Bromley, 2018, 2019
© the chapters their several authors, 2018, 2019

Edinburgh University Press Ltd
The Tun – Holyrood Road, 12(2f) Jackson's Entry, Edinburgh EH8 8PJ

First published in hardback by Edinburgh University Press 2018

Typeset in 10.5/13 Adobe Sabon by
Servis Filmsetting Ltd, Stockport, Cheshire,
and printed and bound by CPI Group (UK) Ltd, Croydon, CR0 4YY

A CIP record for this book is available from the British Library

ISBN 978 1 4744 1460 9 (hardback)
ISBN 978 1 4744 5248 9 (paperback)
ISBN 978 1 4744 1461 6 (webready PDF)
ISBN 978 1 4744 1462 3 (epub)

The right of Elsa Högberg and Amy Bromley to be identified as the editors of this work has been asserted in accordance with the Copyright, Designs and Patents Act 1988, and the Copyright and Related Rights Regulations 2003 (SI No. 2498).

Contents

Acknowledgements	vii
Contributors	viii
Abbreviations	ix

    Introduction: Sentencing *Orlando*   1
    Elsa Högberg and Amy Bromley

1. 'The Queen had come': Orgasm and Arrival   15
    Jane Goldman

2. 'Something intricate and many-chambered': Sexuality and the Embodied Sentence   32
    Anna Frøsig

3. Woolf, De Quincey and the Legacy of 'Impassioned Prose'   44
    Elsa Högberg

4. Rhythms of Revision and Revisiting: Unpicking the Past in *Orlando*   56
    Jane de Gay

5. 'Let us go, then, exploring': Intertextual Conversations on the Meaning of Life   68
    Sanja Bahun

6. '. . . and nothing whatever happened': *Orlando*'s Continuous Eruptive Form   80
    Suzanne Bellamy

7. *Orlando*, Greece and the Impossible Landscape   92
    Vassiliki Kolocotroni

8. Orlando *Famoso*: Obscurity, Fame and History in *Orlando*   104
    Angeliki Spiropoulou

9. Bibliographic Parturition in *Orlando*: Books, Babies, Freedom and Fame — 116
   Alice Staveley

10. The Day of *Orlando* — 128
    Bryony Randall

11. *Satzdenken*, Indeterminacy and the Polyvalent Audience — 139
    Steven Putzel

12. In Amorous Dedication: The Phrase, the Figure and the *Lover's Discourse* — 151
    Amy Bromley

13. A Spirit in Flux: Aestheticism, Evolution and Religion — 162
    Todd Avery

14. Sir Thomas Browne and the Reading of Remains in *Orlando* — 175
    Benjamin D. Hagen

15. The Negress and the Bishop: On Marriage, Colonialism and the Problem of Knowledge — 186
    Randi Koppen

16. *Orlando* and the Politics of (In)Conclusiveness — 198
    Judith Allen

    Aftersentence — 210
    Rachel Bowlby

Index — 217

Acknowledgements

We are immensely grateful to our colleagues, mentors and friends at the Universities of Glasgow and Uppsala, without whom this book would not have taken shape. The vibrant Woolf and modernist studies scene at the University of Glasgow has stimulated and nurtured this project, and very special thanks are due to Jane Goldman in particular. The idea to focus on single sentences as a fruitful way to read Woolf emerged from Jane's pedagogical and scholarly practice, notably in her MLitt course, 'Virginia Woolf Writes Modernity'. In March 2014, she invited us to participate with her students in a public panel discussion for Cryptic Theatre's adaptation of *Orlando*, performed at the Centre for Contemporary Arts in Glasgow. The panel, entitled 'Unlacing *Orlando* in Ten Sentences', enabled extraordinary intellectual creativity, and convinced us to pursue a sentence-based collection on Woolf's novel. We are tremendously grateful to Jane for her warm encouragement and inspirational mentorship on our journey towards its completion.

Two major grants made this project possible: the Swedish Research Council generously funded Elsa's research as a postdoctoral fellow at Uppsala University and the University of Glasgow for three years (2014–17), while the Arts and Humanities Research Council have funded Amy's PhD project at the University of Glasgow (2013–17). These grants not only enabled our individual research, but created the conditions by which we were able to meet and collaborate, and for their support we are extremely grateful. We also wish to thank the editorial and production team at Edinburgh University Press for their indefatigable work at every stage of the publication process.

Finally, we dedicate our warmest thanks to the contributors to this collection: their committed, inspiring and creative responses to this slightly unusual project have brought plenty of joy and pleasure to the editing process. We have been privileged to work with each of them.

Contributors

Judith Allen	University of Pennsylvania
Todd Avery	University of Massachusetts Lowell
Sanja Bahun	University of Essex
Suzanne Bellamy	University of Sydney
Rachel Bowlby	University College London
Amy Bromley	University of Glasgow
Jane de Gay	Leeds Trinity University
Anna Frøsig	Independent Scholar
Jane Goldman	University of Glasgow
Benjamin D. Hagen	University of South Dakota
Elsa Högberg	Uppsala University
Vassiliki Kolocotroni	University of Glasgow
Randi Koppen	University of Bergen
Steven Putzel	Penn State University
Bryony Randall	University of Glasgow
Angeliki Spiropoulou	University of the Peloponnese and University of London
Alice Staveley	Stanford University

Abbreviations

Where the edition is not specified here, each contributor gives this information in an endnote to the first citation from that text.

AROO	*A Room of One's Own*
BA	*Between the Acts*
CSF	*The Complete Shorter Fiction*, ed. Susan Dick (London: Hogarth Press, 1989)
D1–5	*The Diary of Virginia Woolf*, 5 vols, ed. Anne Olivier Bell and Andrew McNeillie (London: Hogarth Press, 1977–84)
E1–6	*The Essays of Virginia Woolf*, 6 vols, ed. Andrew McNeillie (vols 1–4); ed. Stuart N. Clarke (vols 5–6) (London: Hogarth Press, 1986–2011)
F	*Flush: A Biography*
JR	*Jacob's Room*
L1–6	*The Letters of Virginia Woolf*, 6 vols, ed. Nigel Nicolson and Joanne Trautmann (London: Hogarth Press, 1975–80)
MB	*Moments of Being: Autobiographical Writings*, ed. Jeanne Schulkind (London: Pimlico, 2002)
MD	*Mrs Dalloway*
ND	*Night and Day*
O	*Orlando: A Biography*
OH	*Orlando: The Original Holograph Draft*, transcribed and ed. Stuart Nelson Clarke (London: S. N. Clarke, 1993)
PA	*A Passionate Apprentice: The Early Journals 1897–1909*, ed. Mitchell A. Leaska (London: Pimlico, 1990)
RF	*Roger Fry: A Biography* (London: Hogarth Press, 1940)
TG	*Three Guineas*
TL	*To the Lighthouse*
VO	*The Voyage Out*
W	*The Waves*
Y	*The Years*

Introduction: Sentencing *Orlando*

Elsa Högberg and Amy Bromley

A book is not made of sentences laid end to end, but of sentences built, if an image helps, into arcades or domes.

Virginia Woolf, *A Room of One's Own*

If the line is the privileged semantic unit in verse, we could ask whether the sentence plays the same role in prose. Virginia Woolf raises this possibility in *A Room of One's Own* (1929), where the sentence is foregrounded as an aesthetically as well as historically and politically charged entity. The metaphor in the epigraph above figures the sentence as the very material by which the novel can become an art form in its own right, drawing inspiration from the formal qualities of architecture and the visual arts. The prose sentence emerges in this text as an exclusionary property to be handed down through a lineage of male writers, but is appropriated by the woman writer as a 'tool' and 'weapon' with which to transform the novel genre.[1] In Woolf's emphasis on the shape of the book, built from sentences, aesthetic expression converges with a subversive gender and genre politics, and her engagement with the sentence as a material element in the writer's arsenal-toolbox comprises the shape-shifting of literary forms and canons across history.

The metaphors of shape, form and re-forming that pervade *A Room of One's Own* recur throughout Woolf's critical essays, where they inform an aesthetic theory of the sentence in which the idea of morphology is central.[2] Morphology as a concept has roots in scientific investigations of structures and shapes from the fields of biology to linguistics, in which it can also double as 'a history of variation in form'.[3] Woolf was consistently concerned with the morphological variations of literature and the literary sentence. Her fiction engages her critical ideas around literary history and form, and she often described her novels in terms of their architecture. Woolf's sense of morphology is particularly vivid in her dazzling novel-biography *Orlando: A Biography* (1928), a text whose fantastic time-span and multiple, shifting styles set it apart in her *oeuvre*. When Woolf articulated her theory of the literary sentence in *A Room of One's Own*, she had already put it into play in *Orlando*, where fantasy, parody and satire combine to produce a wide spectrum of different sentence types. The geneses of the two texts are intimately linked,[4] and the historical and subversive force ascribed to the sentence in her essay pervades *Orlando*. Shaped by layers of cultural and historical reference, the sentences of *Orlando* enact Woolf's brilliant, modernist rewriting of biography and gender, and the orthodox ways in which they tend to shape life and the body.

The present volume was initiated by the insight that *Orlando* presents a unique experiment with the historical resonances and subversive capacities of the modernist sentence, and that the text is therefore especially suited for a study of the form and structure (the morphology) of its sentences in the wider context of modernist aesthetics. Among Woolf's works, *Orlando*, with its panoramic, hybrid narrative, is particularly concerned with the changing shapes of literature as it morphs over time. Moreover, the shape of *Orlando* as a modernist text separates itself from the shape of individual sentences when we reflect upon the book as a whole, and yet the form and structure of the sentence become a crucial element in the morphology of the book. This intriguing relationship between part and whole informs our decision to curate a collection of essays reading *Orlando* on the level of the sentence. We wondered to what extent new insights can be gained about a literary work, in all its formal, contextual and historical dimensions, via sustained focus on a small linguistic unit such as the sentence. The rich format of the essay collection seems ideal for such analysis, by virtue of including multiple readings of a range of widely different sentences. This book, as far as we have established, is also the first scholarly collection dedicated specifically to *Orlando*. It presents original critical discoveries about Woolf's text, and outlines simultaneously a sentence-based mode of literary analysis that we hope will benefit the field of modernist studies as well as engagements with the literary sentence in other areas. The extraordinary creative and critical potential of such an approach triggered myriad questions. What are the contextual webs woven by the stylistic features of *Orlando*, notably its satire, parody, pastiche and syntactic manipulation that unsettles the boundaries of the sentence? Woolf foregrounds the sentence as a unit by citing, imitating and distorting sentences by various other writers, but what are the social, political and cultural loads carried by these practices? What contexts does this novel engage through its rich allusions to literary works, and how can a close focus on Woolf's modernist sentences open new perspectives on questions of, for

Introduction: Sentencing Orlando   3

example, sex, gender, genre and politically charged modes of reading? We invited a group of sixteen scholars to address such questions in an essay prompted by a single sentence from *Orlando*. In their responses to this invitation, the contributors perform close readings of the form, language and syntax of their chosen sentences, and, through these readings, they engage these sentences' wider aesthetic, cultural and historical resonances. Each essay examines how Woolf's probing of generic, gendered, sexual or racial boundaries plays out on the level of the sentence; together, the chapters yield fresh views on the many interlacing connections between aesthetics and context that shape *Orlando*, and Woolf's writing more broadly.

Combined into one volume, these critical excursions demonstrate that the 'plain sentences' of *Orlando*, as Woolf herself called them, present a far greater reading challenge than one might expect from this 'writer's holiday', this *jeu d'esprit* written 'half in a mock style very clear & plain, so that people will understand every word' (*D3* 164, 177, 162).[5] Woolf also described the book as 'too freakish & unequal [...] Not, I think "important" among my works' (*D3* 177) – works such as *To the Lighthouse* (1927) or *The Waves* (1931), which she repeatedly referred to as rigorous artistic experiments with form and design. This attitude has been reflected in the relative critical neglect of *Orlando*, which stands in contrast to its enormous popularity at the time of its publication – it sold better than any of Woolf's books to date. Contemporary reviews stressed its appearance as a 'lark' (Arnold Bennett, Raymond Mortimer), but also its aesthetic achievement: Rebecca West called it 'a poetic masterpiece of the first rank' and Desmond MacCarthy 'beautiful and original'.[6] For decades, the novel was often omitted from major scholarly works on Woolf, until it began to receive large-scale critical and popular attention with the emergence of LGBTQ studies and queer theory in the 1990s, and Sally Potter's 1992 film starring Tilda Swinton. Thanks to the sustained efforts, during the past thirty years, to claim a central place for *Orlando* in Woolf's *oeuvre*, we are now in a position to recuperate the text as one of her most aesthetically dynamic novels. To this effect, the essays in this collection explore *Orlando*, with its allegedly clear and plain style, as a unique modernist experiment that deserves attention as such. To sentence *Orlando* thereby amounts to several things: pronouncing a deliberate opinion on its aesthetic and contextual complexity, and, in order to perform this critical judgement, examining the text as it was composed, or put into sentences, by Woolf.

In contrast to the associative, and demanding, 'non-subordinating style' of the sentences in *Mrs Dalloway* (1925) and *To the Lighthouse*,[7]

Orlando taught Woolf 'how to write a direct sentence' (*D3* 203). This book, she writes,

> taught me continuity & narrative, & how to keep the realities at bay. But I purposely avoided of course any other difficulty. I never got down to my depths & made shapes square up, as I did in The Lighthouse. (ibid.)

But even if *Orlando*'s sentences might be 'direct', in that they produce an effect of narrative fluidity and control through syntactic subordination, they are no less interesting formally as building blocks of the very particular modernist style she crafted in this 'freakish and unequal' book. In a sense, it is the accessible, fluid style of this text – alongside the fact that its shapes don't 'square up' – that makes it an exceptionally compelling object for a sentence-based study. Through its singular formal hybridity, *Orlando* creates an intricate weave of different types of sentence that engage, imitate, cite, allude to and parody different historical contexts as well as literary works, practices, modes and genres.

If a literary text is a weave, as the etymology of 'text' suggests, then sentences arguably compose its material.[8] The affinities between text and texture permeate *Orlando*: Woolf repeatedly referred to the work as a painter's canvas (*D3* 164, 168, 176), and the numerous tapestries in Orlando's house run as a textile thread through the text. As we examine the sentences that compose this weave or artwork, we find that a syntactically simple sentence like the following observation on the first page: 'The green arras with the hunters on it moved perpetually'[9] is in fact charged with intertextual allusion and a complex gender politics. In beginning a series of references to a tapestry depicting scenes from Ovid's *Metamorphoses*, this sentence foreshadows Orlando's pleasurable metamorphosis from man into woman as well as the novel's ambivalent treatment of the gender polarisation shaping not only the Ovidian subtext, but a long history cutting through *Orlando*'s temporal frame from the Elizabethan era to the 'present day' of its ending: 11 October 1928.[10] This was the day on which the Hogarth Press edition of *Orlando* was published, and later that month Woolf gave the lectures that form the basis of *A Room of One's Own*. As this suggests, the 'plain' and 'direct' sentences that are seamlessly joined together in a continuous narrative are in fact infinitely suggestive, even 'wild';[11] they make the weave of *Orlando* as shifting and alluring as the tapestry that moves at night in the Leicester Gallery at Knole, as described in Vita Sackville West's *Knole and the Sackvilles*: 'the tapestry sways, and the figures on it undulate and seem to come alive'.[12] By examining the shape and texture of Woolf's sentences, we hope, in this volume, to make the figures inspiring and populating

Introduction: Sentencing Orlando 5

Orlando come alive. Through this reading method, we hope to illuminate the many intersecting voices, stories and realities that have been obscured by the persistent notion of *Orlando* as a mere 'joke' or 'writer's holiday'.

The intertextual layering of discourses and voices that emerges through a close reading of sentences such as the one cited above is especially dense in *Orlando*; this weight of reference even made an early reviewer compare the book to T. S. Eliot's *The Waste Land* (1922).[13] The modernist polyphony of *Orlando* emerges from its satirical, parodic mode, where literary and historical figures' voices speak from the page through citation or resonate through allusive echoes, often twisted, transformed and merged with the narrator's voice through mimicry. The discourses of law, sexology, religion, history, poetry and biography are all voiced in this complex fashion. Moreover, the legal and discursive meanings of the word 'sentence' are particularly resonant in *Orlando* through Woolf's subversive treatment of material property, declarations, verdicts, censorship, sexuality and gender – all of which are examined in this volume.

The sentences that weave *Orlando*, in shaping its comic mode particularly, produce a fantastical and at times surreal aesthetic of juxtaposed words, images and ideas. In her essay 'The Sun and the Fish' (1928), Woolf speaks of incongruous sights that 'marry [. . .] morganatically' in the mind (like Queen Victoria and a yellow camel; *E4* 519) – a phrase that illuminates the 'freakish and unequal' aesthetic of *Orlando*.[14] This idea is developed in a later essay on the 'swift marriages' in which unruly words, laden with historically accumulated associations and meanings, compose evocative sentences that call on all the senses of the reader to work with the writer in producing them: 'Thus one sentence of the simplest kind rouses the imagination, the memory, the eye and the ear – all combine in reading it' ('Craftsmanship', 1937; *E6* 94). Words thus conceived are 'highly democratic': 'They do not like to have their purity or their impurity discussed [. . .] there are no ranks or titles in their society' (*E6* 96). *Orlando*, which incorporates 'all variety of human speech and expression' from 'slang and oaths' to 'the jargon of the professions' and 'the gibberish of lovers',[15] can indeed be read as an early experiment in the hybrid, popular style of late works by Woolf such as *Between the Acts*. Yet the book is clearly of its time, and this collection of essays traces multiple simultaneous conversations – many previously unexplored – between the polyphonic, 'morganatic' *Orlando* and key modernist works of the 1920s and early 1930s. In focusing on the 'swift marriages' of words, voices and images by which the sentences of *Orlando* create a dialogue with other writers' sentences – a dialogue extending from the Renaissance into Woolf's present – the contributors sketch a morphology of the modernist sentence.

Methodologically, our ambition to read Woolf via the sentence follows the current reappraisal, in modernist and Woolf studies, of aesthetics and literary form as embedded in diverse contexts, including the historical-material, political, philosophical and cultural. As the editors of the recent collection *Virginia Woolf in Context* recognise, considering Woolf 'in context' is no easy task in the second decade of the twenty-first century; at this juncture of historicist and new aestheticist modernist scholarship, such contextualising work does indeed 'require sophisticated methodologies'.[16] While one (reactionary) version of new formalist criticism has sought to 'bring back a sharp demarcation between history and art, discourse and literature', privileging a pseudo-Kantian notion of aesthetic experience as 'disinterested, autotelic, playful, pleasurable, consensus-generating',[17] the tendency of recent Woolf scholarship has been towards what Marjorie Levinson terms an 'activist formalism' – one that restores the close-reading of aesthetic form to historically and contextually oriented modes of literary critique.[18] Both factions of new formalism nevertheless emphasise pleasure as a central dimension of aesthetics and close textual analysis, and both 'seek to reinstate close reading both at the curricular center of our discipline and as the opening move, preliminary to any kind of critical consideration'.[19] The idea of form as a source of pleasure inspiring the act of reading and analysing literary texts has guided us in the composition of this collection, where we align ourselves with the 'activist' mode of formal analysis. By looking at Woolf's sentences as aesthetically and contextually charged units, the essays highlight the joys that these sentences continue to release through their forms (and re-forming of other material), at the same time as they explore the intersections of aesthetics, politics, discourse and history in *Orlando*'s polyphonic utterances.

Orlando continues to be a source of pleasure for its readers. Indeed, its playful vibrancy makes the text unique in Woolf's *oeuvre*: the book is saturated with the intensely pleasurable impulse that brought it into being, and with the erotic playfulness surrounding its composition as a 'love letter' to Vita Sackville-West.[20] There is, then, an emphasis on play and pleasure both in the style of *Orlando* and in the contributors' approach to it here, from the first chapter by Jane Goldman to Rachel Bowlby's creative Aftersentence. By playing with the novel's playful sentences, this volume offers substantial insights into their extraordinary interweaving of aesthetics and context. Such a project is long overdue,[21] and the recent aesthetic turn has brought about a useful critical focus on the linguistic units composing literary works. Representative studies include Anne Toner's *Ellipsis in English Literature: Signs of Omission* (2015), which offers an account of the marker of unfinished sentences across the history of English literature, and the interdisciplinary revisiting of Ann Banfield's *Unspeakable Sentences: Narration and Representation in the Language of Fiction* (1982) in *Phantom Sentences: Essays in Linguistics and Literature Presented to Ann Banfield* (2008), edited by Robert S. Kawashima, Gilles Philippe and Thelma Sowley.[22] Popular, essayistic works such as Stanley Fish's *How to Write a Sentence: And How to Read One* (2011) and, to some extent, William H. Gass's *Life Sentences: Literary Judgments and Accounts* (2011) explore the idea of the sentence as a minimal and fruitful unit for analysis of literary style. Both are close reading excursions into a random selection of literary works, where the authors delight as much in the shape and form of their primary texts as in their own discovery of these works. But can these excursions serve as an inspirational model for literary scholarship? For a morphology of the modernist sentence?

Sentencing Orlando makes a case for pleasurable, critical explorations of form in modernist fiction that begin on the level of the sentence. Such a practice resonates with Woolf's own ideas about reading, theorised in her literary journalism in the years surrounding the composition of *Orlando*. These ideas shaped the novel, but they also converge in intriguing ways with the aesthetically oriented critical tenets of our time. 'On Re-reading Novels' (1922) is one essay where Woolf claims that a deep appreciation of a novel as a work of art emerges through 'a sudden intensity of phrase' that 'startles us into a flash of understanding [. . .] Later in the same way we are roused by a sentence' (*E3* 340). The narrator of *A Room of One's Own* comes to realise the achievement of the fictional Mary Carmichael's first novel – potentially the first literary exploration of female same-sex desire – in a similar fashion: 'I tried a sentence or two on my tongue [. . .] The smooth gliding of sentence after sentence was interrupted' (*AROO* 104). The initial, intensely pleasurable experience of reading sentences 'at random'[23] is also addressed in 'How Should One Read a Book?' (1926), where Woolf outlines a procedure for assessing the aesthetic quality of a literary text:

> To read a book well, one should read it as if one were writing it. Begin not by sitting on the bench among the judges but by standing in the dock with the criminal. Be his fellow worker, become his accomplice. (*E4* 390)

The later, more rigorous reading phase is described as a form of sentencing, of 'criticising and judging', and yet this capacity to pass sentences on a book depends on the vital, earlier way of reading where 'one's judgement is suspended' (*E4* 396).[24] While Woolf's legal metaphors pertain to the attribution of aesthetic value, the reading process she depicts has a lot to offer literary scholars and teachers of literary subjects today. In this sense, *Sentencing* Orlando cultivates Woolf's emphasis on the pure enjoyment of a good sentence as a precondition for literary criticism. We are hoping thereby to propose a creative model not only for research, but also for classroom engagements with literature – one that cultivates a slow, deep or immersive reading practice that our digital age persistently undermines.[25]

The contributors to this volume provide a vivid demonstration of the original insights into multiple styles and contexts that can emerge from an intense study of a single modernist sentence. The expansive potential of such study is realised in each essay, and together, the chapters span a broad thematic and theoretical scope. With the increasing critical attention to *Orlando* since the 1990s, the predominant focus has been on questions around gender and sexuality, although recent criticism covers a wide range of topics including historiography, race and colonialism, materiality, as well as intertextuality and the literary past. *Sentencing Orlando* contributes to this expanding scholarship by presenting fresh perspectives on these topics and on Woolf's writing more broadly.

One way of organising the chapters in this collection would have been to follow the order of the sentences as they appear in the text, with its linear movement through four centuries. We have chosen instead a course more in keeping with Woolf's critique of linear chronology, where the chapters are arranged according to their subject-matter. This arrangement foregrounds the many intersecting discourses that shape the text; it also follows Woolf's own favoured mode of whimsical and instinctive reading at random. In her essay 'Phases of Fiction' (1929), composed while she was writing *Orlando*, Woolf is less concerned with a teleological understanding of fiction through the ages than with the morphological processes of the common reader's spontaneous appetite for particular styles and tones of writing; for example, the saturation of the senses in Proustian psychological realism requires some light relief by satire and fantasy, much in the same way that *Orlando* followed *To the Lighthouse*. Taking our impetus from Woolf's reading and compositional practice, then, we have constructed our own path through *Orlando*.

In the opening chapter, Jane Goldman focuses on one of the novel's most direct sentences: 'The Queen had come'. While this sentence reports the arrival of a Queen, presumably Elizabeth I, it is also an equally direct report of a woman's orgasm as a *fait accompli*: 'vulgar, bawdy, openly celebrating female autoeroticism', yet 'coded, cryptic, somehow hidden in plain sight'. Taking the multiple queen figures evoked in this 'orgasmic feminist Sapphic coup' as her starting point, Goldman pursues *Orlando*'s queer and queenly genealogy from Mary, Queen of Scots, via Oscar Wilde and Gertrude Stein to Woolf's and Vita Sackville-West's erotic intimacy. Anna Frøsig's chapter also addresses the Woolfian *double entendre* and the wildness underlying the supposedly plain style of *Orlando*. Engaging the phenomenology of Maurice Merleau-Ponty, Frøsig reads the sentences constructing the novel's simultaneously sexual and ethical spaces in terms of the female body. In Woolf's hands, Frøsig suggests, literary form becomes 'something intricate and many-chambered, which one must take a torch to explore, in prose not verse' (*O* 124), and such exploration turns out to be at once intimate and bound up with an ethics of alterity.

The chapters by Elsa Högberg and Jane de Gay take the exploration of literary language and sexuality in other directions. Högberg illuminates Woolf's sensual, lyrical writing in light of its contact with Thomas De Quincey's 'impassioned prose', drawing out the erotic and political dimensions of the book as a gift to Sackville-West. Examining the dream-like, visual and musical aspects of a long sentence at the end of Chapter V, Högberg considers the gender politics involved in Woolf's appropriation of De Quincey's prose style. In Högberg's reading, the lyricism of *Orlando* unravels the time of the legal sentence, and thereby the logic by which aesthetic and material property is passed down an exclusively male line of inheritance. After the rhythmic oscillations of Woolf's De Quincean sentences, Jane de Gay invites us to explore a sentence in which Orlando as a Victorian woman writer is urged by the 'spirit of the age' to reconsider a few poetic lines she has just written. Voicing a passage from Sackville-West's *The Land* (1926), these lines express a barely hidden lesbian eroticism, which is, paradoxically, intensified by intertextual allusions to canonical male writers. Addressing questions of censorship and self-censorship, de Gay demonstrates how *Orlando*'s sentences, with their accretions of past literary styles, encourage a non-linear reading movement that ultimately affirms the free expression of same-sex desire.

Sanja Bahun continues the pursual of intertextual echoes via Woolf's poetic engagement with T. S. Eliot. Bahun's chosen sentence rewrites the opening of 'The Love Song of J. Alfred Prufrock' (1915) and is embedded in a densely allusive passage that also cites Joyce, Forster and Lawrence. With careful attention to rhythm and syntax, Bahun shows how Woolf's rewriting of Eliot invokes and transforms the emerging, predominantly male modernist canon in a vibrant exploration of modern subjecthood and the question: 'How does one represent life?' Suzanne Bellamy also draws attention to the density of reference encompassed by a single sentence from *Orlando*, alighting on intertextual resonances between Woolf, Sackville-West, Stein and Laurence Sterne. The sentence on which Bellamy focuses is 'a very long and daring exercise in linguistic implosion'; through its many-layered parody – notably of Woolf's own writing in *To the Lighthouse* – this sentence undermines the narrative contract sustaining nature writing and mimetic description. However, as Bellamy's reading reveals, it also enacts a Steinian process of composition as explanation, thus shedding light on *Orlando* as a modernist textual and visual experiment that enables new modes of perception.

Tracing the trope of landscape as it appears in Orlando's experience on Mount Athos – a monastic site upon which women were historically forbidden to trespass – Vassiliki Kolocotroni explores the poet Orlando's allegorical and pastoral scene-making impulses. Grounded in the thought of classical scholar Jane Ellen Harrison, Orlando's vision of the Greek landscape enacts a feminist transgression, Kolocotroni argues, at the same time as it problematically appropriates this space and the classical past. Kolocotroni thereby highlights Orlando's ambivalence as 'emblem of an impossibility, a female creature on a sacred, forbidding all-male space'. The spectres of past and future imagined literary spaces also pervade Angeliki Spiropoulou's chapter. Drawing on classical and Renaissance constructions of the hero and the poet, Spiropoulou addresses ideas of literary fame and immortality in *Orlando*. From the caricatured writer Nick Greene, who extols 'La Gloire' above material gain while simultaneously seeking patronage, to the gender politics of anonymity and obscurity, Spiropoulou interrogates the traditional ways in which biography builds fame. Her chapter deftly explores the historically bound nuances of writing for glory, and considers Woolf's own complex relationship to fame in light of *Orlando*'s popular success.

Alice Staveley's and Bryony Randall's chosen sentences both index moments of birth in *Orlando*. In her account of Woolf's labour as a writer and publisher at the Hogarth Press, Staveley connects the labour of mothers and writers, and the delivery of babies and books. Reading the converging deliveries of Orlando's poem 'The Oak Tree', her son, and the manuscript of *Orlando*, Staveley analyses Woolf's invocation of her own 1919 short story 'Kew Gardens' in the novel's final pages. Sounding the resonances of this story's published forms, particularly the limited luxury edition issued in 1927, Staveley argues that the Kew Gardens scene turns the 'narratological modernist motif of closure-as-return into a materialist tribute'. As Randall stresses in her own approach to temporality, writing and delivery, the present moment is revealed at the end of the book to be its publication date, 'Thursday, the eleventh of October, Nineteen hundred and Twenty Eight'. Showing how the concept of the day is as important to *Orlando* as its excursion through a time-span of 400 years, Randall draws on recent theories of narrative temporality, dailiness and the novel to make a compelling case for *Orlando*'s 'final resolution into a concentrated, extended description of a single day as a key part of the text's undoing of traditional history'.

Steven Putzel introduces Roman Ingarden's concept of *satzdenken* – the 'flow of thinking the sentence' – to examine the theatricality of Woolf's sentences. Approaching his selected sentence through audience reception theory, Putzel also engages rich contextual material from Woolf's preoccupation with Elizabethan and Jacobean theatre. His reading historicises textual variants between the first UK and US editions of *Orlando*, and stages for us his own analytic processing of the sentence – which included consulting the opinion of 'a few grammarians', who recommended he 'rewrite the sentence'. Reading a moment from the same theatrical scene of the Great Frost episode, Amy Bromley traces a performative discourse of love in *Orlando*. Drawing on Roland Barthes's creative-theoretical text *A Lover's Discourse: Fragments* (1977), Bromley examines Woolf's multifacted creation of 'figures' via incomplete, fragmentary 'sentence-arias'. Bromley's chapter positions Woolf's dedication of *Orlando* to Sackville-West within a narratological approach to the text's procedures as a love letter and novel-biography, showing how the lover's discourse forms one layer in *Orlando*'s polyphony of discourses.

Todd Avery takes the sentence 'Orlando it seemed had a faith of her own' as a prompt to explore the many expressions of spirituality and religion in the text. He traces through *Orlando* an unconventional, anti-institutional form of 'Woolfian worship' indebted to Walter Pater's aestheticism and Charles Darwin's evolutionary theory. Engaging multiple intersections between modernism and theology, Avery argues that 'the spirituality of *Orlando* emerges from a deep wonder before the mystery, strangeness and absurdity of life'. Avery's reading illuminates the revelatory potential of Woolf's writing, which is also taken up by Benjamin Hagen's chapter. Hagen explores the ways in which Woolf encourages and teaches us to become 'more agile, creative and discerning readers'. Examining a sentence that is also a scene of reading, Hagen addresses some persistent ethical and political questions triggered by Woolf's notion of 'a reader's part' (O 52). He takes on the sentence's challenge to confront issues of colonial violence as it relates to practices of reading and writing, and turns particular focus on the role of Sir Thomas Browne in *Orlando*, whose presence provides a key to Woolf's fascination with ruins and remains.

Calling on thinkers as diverse as Sigmund Freud, George 'Bishop' Berkeley and G. E. Moore, Randi Koppen also identifies a Woolfian reading practice that is alert to dense textual allusion. Her chosen sentence prompts examination of the 'freakish and unequal' aspects of *Orlando* and, more specifically, the 'unequal juxtaposition' of 'biscuits and philosophy, Bishop and negress', in Chapter V. Koppen discusses the manifold allusions encompassed in this sentence – including its dialogue with Woolf's first novel, *The Voyage Out* (1915) – and throws into relief its 'questions of marriage, of language and what we have in common, but also of the colonial origins of modernist aesthetics and life-styles'. Judith Allen, whose chapter closes this volume, explores a politics of inconclusiveness that, she argues, pervades *Orlando*. Attending to the patterning and gender politics of her chosen sentence, with its evocative lists and rhetorical repetitions, Allen highlights Michel de Montaigne's influence on Woolf, and ranges from Mikhail Bakhtin's theory to Gertrude Stein's lists to examine the effects of Woolf's refusal to come to a conclusion. With Montaigne's question 'Que sais-je?' in mind, Allen identifies an essayistic, dialogic mode in *Orlando* resonant with the 'wildness' Woolf infused into this book. Allen thereby reveals something about Woolf's writing that emerges in all the chapters: how it requires keen and active reading practices, asking readers to participate in making meaning, to move nimbly between minute detail and wide horizons of thought and vision, and to read on at least two levels at once. This is the kind of reading practice that the contributors to this volume perform in their excursions into Woolf's plain and poetic, direct and meandering sentences – excursions that, we hope, may open up further avenues for exploring a morphology of the modernist sentence.

Notes

1. Virginia Woolf, *A Room of One's Own and Three Guineas* [1929/1938] (Oxford: Oxford World's Classics, 2008), pp. 99–100.
2. See, for instance, 'On Re-Reading Novels', 'How Should One Read a Book?', 'De Quincey's Autobiography' and 'Craftsmanship'. See also Woolf's engagement with the changing shapes of fiction in 'Mr Bennett and Mrs Brown'/'Character in Fiction', 'Modern Fiction', 'Poetry, Fiction and the Future' and 'Phases of Fiction'.
3. 'morphology, n.', *OED Online*, available at <www.oed.com/view/Entry/122369> (accessed 9 November 2016).
4. *Orlando* was published a few weeks before Woolf gave the talks at Newnham and Girton colleges, Cambridge, which later became *A Room of One's Own*.

5. Woolf wrote on 20 November 1927 about the composition of *Orlando*: 'Do I learn anything? Too much of a joke perhaps for that; yet I like these plain sentences; & the externality of it for a change' (*D3* 164).
6. As Robin Majumdar and Allen McLaurin note in their edited volume *Virginia Woolf: The Critical Heritage* (London and Boston: Routledge and Kegan Paul, 1975), p. 21, the early reviews of *Orlando* were divided between those that saw the book as a mere *jeu d'esprit*, and those that assigned it a central role in the trajectory of her modernist experiments. For a selection of reviews from 1928 to 1930, see pp. 222–54.
7. Stanley Fish, *How to Write a Sentence: And How to Read One* (New York and London: Harper, 2011), p. 76. Fish discusses Woolf on pp. 76–84.
8. The sentence has been considered the minimal productive unit for literary analysis by a range of scholars from Richard Ohman ('Literature as Sentences', *College English*, 27.4 (January 1966), pp. 261–7) to Ann Banfield (*Unspeakable Sentences: Narration and Representation in the Language of Fiction* (Boston and London: Routledge and Kegan Paul, 1982)).
9. Virginia Woolf, *Orlando: A Biography* [1928] (London: Penguin, 1993), p. 11.
10. See Sarah Annes Brown's account of *Orlando*'s Ovidian subtexts in *The Metamorphosis of Ovid: From Chaucer to Ted Hughes* (London: Duckworth, 1999), pp. 201–15.
11. Woolf noted on 20 December 1927: 'I see looking back just now to March that it is almost exactly in spirit [...] the book I planned then as an escapade; the spirit to be satiric, the structure wild' (*D3* 168).
12. Vita Sackville-West, *Knole and the Sackvilles* (London: Lindsay Drummond Limited, 1948), p. 15.
13. See Conrad Aiken's review of *Orlando* in the *Dial*, February 1929, in Majumdar and McLaurin, *Critical Heritage*, p. 236.
14. On a more immediate level, the 'morganatic' aesthetic of *Orlando* fits the theme of illegitimacy and dispossession, which pervades the history of Knole and the Sackville family. See Robert Sackville-West, *Inheritance: The Story of Knole and the Sackvilles* (London: Bloomsbury Publishing, 2010) and Victoria Glendinning, *Vita: The Life of V. Sackville-West* (London: Weidenfeld and Nicolson Limited, 1983).
15. Virginia Woolf, *Orlando* [1928], ed. Maria DiBattista (Orlando: Harcourt, 2006), p. xxxviii.
16. Bryony Randall and Jane Goldman (eds), *Virginia Woolf in Context* (Cambridge: Cambridge University Press, 2012), p. xi.
17. Marjorie Levinson, 'What is New Formalism?', *PMLA*, 122.2 (March 2007), p. 559.
18. Ibid. pp. 559–61.
19. Ibid. pp. 560–1.
20. Woolf wrote on 22 October, as she began to compose *Orlando*: 'I walk making up phrases; sit, contriving scenes; am in short in the thick of the greatest rapture known to me [...] I felt happier than for months [...] & abandoned myself to the pure delight of this farce' (*D3* 161–2). Nigel Nicolson, in *Portrait of a Marriage* (London: Futura Publications, 1974), famously called *Orlando* 'the longest and most charming love-letter

in English literature' (p. 209), even if he, alongside many others until the 1980s, downplayed the eroticism in Woolf and Sackville-West's relationship, and hence the erotic impulse behind *Orlando*. See, for instance, Sherron E. Knopp, '"If I Saw You Would You Kiss Me?": Sapphism and the Subversiveness of Virginia Woolf's *Orlando*', *PMLA*, 103.1 (Jan. 1988), pp. 24–34; and Adam Parkes, 'Lesbianism, History, and Censorship: *The Well of Loneliness* and the Suppressed Randiness of Virginia Woolf's *Orlando*', *Twentieth-Century Literature*, 40.4 (Winter 1994), pp. 434–60.

21. Earlier accounts of the sexual and textual politics of Woolf's 'feminine sentences' tend to pay little attention, if any, to the sentence as an aesthetic unit. See, for instance, Janet Wolff, *Feminine Sentences: Essays on Women and Culture* (Cambridge: Polity Press, 1990) and Sandra M. Gilbert, 'Woman's Sentence, Man's Sentencing: Linguistic Fantasies in Woolf and Joyce', in Jane Marcus (ed.), *Virginia Woolf and Bloomsbury: A Centenary Celebration* (Bloomington: Indiana University Press, 1987), pp. 208–24.
22. Banfield's book was republished, significantly, in the Routledge Revivals series in 2014.
23. The title of Woolf's late, unfinished book on literary history, 'Reading at Random', captures her working method as she embarked on this project.
24. Cf. 'How Should One Read a Book?': 'That pleasure [of reading] is so curious, so complex, so immensely fertilising to the mind of anyone who enjoys it, and so wide in its effects, that it would not be in the least surprising to discover, on the day of judgement [. . .] that the reason why we have grown from pigs to men and women [. . .] and made pavements and houses and erected some sort of shelter and society on the waste of the world, is nothing but this: we have loved reading' (*E4* 398–9).
25. See, for instance, Jonathan Culler, 'The Closeness of Close Reading', *ADE Bulletin*, 149 (2010), pp. 20–5; Mark Hussey, 'How Should One Read a Screen?', in Pamela L. Caughie (ed.), *Virginia Woolf in the Age of Mechanical Reproduction* (New York: Garland Publishing, 2000), pp. 249–66; and David Mikics, *Slow Reading in a Hurried Age* (Cambridge, MA: Harvard University Press, 2013).

Chapter 1

'The Queen had come': Orgasm and Arrival

Jane Goldman

The Queen had come.[1]

These four words surely comprise *the* most direct sentence of *Orlando: A Biography*, the novel that taught Woolf 'how to write a direct sentence' (D3 203). Vulgar, bawdy, openly celebrating female auto-eroticism, orgasmic pleasure, they nevertheless remain coded, cryptic, somehow hidden in plain sight. These plainest of words simply report, in base language of information, the historic arrival of Queen Elizabeth I at Knole in 1573 – if indeed the fictitious Orlando's 'own great house' (*O* 21) is the house that would not be inherited, because of male primogeniture, by the novel's real-life dedicatee, Vita Sackville-West.[2] VSW's book *Knole and the Sackvilles* (1922) does not mention that visit, but clearly states that Knole was 'granted to Thomas Sackville by Queen Elizabeth' thirteen years later in 1586.[3] In context and out, this sentence refuses to oblige any such innocent or literal reading. It is equally a direct, open report of a woman's having achieved orgasm: 'The Queen had *come*'. With orgasm comes sovereign power too: 'The *Queen* had come'. The pluperfect is the *coup de grace*: it was and still is no use arguing or worrying after the fact. An orgasmic feminist Sapphic coup had (has) already happened, so let us face the fact: 'The Queen *had* come'.

'To come' for centuries has meant to 'experience sexual orgasm', its earliest recorded usage in a song, 'Walking in Meadow Green' (1650): 'Then off he came, & blusht for shame soe soone that he had endit'. See too the notorious Earl of Rochester's pornographic collection *Cabinet of Love* (1714): 'Just as we came, I cried, "I faint! I die!"'. An instance of female erotic urgency occurs in the anonymous Victorian memoir *My Secret Life* (c. 1890): '"Shove on", said she, "I was just coming"'. Woolf would have read in Joyce's *Ulysses* (1922) two further lewd examples of coming: 'Suppose you . . . came too quick with your best girl'; 'yet I never came properly till I was what 22'. In 1928, the year of *Orlando*'s publication, D. H. Lawrence's *Lady Chatterley's Lover* (1928), immediately banned for obscenity, furnished two more examples: '"We came off together that time", he said'; 'when I'd come and really finished, then she'd start on her own account'.[4] So far, so taboo, so far so heterosexual. Radclyffe Hall's romantic Sapphic novel *The Well of Loneliness* was also banned for obscenity in 1928, because of one coy utterance: 'that night, they were not divided'.[5]

How *did* Woolf get away with 'The Queen had come'? More direct than the censored Hall's veiled allusion, it is hardly so encoded as Gertrude Stein's surreal refrain 'My wife has a cow', understood by a semi-closeted Sapphic coterie, dormant for decades in her 'cubist' poetry, before outed to academic critical authority as lesbian slang for orgasm.[6] Woolf was acquainted with Stein's work by 1926 when she published 'Composition as Explanation' in the Hogarth Essays Series. Fretting over the reception of *A Room of One's Own* (1929) in case 'attacked for a feminist & hinted at for a Sapphist' (*D3* 362), Woolf (an uncalled defence witness) was composing mock-prurient, arch allusions to Hall's trial, including Mary Carmichael's possibly Sapphic fictitious novel, *Life's Adventure*: 'Chloe liked Olivia. They shared a laboratory together . . .'.[7] The same year comes Woolf's open 'most charming love letter' to an already notorious Sapphist,[8] ignoring the advice of another of the era's famously louche women – 'Keep It To Yourself' (Bessie Smith)[9] – to get away with 'The Queen had come'.

The sentence comes pages into Chapter I, which begins by catching the male Orlando 'in the act of slicing at the head of a Moor which swung from the rafters' (*O* 15). Embodying the Elizabethan period's enterprising colonial impulse, he is duly rewarded by the Queen herself, or a character resembling Elizabeth, whose sovereignty famously transcended *and* exploited her gender. The novel explores the complex gendered, sexualised politics of the ageing monarch's bestowal of propertied power on eternally young Orlando. The Queen's coming to bestow Knole upon Orlando's family is communicated via an erotically charged account of the very landscape Orlando is to enjoy dominion (*jouissance*) over for centuries to come. His view brings luminous colour to a previously 'dark country' of feminine sexuality: 'white clouds had turned red, the hills were violet, the woods purple, the valleys black – a trumpet sounded. Orlando leapt to his feet. The shrill sound came from the valley' (*O* 21). The trumpet heralds an intimate sense of feminine sexuality and of the gender Orlando later inhabits in dress and then in aligned somatic identity:

It came from a dark spot down there; a spot compact and mapped out; a maze; a town, yet girt with walls; it came from the heart of his own great house in the valley, which, dark before, even as he looked and the single trumpet duplicated and reduplicated itself with other shriller sounds, lost its darkness and became pierced with lights. (O 21)

Sexually subversive, this autoerotic vision is replicated by the gender-disruptive discovery of 'his own great house in the valley', previously the Queen's own. Liberated feminine sexuality brings multiple gendering of the 'dark spot', queering Orlando and Queen, accompanied by a fanfare, the 'shrill sound' of which marks clitoral pleasure. It culminates, after the attentions of various servile men, in playfully coded but nevertheless fairly explicit suggestion of orgasm:

> Some were hurrying lights, as if they burnt in empty banqueting-halls made ready to receive guests who had not come; and others dipped and waved and sank and rose, as if held in the hands of troops of serving men, bending, kneeling, rising, receiving, guarding, and escorting with all dignity indoors a great Princess alighting her chariot. Coaches turned and wheeled in the courtyard. Horses tossed their plumes. The Queen had come. (O 21)

Mounting excitement in that rhythmic catalogue of participles denoting arousal ('bending [...] rising') meets explosive climax in perfect tenses ('turned [...] tossed'). This change of syntactic pace echoes Stein's technique in 'As a Wife has a Cow/ A Love Story'. The sexual pun in that final report is fittingly Elizabethan. The trumpeting's coded reference to feminine sexual pleasure is confirmed at the novel's mid-point, where Orlando's sex change is likewise trumpeted: 'The trumpeters [...] blow one terrific blast', and the 'trumpets pealed Truth! Truth! Truth! we have no choice left but confess – he was a woman' (O 126). This trumpet blast heralding female sovereignty is a feminist counterblast to John Knox's *The First Blast of the Trumpet Against the Monstrous Regiment of Women* (1558), a misogynist anti-Marian attack on women's sovereignty, not least targeting Mary Queen of Scots (hereafter MQS), but also unsettling Elizabeth I.[10] Five asterisks mark this, the novel's bifurcating point where feminism blows her own trumpet (O 126). In everything prior, Orlando is a man; everything after, a woman. Yet already multiple gender possibilities are announced by that first trumpet.

'A Queen' and a 'wild goose' are the portents at the novel's close (O 295). Woolf's steamy correspondence with VSW suggests sophisticated coding of this goose imagery with an erotics of Woolf's signature, V. The draft version, shown to VSW, reads: 'by came flying, in the shape of a v, each with a long neck outstretched, wild geese' (OH 284–5). So,

Leslie Hankins observes, Woolf 'coded her love for Vita between the draft and the published version', itself 'packed with innuendo'.[11] 'The "V" and Woolf's careful manipulation, flaunting and hiding that image and signature' speaks to her lover while 'veil[ing] it from others'.[12] Compare the love letters. 'Dearest Honey', she wonders, 'what would happen if I let myself go over? Answer me that. Over what? you'll say. A precipice marked V' (L3 351–2). Caution and coding have indeed been abandoned in *Orlando*. Whereas Hall's coy 'that night, they were not divided' has us guessing at the threshold, spying through keyholes, blushing and prurient, and Stein's coded 'wife has a cow' puts us firmly on one side or the other of the closet door – inside (smirking) or outside (baffled) – the much more openly saucy Woolf dares to throw readers over that precipice marked V with that most direct of all her sentences: 'The Queen had come'.

But which Queen had come? 'The Queen', queer queens, and the wild(e) goose

This spoof biography/love letter plays on intertwining her lover's initials and Woolf's own – VSW and VW.[13] Knole, *Orlando*'s main locus and Woolf's lover's house, is everywhere inscribed (fireplaces, beams, walls and other architectural features) with a 'double-V design', an apotropaic mark traditionally carved by workmen to ward off witches and introduced during renovations to Knole after it passed to the Sackvilles in 1604. This 'Marian symbol invoking the protection of Mary the Mother of God', standing for "Virgo Virginum", became surprisingly popular 'during the post-Reformation given that the cult of worship surrounding Mary was no longer officially sanctioned'.[14] Woolf co-opts for unchaste purposes, then, this Marian double V to unite Virginia and Vita as 'VV', which, read as 'W', also unites West and Woolf. Turned upside down, that 'W' becomes 'M'. 'M' for Mary? But which Mary?

Orlando is simultaneously a love letter to all women; to the multiplicitous erotic life of women; to emergent modern claims on sovereignty by women. 'Queen', a most cherished, repeated word in the novel, communicates the latter so well, consistently a term recognising a woman's power and significance *and* only one consonant away from 'Queer' – another key term in *Orlando*. As queen is also longstanding slang, since the eighteenth century, for 'male homosexual, typically one regarded as ostentatiously effeminate',[15] we cannot rule out its embrace as co-extensive with a lesbian-gay-queer continuum. This mock biography's intended 'main note' was 'satire', so it may constitute a veiled

'The Queen had come'   19

wink at the queerness unleashed by the scandalous trial of Oscar Wilde: '– satire and wildness', Woolf clarifies to her diary (*D3* 131). Is there a silent 'e' in her 'wildness', also appending 'wild' in the 'single wild bird [. . .] The wild goose' that springs up 'over [the] head' of Orlando (*O* 295), but by no means over the heads of Woolf's readers? Another satiric target is Woolf's 'own lyric vein' (*D3* 131). The verticality of lyric exclamation is certainly sent up by that wild goose springing up at the 'twelfth stroke of midnight', heralding the novel's end, perhaps delivering a double goosing to the backsides of 'Orlando' and *Orlando*. Given Orlando's legendary trans-sexual morphology, Woolf pointedly seems to repeat this possibly slang 'goose', meaning 'poke, tickle' '(a person) in a sensitive part, esp. the genital or anal regions' and 'more specifically, = fuck'.[16] We might speculate on which genital or anal orifice precisely such a goosing is delivered.

A goose flies up too into the 'phantom' scene on the final page, itself a phantom reprise of the first encounter with the word 'Queen' ('The Queen had come'):

> There stood the great house with all its windows robed in silver. Of wall or substance there was none. All was phantom. All was still. All was lit as for the coming of a dead Queen. Gazing below her, Orlando saw dark plumes tossing in the courtyard, and torches flickering and shadows kneeling. A Queen once more stepped from her chariot. (*O* 295)

This passage reprises the first scene's 'great house' in muted, telegraphic after-images, 'dark plumes tossing' no longer tossed by horses, the simile of 'hurrying lights, as if servants' (*O* 21) compressed now to metaphoric personification: 'torches flickering and shadows kneeling'. The third-person possessive assigned to Orlando has switched gender ('his' becomes 'her'). But for whom is this flickering, chiaroscuric, genuflection? The scene is 'lit for the coming of a dead Queen', transforming the pluperfect of the first arrival ('The Queen had come') from past completed action to the present-future continuum of 'the coming'; from the arrival of '*The* Queen' to the anticipated 'coming of *a* [. . .] Queen', and an already dead one at that. Yet now she lives: 'A Queen once more stepped from her chariot'. But which Queen might be restored? We cannot even be sure of which Queen is signified in her first appearance in the book, in 'The Queen had come'.

Attentive literalists, of course, may be goosing in another sense ('hissing') at suggestion of a queer queen. 'The Queen' ought only to be Elizabeth. But Woolf chose not to write explicitly 'Queen Elizabeth had come'. With clear self-licence for 'satire and wild(e)ness', as well as for lyric verticality, it would surely impoverish the sentence considerably

20   Jane Goldman

to take it so flatly. What anyway does 'Queen Elizabeth [I]' signify to modern readers; what legends trail in her wake? Her struggle over sovereignty with her cousin, MQS, and her unsisterly ordering of her execution? 'The Queen' – even without specification of which Queen – opens the historical power struggles between Catholic and Protestant, and further valences of Mariolatry, the Marian, of Mary, Queen of Heaven, mother of the messiah. Attempting precise historical dating of *Orlando*, attentive literalists are obliged to fathom *which* Queen. Only readers born after the accession of Queen Elizabeth II require the numeral on the first. Yet, even in 1928, 'the Queen' might be a Spenserian double of Elizabeth (Woolf knew well *The Faerie Queene*). Readers would still need to fathom whether this visit is before or after she ordered the execution.

Teasing reverse reference to unsisterly decapitation occurs in Orlando's meeting with 'the Queen':

> his mind was such a welter of opposites – of the night and the blazing candles, of the shabby poet and the great Queen, of silent fields and the clatter of serving men – that he could see nothing; or only a hand [...] the Queen herself can have seen only a head. (O 23–4)

The spectre of Elizabeth is further raised, as 'a dead Queen', by allusion to the head of her wax effigy that went with her funeral hearse to Westminster Abbey where it still resides:

> But if it is possible from a hand to deduce a body, informed with all the attributes of a great Queen, her crabbedness, courage, frailty, and terror, surely a head can be as fertile, looked down upon from a chair of state by a lady whose eyes were always, if the waxworks at the Abbey are to be trusted, wide open. (O 23)

Woolf echoes her own essay 'Waxworks at the Abbey' (1928), composed alongside *Orlando*.[17] Here waxy Elizabeth 'dominates the room as she once dominated England [....] a drawn anguished figure [...] immensely intellectual, suffering, and tyrannical. She will not allow one to look elsewhere' (E4 540, 541). Has she held the gaze too of readers of *Orlando* at the expense of noticing its numerous references to MQS?

Feminine sovereignty is unstable here. 'The Queen', a moveable term of office, is a slippery, multivalent signifier in *Orlando*, slippery enough to embrace both Queen Elizabeth and Mary. The loose play of the deictic 'The' cannot be ignored. 'The Queen' could be one of those 'Kings and Queens of impossible territories' making up 'the personages of [Orlando's poetic] drama' (O 18), two pages earlier. Who is to say that in such fictions, it is not a revenant, messianic, MQS who 'had come'? Nor can we ignore the reverberations of the 'coming' of messianic, revenant 'dead poet' Judith Shakespeare, who 'will put on the body she has so often laid down' (*AROO* 172). This prophecy comes itself in a multiply-voiced text ventriloquised through three personae from a famous Scottish ballad on infidelity and infanticide at the court of MQS, variously rendered as 'The Four Maries', 'The Queen's Mary' or 'Mary Hamilton': 'call me Mary Beton, Mary Seton, Mary Carmichael or by any name you please' (*AROO* 8). Surely some queer queen is at hand – or some 'minor tyrant mimicking the Red Queen', as Gillian Beer deems Lewis Carroll's Duchess.[18]

The granite-like fact of Elizabeth's historic gift of Knole, recorded in *Knole and the Sackvilles*, like Quentin Crisp's superbly queening performance in Sally Potter's film, encourages us to read the coming as that of Good Queen Bess. Yet how one Queen haunts the other. VSW's 'Chronological Table', for example, for Knole and her ancestor Thomas Sackville, Lord Buckhurst (1536–1608), starkly reveals its gifting in the very same year as Mary's execution:

1586 *Execution of* MARY *Queen of* SCOTS
1586 *Given* KNOLE *by* QUEEN ELIZABETH[19]

Buckhurst, not 'in the Star Chamber at Westminster when she was condemned' was yet

> sent to announce the sentence to death, and received from her in recognition of his tact and gentleness in conveying this news the triptych and carved group of the Procession to Calvary now on the altar in the chapel at Knole.[20]

Knole, one Queen's gift, is pregnant with the gift of her executed rival. Crucial to *Orlando* is Buckhurst's relinquishing of 'what might have been a first-rate literary career for a second-rate political one': 'Poetry – a frivolous pursuit – had long since been left behind. The poet had become the statesman'.[21] Woolf reverses this move.

Knole and the Sackvilles shows just how significant to its poet author, barred from inheriting on gender grounds, is the altar gifted to Knole by MQS. Here is the heart of the house: 'small and very much bejewelled. Tapestry, oak, and stained glass – the chapel smoulders with colour'.[22] No fan of its later adornments – 'the hand of the nineteenth century fell rather heavily on the chapel' – VSW recommends turning 'your back on them' to 'look down the little nave to the altar where Mary Queen of Scots' gifts stand under the Perpendicular east window. All along the left-hand wall hangs the Gothic tapestry'.[23] The chapel's tapestries show 'scenes from the life of Christ' in 'ungainly' figures. VSW repeats

Horace Walpole's irreverent account of '"Saint Luke in his first profession [...] holding a urinal"', before nodding to 'other tapestries in the house' which 'alas, had to be sold, and are now in America'.[24] All Biblical scenes, these are not explicitly described in *Orlando*. A green-blue 'arras' or 'tapestry', is a running motif, 'mov[ing] perpetually' (*O* 16) in the winds blowing through the vast house throughout Orlando's life, sometimes depicting pagan hunting scenes, such as Apollo's pursuit of Daphne, fluttering images of a frozen chase from 'the green arras with the hunters on it' (ibid.) to the tapestry where 'still the hunter rode; still Daphne flew' (*O* 285).[25] Orlando, at the close, locates this in the room 'where the heart of the house still beat' and where she 'watched the tapestry rising and falling on the eternal faint breeze which never failed to move it' (*O* 285). The first tapestry flutters in the vacillating wind that makes the 'skull [swing] to and fro' (*O* 16). Consider the novel's first sentence where Orlando, ironically introduced as 'He – for there could be no doubt of his sex', is 'slicing' at the Moor's head that 'swung from the rafters [...] in the breeze which never ceased blowing through the attic rooms of the gigantic house of the lord who had slain him' (*O* 15). Is there symbolic causal relation between the Moor's murder and the ill winds blowing through his murderer's house? For some ancestor of the fictitious Orlando 'had struck it from the vast Pagan who had started up under the moon in the barbarian fields of Africa' (ibid.). Did a Sackville-West ancestor ever commit such a decapitation, we might legitimately wonder? And if the sex of Orlando turns out to be in doubt, and more than merely under the 'disguise' of 'fashion', when later 'He' swings to 'She', how accurate, moreover, we might wonder in parallel, is the gender pronoun assigned to the head he is 'slicing' at? Or perhaps decapitation became habitually associated with the house? Does the 'vast Pagan' hint at the Pagan idolater, MQS, as caricatured by Knox?[26]

'You perambulate miles of galleries; skip endless treasures', Woolf remarks on first visiting a lifeless 'preserved' Knole in July 1924, finding 'chairs that Shakespeare might have sat on – tapestries, pictures, floors made of the halves of oaks', but 'the extremities & indeed the inward parts are gone dead. Ropes fence off half the rooms [...] life has left them' (*D2* 306). But the Chapel gets her attention: 'Mary Stuart's altar, where she prayed before execution. "An ancestor of ours took her the death warrant" said Vita' (ibid.). That MQS herself was never at Knole is elided here, the altar being her bequest to the Sackville ancestor who so gently delivered her death warrant. Woolf now turns at this very point in her diary to describe her lover and, in close connection with this scene, to how precisely she is enamoured of her physique:

All these ancestors & centuries, & silver & gold, have bred the perfect body. She is stag like, or race horse like, save for the face, which pouts, & has no very sharp brain. But as a body hers is perfection. (ibid.)

In effect, Woolf's amorous appraisal here is a kind of verbal decapitation – the face, the brain, and implicitly the head, are dismissed.

VSW, however, whose middle name was Mary, enjoyed her own personal, private angle of access to this cherished site, aflutter with tapestries, and 'strange and lovely during a midnight thunderstorm: the lightning flashes through the stone ogives of the east window, and one gets a queer effect, unreal like colour photography, of the colours lit up by that unfamiliar means'.[27] She recalls the 'flight of little private steps' from her 'bedroom straight into the Family Pew', boasting powerful childhood memories: 'I used to "take sanctuary" there when I had been naughty: that is to say, fairly often. They never found me, sulking inside the pulpit'.[28] She was married there on 1 October 1913. Little wonder, with its 'gifts' from MQS, herself a Daphne of sorts, and its associations for VSW with her ancestor's part in the fate of MQS, with her own sense of personal sanctuary, her infantile transgressions and her wedding, the chapel features so powerfully in *Orlando*.

Returning home, Orlando roams past swaying tapestries, and like VSW, 'bathed her hand, as she had loved to do as a child, in the yellow pool of light which the moonlight made falling through the heraldic Leopard in the window' (O 157). Her sojourn around the house concludes when 'at length, tired out, she entered the Chapel and sank into the old red arm-chair in which her ancestors used to hear service' (ibid.). Here Woolf's novel somewhat comically describes a sacred relic of MQS's not mentioned by VSW or other sources:

> There she lit a cheroot ('twas a habit she had brought back from the East) and opened the Prayer Book. It was a little book bound in velvet, stitched with gold, which had been held by Mary Queen of Scots on the scaffold, and the eye of faith could detect a brownish stain, said to be made of a drop of the Royal blood. But what pious thoughts it roused in Orlando, what evil passions it soothed asleep, who dare say, seeing that of all communions this with the deity is the most inscrutable? [. . .] In the Queen's prayerbook, along with the blood-stain, was also a lock of hair and a crumb of pastry; Orlando now added to these keepsakes a flake of tobacco, and so, reading and smoking, was moved by the humane jumble of them all – the hair, the pastry, the blood-stain, the tobacco – to such a mood of contemplation as gave her a reverent air suitable in the circumstances, though she had, it is said, no traffic with the usual God. (O 157)

The 'Queen's prayerbook' resembles one now held in the Collection of Stuart Relics at Stonyhurst College, Lancashire. 'The Book of Hours

24   Jane Goldman

of Mary, Queen of Scots', Jan Graffius tells us, sports a 'most unusual' 'double piled velvet' binding, 'deep vermilion red silk damask' and 'gold tassels'.[29] Woolf's playfully unstable text about vacillating and unstable identities, then, invokes a prayerbook not to begin with the property of MQS, but of her cousin, another Queen Mary whose name appears in 'silver gilt and enamelled metal letters':

> how did it pass to her cousin, Mary, Queen of Scots, the only other woman who could have fulfilled the criteria for its ownership, namely a Catholic queen called Mary, with Tudor family associations and a claim to the crown of England?[30]

If the name on this one signifies an unstable, shifting feminine sovereignty applicable to more than one historic person, the legendary book itself is also not at all singular. There are extant 'two other prayer books' with a claim 'to have been on the scaffold with Mary', perhaps 'several' more.[31]

Orlando's readers cannot be sure of the provenance of the book in its fictitious protagonist's hands. This is surely Woolf's satire on religious relics. She nevertheless, albeit humorously, offers up the accidental tobacco crumbs of Orlando's clumsy communion with its pages as further secular but reverenced accretions along with the martyred Queen's purported hair and blood. 'Communion' with 'the Queen's prayerbook' paradoxically leads Orlando to counter notions of absolute divine right, heredity power through bloodlines, and the absolutism of monotheism: 'Nothing, however, can be more arrogant, though nothing is commoner than to assume that of Gods there is only one, and of religions none but the speaker's. Orlando, it seemed, had a faith of her own' (O 157). Her poem's overused sibilant alliteration and present participle become 'sins' in Orlando's secular poetics: 'To evade such temptations is the first duty of the poet [. . .] for as the ear is the antechamber to the soul, poetry can adulterate and destroy more surely than lust or gunpowder' (O 158). Occupying 'the place for believing in Devils' or the position of the binary, Manichean theology that follows from Christian monotheism, Orlando shifts paradigms from singular religious belief to a multiplicitous aesthetics of words, letters, syllables and syntactic morphology. Scorn for the letter S's satanic and Edenic associations (and there are 'still too many' in her poem, 'The Oak Tree') is wittily followed by a sentence with seven sybillant sounds *and* the 'present participle' which 'is the Devil himself, she thought, now that we are in the place for believing in Devils' (O 157–8). Orlando celebrates the materiality, the poetry, and the very print of the prayerbook in her hand, and is close to saying that the only believed 'devil' in this 'place' (the book, the chapel, the house, the person) is a printer's devil. For as Woolf well knew, having more or less been one herself for her own Hogarth Press, a printer's devil is the often ink-bespattered apprentice in a printing office.

The *OED* cites Joseph Moxon's *Mechanick exercises; or, The doctrine of handy-works. Applied to the art of printing* (1683): 'These Boys do in a Printing-House, commonly black and Dawb themselves: whence the Workmen do Jocosely call them *Devils*; and sometimes *Spirits*, and sometimes *Flies*'. A printer's devil might be a girl too. See Boswell's *Life of Johnson* (1781), a book Woolf knew intimately:

> He had married a printer's devil . . . Reynolds: 'I thought a printer's devil was a creature with a black face and in rags'. Johnson: 'Yes, Sir. But I suppose, he had her face washed, and put clean clothes on her'.[32]

Printer's devil became in the nineteenth century derogatory for one 'employed by an author or writer to do subordinate parts of his literary work under his direction; a literary "hack" [. . .] one who does work for which another receives the credit or remuneration or both'.[33] This figure haunts Orlando and *Orlando*. Nicholas Greene, for example, resembles and shares the first name of equally prolific and financially motivated, 'opportunist' writer Nicholas Breton (1554/5–c. 1626), notorious for his timely Gunpowder Plot verse, 'An Invective Against Treason' (1616).[34] Compare Orlando above on 'poetry' and 'lust or gunpowder'.

Orlando early supplants religion with art: 'his prayer was, no doubt, a poem said aloud' (O 114). Female Orlando's conversion to poetry's call is staged at the altar of MQS with purported prayer book in hand – precisely where VSW relates her ancestor Buckhurst's recanting of poetic ambition, after serving the death warrant on MQS. Where Buckhurst relinquished a possibly 'first-rate literary career for a second-rate political one', Orlando abandons politics and religion for poetry. VSW's observation – 'Poetry – a frivolous pursuit – had long since been left behind. The poet had become the statesman'[35] – is reversed in similarly Marian context where MQS's prayer book is Orlando's touchstone for 'development of her soul':

> 'This is better than Turkey. Hair, pastry, tobacco – of what odds and ends are we compounded', she said (thinking of Queen Mary's prayer-book). 'What a phantasmagoria the mind is and meeting-place of dissemblables! At one moment we deplore our birth and state and aspire to an ascetic exaltation; the next we are overcome by the smell of some old garden path and weep to hear the thrushes sing'. (O 157)

The gender crisis or discontinuity of a woman's call to poetry, itself always already patriarchal, is pressed by the abruptly juxtaposed sentences: 'The poet's, then, is the highest office of all, she continued. His words reach where others fall short' (O 158). The full stop prevents her continuing after 'continued', initiating 'His words'. MQS's relic intervenes between Orlando's provisional sense of self-development and her dead antecedents: '"I am growing up," she thought [. . .] "I am losing some illusions," she said, shutting Queen Mary's book, "perhaps to acquire others," and she descended among the tombs where the bones of her ancestors lay' (ibid.). Shutting the martyr's prayerbook, is Orlando invoking her as poet (for MQS was a poet too)? The celebration of a materialist, collagistic, multivalent poetics, anchored in the memory of the prayerbook, itself an object in the world among pastry and tobacco crumbs, culminates in Orlando's starting 'afresh upon "The Oak Tree"' (O 161).

Scenting 'the wind' blowing through novel and house, the lovers Orlando and Shelmerdine are prompted to marriage vows, taken in a fictionalised version of the chapel where VSW wed Harold Nicolson. VSW's 'queer effect' of 'midnight thunderstorm' and 'lightning flashes' in the chapel reverberates in Woolf's 'lightning playing', 'rain pouring', 'clap of thunder' muting 'the word Obey', and eliding the 'golden flash' of the 'ring pass[ing] from hand to hand' (O 235–6). A queer queen, a queer MQS, is again invoked in these tumultuous, secular, poetic nuptials, where words break like confetti 'in a shower of fragments to the ground' (O 236), and over which Mr Dupper presides with 'Queen Mary's prayer book in his hands' (O 235). Woolf's fictitious 'Queen Mary's prayerbook' emphasises the import of Knole's revered Marian altar. What does it mean to be custodian of such a relic, particularly one whose ancestor was bequeathed it by the very Queen whose execution he also helped to arrange? What does it mean to say a prayer at such an altar now installed in the very house that was gifted by the rival Queen who ordered the execution? To whom does one pray in such a doubled queenly context?

The novel written in tribute to a woman descendent denied, on grounds of her sex, inheritance of house, chapel, altar (possibly prayer book too), closes with a reprise annunciation of the 'coming of a dead Queen'. A mutation of the earlier sentence on a past woman's royal arrival, 'The Queen had come', it anticipates further mutation, in *A Room of One's Own*. The Marian trope here announces the coming of the common citizen-poet, Shakespeare's sister. Thus the 'great Queen' is deposed by the 'shabby poet' of Orlando's first royal encounter. Both instances of queenly coming may construe Orlando, then, narcissistically watching her own arrival.

The queer queenly genealogy of Orlando and *Orlando: A Biography*

The novel's subtitle might well be 'A Bibliography', given its intermixing of biography, genealogy and textual genesis. Its key sentence on sovereignty, 'The Queen had come', is radically unstable. Multiple is the legendary prayer book taken to the scaffold by one of the many Queens the sentence possibly invokes; multiple is Orlando, whose point of view dominates the sentence, having gloriously 'a great variety of selves to call upon' (O 278). So too, *Orlando*, the text hosting this sentence, is multiple – even in the first edition, where a substantive variant occurs between impressions in another sentence that nevertheless has direct significance for readings of 'The Queen had come'.

Orlando's earliest hope is to belong 'to the sacred race rather than to the noble', to be 'by birth a writer, rather than an aristocrat' (O 78). Orlando is to write him- or herself into poetic sovereignty, into a lineage requiring not ancestral blood but universal ink. The novel has its own contradictory family tree (stemma), calling upon a variety of *Orlando*s, all of whom have a claim to be sovereign text or Queen text or the text who 'had come', as well as the returning Queen text. No textual variant exists for 'The Queen had come'. But this sentence, haunted by multiple sovereignties, is illuminated by a startling substantive textual variant I found on a name in a clause in another sentence altogether.

Orlando's gender reassignment is preceded by a period of pupation 'in profound slumber' (O 121) during which his secretaries discover a 'deed of marriage' in his 'state papers'. This fictional document of Orlando's marriage to 'Rosina Pepita, a dancer, father unknown, but reputed a gipsy' (O 122), collapses a number of generations of VSW's real antecedents into the fictive marriage of someone resembling her notorious gipsy grandmother to her own fictional counterpart. 'Rosina Pepita' shares her second name with Pepita, VSW's grandmother, properly named Josefa Durán (1830–71). VSW later published a book on this exotic forebear, *Pepita* (1937). Pepita was the Spanish dancer with whom VSW's grandfather, Lionel Sackville-West (1827–1908) co-habited until her death. They never married. The 1910 court case brought by VSW's mother's siblings (the grandfather's illegitimate children) established this granite-like fact. They unsuccessfully argued claim to Knole, disputing the legality of their mother Pepita's only recorded marriage (at twenty to Juan de la Oliva, a dancer), asserting she was legally their father's wife. Because VSW's mother had married her first cousin, legitimate heir to Knole, Lionel Edward Sackville-West (1867–1928), 'it was in her interests to contest the lawsuit, even though doing so meant publicly acknowledging her own illegitimacy [...] Henry lost, after Vita's parents produced a certificate of marriage between Pepita and Juan de la Oliva dated 1853'.[36]

Pepita, in Spanish 'pumpkin seed', is a traditional nickname for the formal Josefina, the feminine form of Joseph, meaning God shall add or increase. If Woolf's famous theory of biography as 'granite and rainbow', referenced in *Orlando* (O 73), is applied to Rosina Pepita, then Pepita is the granite-like fact sourced in VSW's historic ancestry. But Rosina was not a name of Vita's grandmother. With no link to that ancestry at all, it appears a rainbow-like imaginary embellishment by Woolf. Rosina, a popular girl's name in Italy and Spain, appears nowhere else in Woolf's writings. It is a Latinate name meaning 'rose' and carrying too associations with the Virgin Mary. Perhaps Woolf's fictional coupling of Rosina (associated with Mary) and Pepita (an informal feminine version of Joseph) is a humorous nod to the Biblical couple Mary and Joseph, the earthly parents of Jesus Christ, already caricatured as warring rooks by Mrs Ramsay in *To the Lighthouse* (1927): 'the father rook, old Joseph [...] and Mary were fighting'.[37] Her son Jasper foreshadows Orlando's heretical doubts, where he 'rather liked her stories about Mary and Joseph [...] But how did she know that those were Mary and Joseph?' (*TL* 128).

Orlando in print makes fascinating, substantive (textual) genetic mischief with this material. 'Rosina Pepita', page 122 of the first British edition, published October 1928, becomes, on page 122 of the second impression (later that month) *and* of the third impression (December 1928): 'Rosina Lolita'! Why? Is it a printer's error, or even a printer's devil's error? Or willed variant at the author's instruction, herself an arch printer's devil? Consider as circumstantial evidence for the latter the 'bitter letter' about *Orlando* from VSW's mother (Pepita's daughter) on the very same day Woolf also notes: 'We've got to reprint –' (*L3* 548).[38] Lolita appears too in the Tauchnitz edition of early 1929. But barring a flirtatious appearance on a sample printer's page, she vanishes to be replaced by Pepita in the Uniform edition (1930). The substantive variant Lolita, a version of Lola, in Spanish means 'sorrows of the Virgin Mary'. It is not associated with VSW's grandmother. Lolita occurs nowhere else in Woolf's writings, although Lola occurs once – in gossip in *The Voyage Out* about a 'prostitute', 'Signora Lola Mendoza, as she calls herself, cross[ing] the passage in her nightgown'.[39]

The swapping of three letters ('Pep' to 'Lol'), hermetically recoding Pepita as Lolita, loses the granite-like factual link, then, to VSW's grandmother in three printings of the novel. So how do we read the fictional rainbow name Lolita, now added to the other one? Rosina Pepita may suggest an XY chromosome (a system discovered in 1905): Rosina = Mary (X), Pepita = Joseph (Y). A prototype perhaps of new millennial 'sexting', this conjures the image of rose with seed, in turn coaxing a lewd parsing of 'The Queen had come' (following David Bradshaw's reading instincts for innuendo).[40] Rosina Lolita, contrarily doubling, compounds fictive, distaff Marian references, suggesting the XX chromosome. Rosina Pepita discloses Mary and Joseph, Rosina Lolita discloses Mary and Mary, a kind of increased thinking and writing back through self-replicating, parthenogenetic, Marian mother lines. The temporary change of typeface, whether due to printer's devil's error or authorial intervention, ironises further its syntactic context, the long sentence concerning certification of identity and property rights in the deed of marriage between Orlando (now suspended between man and woman: XY/XX) and Rosina Pepita (XY) or Rosina Lolita (XX).[41]

'The Queen had come' is a queer annunciation, then, heralding, contra Knox, (orgasmic) arrival of multiple queer queens. The book's shortest encapsulation of its own entire plot and movement, it inscribes a shift, or disruption, in universal sovereign identity or subjectivity from singular masculine to multiplicitous feminine. This novel's related self-conscious glancing instances of variant ancestral names, derailing past granite facts and pointing up its own rainbow status as a textually unstable, yet material, printed book, herald the coming of a queen inextricably linked to the coming of a poet, or at least of a printer's devil.

I dedicate this essay to the memory of Dr Jim Stewart (1952–2016), my esteemed colleague in Woolf studies and that rare and great talent indeed – scholar, poet and printer's devil.

Notes

1. Virginia Woolf, *Orlando: A Biography* (London: Hogarth Press, 1928), p. 21.
2. Henceforth in this chapter 'VSW'.
3. See Robert Sackville-West, *Inheritance: The Story of Knole and the Sackvilles* (London: Bloomsbury Publishing, 2010), pp. 7–8, 14.
4. 'come, v.', *OED Online*, available at <www.oed.com/view/Entry/36824> (accessed 19 May 2017).
5. Radclyffe Hall, *The Well of Loneliness* (New York: Sun Dial Press, 1928), p. 285.
6. Gertrude Stein, 'As a Wife has a Cow/ A Love Story', *transition*, 3 (June, 1927), pp. 10–14.
7. Virginia Woolf, *A Room of One's Own* [1929] (London: Hogarth Press, 1929), p. 109.

8. Nigel Nicolson, *A Portrait of a Marriage* (London: Weidenfeld, 1967), p. 107.
9. Bessie Smith, 'Keep It To Yourself' (Columbia Records, 1930).
10. On the British Museum's published catalogue list under the category 'Women. Characteristics', a list to which Woolf pointedly refers in *A Room of One's Own*, see Susan David Bernstein, *Roomscape: Women Writers in the British Museum from George Eliot to Virginia Woolf* (Edinburgh: Edinburgh University Press, 2013), p. 165. For Knox's Anti-Marianism, see Gabriel Torretta, 'Our Lady Reconsidered: John Knox and the Virgin Mary', *Scottish Journal of Theology*, 67.2 (May 2014), pp. 165–77.
11. Leslie Hankins, 'Orlando: "A Precipice Marked V": Between "A Miracle of Discretion" and "Lovemaking Unbelievable: Indiscretions Incredible"', in Eileen Barrett and Patricia Cramer (eds), *Virginia Woolf: Lesbian Readings* (New York: New York University Press, 1997), p. 181.
12. Ibid.
13. Before marriage Woolf's initials were AVS: Adeline Virginia Stephen.
14. James Wright, '"The Instruments of Darkness Tells Us Truths": Ritual Protection Marks and Witchcraft at Knole, Kent' (2015), available at <www.gresham.ac.uk/lecture/transcript/print/ritual-protection-marks-and-witchcraft-at-knole-kent> (accessed 4 May 2017).
15. 'queen, n.', *OED Online*, available at <www.oed.com/view/Entry/156212> (accessed 19 May 2017).
16. 'goose, v.', *OED Online*, available at <www.oed.com/view/Entry/80030> (accessed 19 May 2017).
17. See Leena Kore Schröder, 'Waxing into Words: Virginia Woolf and the Funeral Effigies at Westminster Abbey', *Virginia Woolf Miscellany*, 85 (2014), pp. 15–19.
18. Gillian Beer, *Alice in Space: The Sideways Victorian World of Lewis Carroll* (Chicago and London: University of Chicago Press, 2016), p. 49.
19. Vita Sackville-West, *Knole and the Sackvilles* (London: Heinemann, 1922), p. vii.
20. Ibid. p. 35.
21. Ibid. pp. 32, 35.
22. Ibid. p. 16
23. Ibid.
24. Ibid. pp. 16–17.
25. See also O 44, 103, 109, 156.
26. See Andrew Lang, *John Knox and the Reformation* (London: Longmans, 1905): 'The churching of women, they said, is both Pagan and Jewish', available at *Project Gutenberg*, <www.gutenberg.org/files/14016/14016-h/14016-h.htm> (accessed 23 May 2017).
27. Sackville-West, *Knole*, p. 17.
28. Ibid.
29. Jan Graffius, 'The Stuart Relics in the Stonyhurst Collections', *British Catholic History*, 31.2 (October 2012), pp. 147–69.
30. Ibid.
31. Ibid.
32. 'devil, n.', *OED Online*, available at <www.oed.com/view/Entry/51468> (accessed 19 May 2017).

33. Ibid.
34. *The Oxford Dictionary of National Biography Online*, available at <www.oxforddnb.com/view/article/3341> (accessed 8 May 2017).
35. Sackville-West, *Knole*, pp. 32, 35.
36. See Suzanne Raitt and Ian Blyth (eds), *Orlando: A Biography* (Cambridge: Cambridge University Press, forthcoming 2017).
37. Virginia Woolf, *To the Lighthouse* (London: Hogarth Press, 1927), p. 126.
38. I thank Stephen Barkway for pointing this out.
39. Virginia Woolf, *The Voyage Out* (London: Duckworth, 1915), p. 290.
40. David Bradshaw, 'Winking, Buzzing, Carpet-Beating: Reading *Jacob's Room*' (Southport: Virginia Woolf Society of Great Britain, 2003), p. 9.
41. 'It was nothing less, indeed, than a deed of marriage, drawn up, signed, and witnessed between his Lordship, Orlando, Knight of the Garter, etc., etc., etc., and Rosina Pepita, a dancer, father unknown, but reputed a gipsy, mother also unknown but reputed a seller of old iron in the market-place over against the Galata Bridge' (O 122).

Chapter 2

'Something intricate and many-chambered': Sexuality and the Embodied Sentence

Anna Frøsig

> Slowly there had opened within her something intricate and many-chambered, which one must take a torch to explore, in prose not verse; and she remembered how passionately she had studied that doctor at Norwich, Browne, whose book was at her hand there.[1]

Woolf wrote in her diary that *Orlando* taught her 'how to write a direct sentence' (D3 203). It was intended as 'an escapade' from her 'serious poetic experimental books whose form is always so closely considered' (D3 131): *Jacob's Room, Mrs Dalloway* and *To the Lighthouse* – works which openly explore the nature of consciousness and the problem of alterity while probing the boundaries of literary representation. Written around the same time as her polemic *A Room of One's Own*, the whimsical *Orlando* has been the object of studies of sexuality, gender, and gender politics, performativity and genre. Underlying and uniting these questions, however, is the novel's interrogation of what constitutes the sameness and difference of a gendered mind, and in many ways *Orlando* is both the embodiment of Woolf's sexual aesthetics and of her philosophy of mind.

With its 'satirical' spirit and 'wild' structure (D3 131), *Orlando* is a highly political work engaging questions of sexual identity, gender inequality, and personal freedom. As Pamela L. Caughie has argued, *Orlando*'s modernist narrative provides 'a different temporality of embodiment' to offer 'new configurations of gender and sexual identity'.[2] These reconfigurations take place at the level of language as well as that of plot, making *Orlando* an aesthetically challenging work on a par with Woolf's other, more formally experimental novels, despite its ostensibly 'plain' style, written 'so that people will understand every word' (D3 162). The novel's play with metaphor and synecdoche in particular destabilises the boundaries between identity and otherness, body and mind, and questions both the ontological and ethical adequacy of simple gender binaries. Patricia Waugh has shown how Woolf's literary aesthetic sought to overcome Cartesian dualism by 'banishing the soul' as a 'closed individuality', favouring instead an 'extended or distributed idea of mind'.[3] This refusal to accept binary oppositions follows from a deeper concern with the relationship between mind and body in *Orlando* – a relationship which, I propose, is at the heart of its textual exploration of gender, sexuality and sexual identity.

My chosen sentence occurs as Orlando returns in the early days of the eighteenth century from Turkey 'in a highly ambiguous condition, uncertain whether she was alive or dead, man or woman, Duke or nonentity' (O 153). Taking up residence at her country house during the lawsuits that will determine her sex and her rights to titles and estates, she explores – for the first time as a woman – her ancestral home, and settles down to review, 'as if it were an avenue of great edifices, the progress of her own self along her own past' (O 159). As she thinks back to her early sexual experiences with the Russian princess, the depression that followed, and the affair with Nick Greene, she sees how 'something' within her being began to unfold: 'a spirit capable of resistance' (O 160). With its spatial imagery of interior 'chambers' and hints to the unknown 'something' maturing into a state of receptivity, the sentence metaphorically presents, and enters, the vulva, suggesting that the female sexuality must be known through its *form*: both in its somatic physicality and in its literary form 'in prose not verse' (ibid.). As the sentence continues with Orlando's passion for reading and the reference to prose writer Thomas Browne,[4] literary tradition is at once suggested as the 'torch' by which subjectivity can be illuminated, and questioned on its ability to capture 'something' essentially female: while Orlando's youthful admiration for great men of letters has shaped her hitherto male identity, the absence of a strong female literary tradition to guide her becomes evident upon her change of sex. This absence, however, also becomes an opportunity to explore the unknown and to create something from it – to write forth the female sexual body as a subject through a reshaping of language. With Browne's book now 'at her hand', Orlando's command of his text signals at once women's appropriation of established literary genres and the autonomous agency of the female body, at liberty as she is to take up or put down what male-centred tradition has to offer her.

In *A Room of One's Own*, Woolf observes that as late as the nineteenth century, the female writer found 'no common sentence ready for her use',[5] and no formal structure that could adequately express the female sexuality. With 'sentences built [. . .] into arcades or domes' and a literary tradition steeped in 'the weight, the pace, the stride of a man's mind', form and genre were gendered expressions of their time (*AROO*

89, 88). If, as Woolf argues, 'the book has somehow to be adapted to the body' to obtain the 'freedom and fullness of expression' which makes it art, then sentence and genre had to be rewritten in a female voice. For the female writer 'the novel alone was young enough to be soft in her hands' (*AROO* 89–90); it was a genre that could be moulded to the body by the body through the hand's power to hold and to express – both metaphorically and literally, as the text would be written by hand. For Woolf, then, the body offers a structuring principle for both gender identity and aesthetics, and freedom of (sexual) movement becomes central to intellectual liberation: 'No doubt we shall find [the female writer] knocking [the novel] into shape for herself when she has the free use of her limbs; and providing some new vehicle, not necessarily in verse, for the poetry in her' (*AROO* 90). To equate bodily movement with the form of the sentence becomes a way to read metaphor not only as image but as an embodiment in shape and rhythm, giving concrete physical form to poetic expression. With its expansive movement across the boundaries of lines and pages, prose offers the unbroken continuity needed to express an embodied mind, allowing with its subtle and sometimes mid-sentence shifts in grammatical subject and focalisation the simultaneous representation of the body as both subject and object. The slow pacing of the sentence I have chosen provides in the mounting pulse of an unexpected sexual experience a formal template for the illumination of female subjectivity: as the sentence unfolds in progressively shorter clauses, it halts its breath as it comes up against the semi-colon which marks the end of the exploration, and finally lengthens again in release.

The image of the torch reappears in *A Room of One's Own* in a discussion of how to render female same-sex relationships: if the writer 'knows how to express it she will light a torch in that vast chamber where nobody has yet been' (*AROO* 98). But the phrasing is ambiguous. Will the right expression illuminate hidden depths in the narrative, or will its suggestiveness ignite a physical burning in places the reader has not yet discovered in herself? The sentence in *Orlando* carries a similar double meaning, raising questions about knowing oneself and knowing another, for who is it that must explore – Orlando herself, the narrator, or the reader? With its suggestion of sexuality as form, the imperative of this sentence seems to propose something very physical: to come to know the self, whether one's own or somebody else's, it is the body that must be explored.

I see a clear convergence here with the French philosopher Maurice Merleau-Ponty's claim that the body is 'a provisional sketch of my total being'.[6] Perception, for Merleau-Ponty, is 'the archetype of the originating encounter, imitated and renewed in the encounter with the past, the imaginary, the idea',[7] providing a structure for all the ways we can possibly engage with the world – physically, emotionally and intellectually. The perceptual encounter, which entails the meeting between a body and an object of perception, is in its essence relational, and the fact that we can also take ourselves as objects of perception places the body in a double role as both subject and object, making the relationship between subjectivity and objectivity permeable and potentially reversible. As Louise Westling points out, Woolf and Merleau-Ponty were 'responding from within the same modernist intellectual milieu [. . .] to the same developments in physics, and the same twentieth-century impulse to overthrow or move beyond the Cartesian separation of subject and object'.[8] The affinity between Woolf's and Merleau-Ponty's intellectual projects lies in their attempts to formulate how the body is situated in space and time, and Woolf explores aesthetically what Merleau-Ponty calls the 'chiasm' or 'intertwining' between flesh and world.[9] As Waugh has noted, Woolf experimented with a literary representation of consciousness as organised by and embedded in 'the rhythms of places, spaces and bodies',[10] and metaphors for the body pervade *Orlando*. The image of the vulva in the description of the natural world's 'clefts' and 'folds' (O 224) suggests how bodily being is extended in the perception of the natural world.

This notion of the world as living flesh gives rise to Woolf's metaphoric play with sexualising space in displacing descriptions of sexual pleasure from the body to the surrounding space. According to Laura Doyle, whose 1995 essay on *To the Lighthouse* made a strong case for reading Woolf alongside the phenomenology of Merleau-Ponty, 'Woolf feminizes the "intercorporeality" of being and sexualizes the intercourse of body and world', thereby corporealising 'the spaces rendered empty by patriarchal culture and thought'.[11] The same is true of *Orlando*, where the oak tree on Orlando's estate stands as an openly phallic presence complementing the female imagery of the mind as a fertile 'pool' of 'darkness where things shape themselves' (O 294), reminding us that Orlando's attachment to the physical is neither purely female nor male: 'The tree had grown bigger, sturdier, and more knotted since she had known it [. . .] She liked to attach herself to something hard' (O 291). The autoerotic impulse to explore the boundaries of one's bodily being through an intimacy with the natural world hints at a primary perceptual structure in sexual identity, which holds both for Orlando the woman and Orlando the boy.

While the sexual body becomes the structuring principle for Orlando's perception of the world, the changing form of the body invites an intimate identification with that which is not the self, thus driving a metaphorical play in which the boundaries between the body, the mind, and their external situation become permeable. As Woolf argues in *A Room of One's Own*, 'the androgynous mind is resonant and porous,' transmitting 'emotion without impediment' (*AROO* 114), and perhaps it is this porosity which gives Orlando's metaphorical intercourse with the world its suggestive power. As a boy, Orlando

> loved [...] to feel the earth's spine beneath him; for such he took the hard root of the oak tree to be [...] it was anything indeed, so long as it was hard, for he felt the need of something which he could attach his floating heart to; the heart that tugged at his side; the heart that seemed filled with spiced and amorous gales every evening about this time when he walked out. To the oak tree he tied it and as he lay there, gradually the flutter in and about him stilled itself [...] as if all the fertility and amorous activity of a summer's evening were woven web-like about his body. (*O* 20–1)

The imagery of motion and sensual receptivity suggests the dynamics of orgasm, which provides aesthetic possibilities for shaping the sentence to sexual experience as the 'flutter' of the shorter and more rhythmically abrupt clauses come to rest along with the textual rhythm in the heaviness of the body. Orlando's material situation acquires a meaning structured by sensation; the sexed body not only marks identity, but creates it through the structure of erotic perception.

A parallel can be drawn here to Merleau-Ponty, for whom sexuality is 'a form of original intentionality' which expresses the subject's 'manner of being towards the world'.[12] Analogically, when Woolf argues that the female sentence must be adapted to the body, she also makes the form of her own sentences express the gendered existence of her subject. In writing *Orlando*, she portrays a self 'in process of fabrication' (*O* 160), but Orlando's ambiguously sexed body highlights the unstable relationship between gender identity and the life of the mind on the one hand, and identity and sex on the other: 'she seemed to vacillate; she was a man; she was a woman; she knew the secrets, shared the weaknesses of each' (*O* 145). Alternating with equal weight between the sexes, the sentence seems to vacillate as much as its subject, finding stability only in the female pronoun and the stable pulse of the rhythm. The female identity that Orlando gradually acquires after her change of sex is a formal construction which at its heart contains a sense of alterity, as Orlando both is and is not what her identity prescribes – a paradox foreshadowed in the precarious male identity governing the first half of the novel.

Throughout *Orlando*, this paradox is bound up with sexual desire. Nancy Cervetti has pointed out how 'the text marks seductiveness as independent of gender; it seems to be the very uncertainty that characters find so seductive'.[13] Such indeterminacy becomes a way to suspend the objectification of gender as a question of either identity or non-identity, thus breaking down the absolute boundary between self and other. Woolf's female gendering of the sentence is therefore less about erasing the male influence than about drafting a complementary alternative to a sentence already gendered male by default. In creating this 'marriage of opposites' within a single identity (*AROO* 121), Woolf creates in *Orlando* the androgynous space of indeterminacy between the 'purely' male or female mind where there is room for the 'suggestive power' (*AROO* 118) she finds lacking in masculine prose.

Through her formal play with embodied minds and gendered sentences, Woolf places sexuality at the centre of the problem of subjectivity and otherness. Witnessing the orgasmic arrival of Queen Elizabeth – 'The Queen had come' (*O* 21) – Orlando rushes in to greet her: 'He was ready. He was flushed. He was excited. But he was terribly late' (*O* 22). His bodily readiness and response are mirrored in the even, staccato sentences with their masculine, forceful beats. Short of breath, the sentences seem to lose their footing over a 'but' as their length spirals out of rhythm and out of control for the adolescent Orlando who reaches his destination 'only just in time to sink upon his knees and, hanging his head in confusion, to offer a bowl of rose water to the great Queen herself. Such was his shyness that he saw no more of her than her ringed hand in water; but it was enough' (*O* 23). For Merleau-Ponty, the hand constitutes the prime example of our being in the world because it represents how we are at once subjects and objects. With our hand we are able to touch and manipulate external objects and to receive sensations; this makes the hand a vehicle of subjectivity. But it can also be felt and manipulated by our other hand, which turns it into an object, and this is where self-consciousness arises – that is, consciousness of ourselves not only as experiential agents, but also as objects for the experience of others.[14]

The experience of otherness, then, is lived through the 'erotic structure' of perception since the subject belongs to 'the body of another through sexuality'.[15] The gestures of the sexed body express the 'autonomy and dependence' of the relationship between self and other,[16] giving subjective desire its bodily form. Read in this light, the Queens's hand signifies both subjectivity and otherness, and Orlando's experience of it conveys the formation of his sexual identity. Orlando's submission to the Queen would seem total, but as he evades her eye he gains something else: sheltered from the view of her as a whole, the seemingly dismembered hand presents itself to him synecdochically as an object, restoring to him a sense of subjectivity because he acts for a moment as the perceiver and not the perceived. The restoration of power to Orlando awakens his senses and imagination:

> a hand, he guessed, attached to an old body that smelt like a cupboard in which furs are kept in camphor [. . .] All this he felt as the great rings flashed in the water and then something pressed his hair – which, perhaps, accounts for his seeing nothing more likely to be of use to a historian. (O 23)

The narrator coyly reminds us that everything always means 'something else' (O 131), and that different images are often used interchangeably to mean 'exactly the same thing' (O 258). These observations capture the swift transitions between metaphor and metonymy in *Orlando*. As Makiko Minow-Pinkney has argued, 'no metaphor can condense into a single image [Orlando's] constant transgression of sexual boundaries; it can only be presented in metonymical displacement, a sliding of one form into another'.[17] In this sense, Woolf's use of synecdoche rather than metaphor in the depiction of Orlando's meeting with the Queen destabilises the sexual identity of each subject as the hand embodies no particular sex in itself, allowing the imagination to attach any body to it.

If the masturbatory implications of a hand in water are initially veiled, they are still 'enough' to be suggestive, and here the text slides between metonymic and metaphoric substitution. As Patricia Cramer writes, Woolf 'imagined erotic love in concert, not conflict, with the body', and her 'lesbian epiphanies' in particular are 'metaphoric and transformational, but recognisably embodied in the vulva'.[18] When Orlando's head is pressed downwards and beyond the limits of decency, the point of view is momentarily reversed via synecdoche: 'By the same showing, the Queen herself can have seen only a head,' her eyes 'wide open' (O 24). Orlando, it would appear, is giving head. The image of furs and ecstasy is repeated a few pages later, this time without disguise – and when the remarks on Elizabethan hygiene are taken into account, the metaphoric translation of pubic hair into old furs seems almost laughably plain:

> she pulled him down [. . .] and made him bury his face in that astonishing composition – she had not changed her dress for a month – which smelt for all the world, he thought [. . .] like some old cabinet at home where his mother's furs were stored. He rose, half suffocated from the embrace. 'This', she breathed, 'is my victory!' – even as a rocket roared up and dyed her cheeks scarlet. (O 26)

As this orgasmic passage indicates, Woolf's exploration of female sexuality through metaphor suspends the body between the seductive poles of objectification and intimacy; between the exterior perception which objectifies it and the subjective experience of exploring another through the body and the imagination.

Since the sexual body structures the encounter with the other, gendered existence becomes both a barrier and a necessity to the differentiation and autonomy of the self. The erotic structure of perception opens up the complexity and 'many-sidedness of the problem of other minds' which makes the philosopher Martha Nussbaum claim that Woolf 'tackles a venerable philosophical problem' in her works.[19] For Woolf, Nussbaum suggests, the problem of other minds is 'an ethical problem [...] produced by the motives and desires with which we approach beings who are both separate from us and vital to our projects'.[20] These questions are no less pervasive in *Orlando* than in *To the Lighthouse*, the 'serious poetic' work on which Nussbaum focuses. In *Orlando*, they are explicitly brought to bear on a sexual and gendered dynamic of autonomy and possession. The legal question of a woman's right to her own estate in particular shapes the novel's interrogation of our ethical right to define another's sexual identity – a problem which Woolf explores through the gendering of literary form.

As a metaphor for the body as at once subject and object, the male Orlando's ancestral house lies still in anticipation of the Queen's arrival like a great body of stone, marking a definite place in a textual negotiation of female space and autonomy. While the action is announced in short sentences, each governed by a single verb, the exterior walls of the house are syntactically connected to hint at the 'many-chambered' intricacies crying out be discovered:

> a trumpet sounded. Orlando leapt to his feet. The shrill sound came from the valley. It came from a dark spot down there; a spot compact and mapped out; a maze; a town, yet girt about with walls; it came from the heart of his own great house in the valley. (O 21)

Here, a paradox arises: what the young Orlando discovers is something unknown, intricate and external, and yet it is *his*. Described like the female body, the reproductive organs a 'maze' closed in by 'walls', the house suggests the female sexuality as a space which is foreign and object-like to Orlando, yet something which, like the house, will come to be his. The sentences depart from the staccato of masculine arousal as the youthful male 'leaps' into action at the sound of the coming female, revealing in uneven textual waves the clitoral spot which is 'compact' but rhythmically 'mapped out', connected by the semi-colons to the rest of the 'maze' that is the vulva. Orlando sees lights turned on 'in empty banqueting-halls made ready to receive guests who had not come' while other lights 'dipped and waved and sank and rose,' the house pulsating in a sexual rhythm towards the climax: 'The Queen had come' (O 21). With the spatial qualities of the vulva, the house, like the body, opens itself as an unknown but receptive site, into which those who rule or are invited can 'come'. Yet Orlando, who is not of age, is not at this point in a position to invite anybody inside, partly because he does not preside over his family's house, and partly because he does not have a woman's body. But with experience comes the change of sex as the youthful, masculine objectification of the woman's body is replaced by the mature woman's autoerotic experience of living in a female body.

Throughout the text, the struggle between an autonomous definition of sexuality and the objectifying pressures of alterity is embodied by the hand, which continues to suggest Orlando's own voice as well as a foreign subjectivity. To the female Orlando, the Victorian institution of marriage, in which 'the whole world was ringed with gold' (O 217), is oppressively limiting: 'there was something in this indissolubility of bodies which was repugnant to her' (O 219). The seamless coupling of husband and wife like two complementary halves fitting neatly together erases the distinction between self and other, and to feel the boundaries of one's own body, it seems, is necessary to the sustenance of identity. Yet the flourishing autonomy of the self also rests on an intimacy with that which it is not, but it becomes a matter of touch, not of possession, in a dance between solidity and sensation: 'High battlements of thought, habits that had seemed durable as stone, went down like shadows at the touch of another mind and left a naked sky and fresh stars twinkling in it' (O 160). With sexuality always present 'like an atmosphere',[21] there is for Orlando a striking consonance between sensation and mind as the body interferes with rationality, turning questions of matrimony into a matter of bodily autonomy: 'Her ruminations [. . .] were accompanied by such a tingling and twangling of the afflicted finger that she could scarcely keep her ideas in order' (O 219). But during her marriage ceremony something changes, for 'no one heard the word Obey spoken or saw, except as a golden flash, the ring pass from hand to hand' (O 236). As her own hand and the hand of the other collaborate and blur the logic of possession, sexual equality and independence become possible, subverting 'the legal and political construction'[22] of the gendered body. The liberation of Orlando's sexual identity is mirrored in her claim to material rights: when Orlando, now as a woman, enters 'into the undisturbed possession of her titles, her house, and her estate' (O 230), she also claims ownership of her sexuality and her body.[23]

This dynamic is performed in the novel through the act of literary creation: in writing about Orlando writing, Woolf explores how bodily experience is at once translated and transformed into art. Anticipating what Woolf would later describe as the 'cotton-wool' of daily life (MB 72), the narrator dismisses the biographer's task to record 'this mere wool-gathering; this thinking; this sitting in a chair day in, day out' of Orlando's writing practice (O 241). But as the textual exploration of the bodily process of writing reveals the 'territory' between 'the primacy of perception and expression', the 'space of creative production itself' is exposed, as Ariane Mildenberg has put it.[24] In *Orlando*, the body is shown to be as crucial to the process of making art as it is to the imaginative investigation of the object of art, and as it turns out, wool-gathering is a lot livelier than sitting in a chair suggests. As Melba Cuddy-Keane points out, 'the striking feature of Woolf's embodiment is the literal correlation between motion and emotion',[25] and the liberation of Orlando's mind from the confines of historically strict gender identity in the nineteenth century appears to be synonymous with the liberation of the body:

> what is more irritating than to [. . .] witness her sighs and gasps, her flushing, her palings, her eyes now bright as lamps, now haggard as dawns – what is more humiliating than to see all this dumb show of emotion and excitement gone through before our eyes when we know that what causes it – thought and imagination – are of no importance whatsoever? (O 241)

Writing about a woman writing, we can conclude, looks a lot like writing about sex. The irony in this dismissal of 'thought and imagination', of which the text itself is the product, reminds us that bodily experience and identity are equally shaped *by* the mind in a process of mutual constitution. Rachel Hollander has argued that for Woolf the 'imagination is central to the attempt to know another person',[26] but it is not only knowledge of the other which rests on an imaginative intimacy; so does knowledge of the self. When Orlando eventually comes to write and think freely, the words come to her like an exploration of the body through 'the free use of her limbs' (*AROO* 90):

> she plunged her pen neck deep in the ink. To her enormous surprise, there was no explosion. She drew the nib out. It was wet, but not dripping. She wrote. The words were a little long in coming, but come they did. (O 238)

With the 'coming' of words, the prose seems to finally have caught up with the slow opening of the chambers within Orlando, the masturbatory language of 'plunge' and 'wet' unmistakeably female – there is no explosive ejaculation but a slower, steadier form of release, mirrored in the uneven but rhythmic expansion and contraction of the sentences' length. The lines she has penned are blatantly suggestive of the vulva: 'the snaky flower, / Scarfed in dull purple' is where her explorations in the 'springing grass' of body hair have led her (O 238).

Ultimately, breaking her ankle and becoming engaged to the equally androgynous Shelmerdine on the moor has both secured Orlando's property and led her to rediscover her writing voice and her female sexuality: 'For it would seem – her case proved it – that we write, not with the fingers, but with the whole person' (O 219). Likewise, the potential for freedom of gender identity arises in the flow of Woolf's prose, where the formal possibilities for continuity and rupture between the sexes and the sentences are endless, with rhythmic oscillations between hard thrusts and slow openings embodying a restless indeterminacy. The prose explorations of *Orlando* reveal a body which contains its own alterity, loosening the boundaries between self and other; for is being explored by another not to feel oneself, and is the exploration of oneself not to feel one's otherness?

Notes

1. Virginia Woolf, *Orlando: A Biography* (London: Hogarth Press, 1928), pp. 159–60.
2. Pamela L. Caughie, 'The Temporality of Modernist Life Writing in the Era of Transsexualism: Virginia Woolf's *Orlando* and Einar Wegener's *Man into Woman*', MFS Modern Fiction Studies, 59.3 (2013), pp. 519–20.
3. Patricia Waugh, '"Did I Not Banish the Soul?" Thinking Otherwise, Woolf-Wise', in Derek Ryan and Stella Bolaki (eds), *Contradictory Woolf: Selected Papers from the Twenty-First Annual International Conference on Virginia Woolf* (Glasgow: Clemson University Digital Press, 2011), p. 23.
4. See Benjamin D. Hagen's chapter in this volume on Woolf's engagement with the work of Thomas Browne (pp. 175–85).
5. Virginia Woolf, *A Room of One's Own* [1929] (London: Penguin, 2004), p. 88.
6. Maurice Merleau-Ponty, *Phenomenology of Perception*, trans. Colin Smith (London: Routledge, 2002), p. 231.
7. Maurice Merleau-Ponty, *The Visible and the Invisible*, trans. Alphonso Lingis (Evanston: Northwestern University Press, 1969), p. 158.
8. Louise Westling, 'Virginia Woolf and the Flesh of the World', *New Literary History*, 30.4 (1999), p. 856.
9. Merleau-Ponty, *The Visible*, p. 131.
10. Waugh, 'Thinking Otherwise', p. 30.
11. Laura Doyle, '"These Emotions of the Body": Intercorporeal Narrative in *To the Lighthouse*', *Twentieth Century Literature*, 40.1 (1994), pp. 54, 43.
12. Merleau-Ponty, *Phenomenology*, pp. 182–3.
13. Nancy Cervetti, 'In the Breeches, Petticoats, and Pleasures of Orlando', *Journal of Modern Literature*, 20.2 (1996), p. 168.
14. Merleau-Ponty, *The Visible*, p. 133.
15. Merleau-Ponty, *Phenomenology*, pp. 181, 185.
16. Ibid. pp. 180, 194.

17. Makiko Minow-Pinkney, *Virginia Woolf and the Problem of the Subject* (Edinburgh: Edinburgh University Press, 1987), p. 131.
18. Patricia Morgne Cramer, 'Woolf and Theories of Sexuality', in Bryony Randall and Jane Goldman (eds), *Virginia Woolf in Context* (Cambridge: Cambridge University Press, 2012), p. 135.
19. Martha C. Nussbaum, 'The Window: Knowledge of Other Minds in Virginia Woolf's "To the Lighthouse"', *New Literary History*, 26.4 (1995), pp. 733, 732.
20. Ibid. 732.
21. Merleau-Ponty, *Phenomenology*, p. 195.
22. Cervetti, 'In the Breeches', p. 172.
23. For an account of the correlation between Woolf's subversion of primogeniture and an assertive female sexuality, see Elsa Högberg's chapter in this volume (pp. 44–55).
24. Ariane Mildenberg, 'Openings: Epoché as Aesthetic Tool in Modernist Texts', in A. Mildenberg and Carole Bourne-Taylor (eds), *Phenomenology, Modernism and Beyond* (Oxford: Peter Lang, 2010), p. 51.
25. Melba Cuddy-Keane, 'Movement, Space, and Embodied Cognition', in Allison Pease (ed.), *The Cambridge Companion to To the Lighthouse* (Cambridge: Cambridge University Press, 2015), p. 62.
26. Rachel Hollander, 'Novel Ethics: Alterity and Form in "Jacob's Room"', *Twentieth Century Literature*, 53.1 (2007), p. 43.

Chapter 3

Woolf, De Quincey and the Legacy of 'Impassioned Prose'

Elsa Högberg

> He saw her, and heard her coming to him with the crocus and the jay's feather in her breast, and cried 'Orlando', which meant (and it must be remembered that when bright colours like blue and yellow mix themselves in our eyes, some of it rubs off on our thoughts) first the bowing and swaying of bracken as if something were breaking through; which proved to be a ship in full sail, heaving and tossing a little dreamily, rather as if she had a whole year of summer days to make her voyage in; and so the ship bears down, heaving this way, heaving that way, nobly, indolently, and rides over the crest of this wave and sinks into the hollow of that one, and so, suddenly stands over you (who are in a little cockle shell of a boat, looking up at her) with all her sails quivering, and then, behold, they drop all of a heap on deck – as Orlando dropped now into the grass beside him.[1]

Part of the beauty of this sentence is its sensually playful tribute to Vita Sackville-West, and its resonance with Woolf's private image of her friend and lover: 'Vita very free & easy, always giving me great pleasure to watch, & recalling some image of a ship breasting a sea, nobly, magnificently, with all sails spread, & the gold sunlight on them' (D3 146). In another diary entry, the image of Sackville-West as 'some tall sailing ship' triggers a vision of her ancestral home Knole (D3 125), an association that also inspires the long, lyrical sentence upon which my chapter focuses. This sentence appears a few pages after Orlando's reception of a document containing multiple legal verdicts, or sentences:

> 'The lawsuits are settled [. . .] Turkish marriage annulled [. . .] Children pronounced illegitimate [. . .] Sex? Ah! What about sex? My sex', she read out with some solemnity, 'is pronounced indisputably, and beyond the shadow of a doubt [. . .] female' [. . .] Whereupon she appended her own signature beneath Lord Palmerston's and entered from that moment into the undisturbed possession of her titles, her house, and her estate. (O 176–7)

Insofar as Woolf wrote *Orlando* as a 'new biography' of Sackville-West – an artful manipulation of 'granite-like' fact and 'rainbow-like' personality and fiction 'into one seamless whole'[2] – the combination of legal sentences in this passage would have been a near-impossibility in the history of the Sackville-Wests, not only in the mid-nineteenth century (Lord Palmerston was prime minister 1855–65), but as late as 1928, when Vita, at her father's death, was barred from inheriting Knole because of her sex. The echo of the 1910 family lawsuit, after which her father came into 'undisturbed possession' of the house and peerage,[3] is woven together with the grand fiction of the female Orlando's inclusion in a centuries-long tradition of primogeniture.[4]

How, then, does the settling of the novel's lawsuits relate to the poetic sentence with which we began? This sentence forms the climax of a passage at the end of Chapter V, which opens with Orlando escaping the celebration of her triumph to spend time with Shelmerdine in the woods:

> So fine was the weather that the trees stretched their branches motionless above them, and if a leaf fell, it fell, spotted red and gold, so slowly that one could watch it for half an hour fluttering and falling till it came to rest at last, on Orlando's foot. (O 177)

The image of the leaf that, falling, suspends and expands time introduces a poetic sequence that has a similar effect on the more prosaic narrative surrounding it. Two events frame this sequence: Orlando's reception of the legal document, and her marriage to Shelmerdine. I propose that a close focus on the climactic sentence beginning 'He saw her, and heard her coming to him' opens up new perspectives on the lyricism of *Orlando*, which I see as vital in Woolf's creation of this text as a loving gift to Sackville-West. On a biographical level, this sentence and the poetic, dream-like narrative in which it figures suspend the 'granite-like' legal framework of primogeniture. Aesthetically, Woolf's sentence unravels the time of the legal sentence and generates its own temporality: the unbounded time of the gift, female sexual pleasure, and gender equality.[5] Central to this lyrical experiment, I suggest, is her engagement with romantic writer Thomas De Quincey and, more specifically, his 'Dream-Fugue' – the third section of 'The English Mail-Coach' (1849).

But what could De Quincey's angst-ridden opium dreams have to do with Woolf's erotically charged meeting of lovers? The passage surrounding this sentence resonates with clear echoes of 'Dream-Fugue':[6] she closely mimics its maritime imagery, its sudden shifts in tone, mood and pacing, as well as its striking musical and visual qualities. Woolf read De Quincey with ambivalent fascination; her essays praise his groundbreaking poetic prose experiments, his reinvention of autobiography and the formally rigorous musicality of his sentences, but she was also alienated by his masculine verbosity and abstraction.[7] In *Orlando*'s

Preface, De Quincey is acknowledged as one of the 'friends' helping her write the book,[8] and in *A Room of One's Own*, he figures again, this time in a list of exclusively male authors who 'never helped a woman yet, though she may have learnt a few tricks of them and adapted them to her use'. In his double role as inspirational friend and guardian of the 'man's sentence',[9] De Quincey triggers a broader tension in Woolf's assessment and fictional treatment of past male writers. The sentence emerges repeatedly in Woolf's polemic as property to be handed down an exclusionary male line of descent, and poetic prose is declared the medium by which the woman writer must claim and reshape the literary sentence (*AROO* 99–101).

Woolf's gender politics of the sentence explains at least partly why De Quincey's legacy had such impact on her work from *Mrs Dalloway* to *The Waves*. While critics have begun to explore De Quincey's influence on Woolf's 'serious poetic experimental books' (*D3* 131),[10] I would like to consider her appropriation of his sentence style in *Orlando* as an act of mimicry with aesthetic as well as political consequences. If we begin to consider this pleasurable 'writer's holiday' (*D3* 177) as central to her poetic prose experiments of the period 1922–31, we can detect a playful, yet rigorously crafted lyricism that operates on the level of the sentence as a form of not quite legitimate gift: Woolf takes aesthetic property that is not fully hers – the male sentences of De Quincey and others – and transforms it in order to make a symbolic gift for her female lover of material property that she cannot inherit. In recasting the legacy of the literary sentence in terms of the gift, *Orlando* suspends and revises the logic of property and inheritance.[11]

Among Woolf's novels, *Orlando* ventures a particularly daring exploration of the poetic prose sentence as an intervention into the premises of heritage. Her lyrical sentence figuring Orlando and Shelmerdine's encounter forms the textual climax of a passage written in De Quinceyan 'impassioned prose' – his term for writing capable of conveying heightened emotional states in which 'time is miraculously prolonged and space miraculously expanded'.[12] In Woolf's words, such prose combines 'the rapid passage of events and actions' and 'the slow opening up of single and solemn moments of concentrated emotion'.[13] She thus alternates her pacing of this episode in a manner that strongly recalls 'Dream-Fugue', with its sudden transitions from suspense and stillness to agitated, rapid motion. Opening with the image of the slowly falling leaf, a lyrical sequence suspends the fast-paced narration of the lawsuit celebrations. Then, immediately after the sentence where Orlando approaches Shelmerdine 'as if she had a whole year of summer days', the pacing shifts abruptly as 'a leaf which had started to fall slowly enough from a tree-top whipped briskly across Orlando's foot' (*O* 180). The south-western wind makes the couple run to the chapel on Orlando's estate, where a tumultuous wedding scene takes place before Shelmerdine rides off to put out to sea. In De Quincey's dream narratives, Woolf argues, some of the autonomy of poetry is conferred onto the prose work so that 'we can draw all our pleasure from the words themselves',[14] and this dynamic is central to her own lyrical episode at the end of Chapter V, which prolongs indefinitely the sentencing of Orlando – and Sackville-West – as the legitimate owners of their estate.

The whole sequence challenges a persistent notion of *Orlando* as a book written 'half in a mock style very clear & plain' (*D3* 162) by demonstrating a De Quinceyan 'gift of composition'; his legacy of impassioned prose entails the composition of dream-like visual 'scenes' as well as a musical aesthetic virtuosity.[15] Woolf's brief scenes emulate De Quincey's, where 'the emotion is [...] brought slowly by repeated images before us until it stays, in all its complexity, complete'.[16] Her technique here is to evoke affects and moods through vivid images associated with the names of Orlando and her beloved – 'Mar', 'Bonthrop', 'Shelmerdine' – a form of repetition through variation resembling musical themes. The result is a De Quinceyan, impersonal lyricism that is different from the writer's effusion of private emotion;[17] while Woolf's passion for Sackville-West emerges clearly in her depiction of Orlando and Shelmerdine's intimacy, this passage is crafted so as to convey the autonomous pleasure created by 'the words themselves'. And this pleasure is particularly intense – and intensely political – in her appropriation of De Quincey's measured sentences, to which she frequently returns in 'De Quincey's Autobiography': 'Nobody tunes the sound and modulates the cadence of a sentence more carefully and more exquisitely' (*E5* 455).

In a polyphonic prelude to the climactic sentence quoted in epigraph to this chapter, a jay shrieks 'Shelmerdine', whereupon Orlando mimics the jay, calling 'Shelmerdine' in turn. Then, in the sentence where Shelmerdine answers her call, an intense emotional state is not only evoked; it is staged by the narrator in painstaking parentheses, framing the scene in a provocatively teasing way. Through this cheeky staging act, which asserts the biographer's illicit presence at this dyadic encounter, Woolf overtly claims her position as Sackville-West's biographer and lover – and rival of her many erotic relations with other women.[18] The direct address by a meddling third person has a distancing effect, but it also induces us to feel a mounting excitement, which reaches its full intensity when we are made to see with Shelmerdine. The generic 'you' marks the erotic climax of the sentence: 'and so, suddenly stands over you (who are in a little cockle shell of a boat, looking up at her) with all her sails quivering'. It is not only the stumbling syntax that creates a breathless, orgasmic suspense here, following the steady sexual rhythm suggested by the ship 'breaking through', riding and 'heaving':[19] so too does the image of the overpowering ship with quivering sails standing dangerously close to the frail boat, and, finally, the uncertainty about this 'you', which seems to include me (Woolf's reader) along with Shelmerdine, Orlando's biographer, Sackville-West's husband Harold Nicolson (the model for Shelmerdine), her female lovers, and Woolf herself. In casting this sentence as a De Quinceyan dream vision, Woolf cannily uses striking visual images (the bright colours of the crocus and jay's feather; the movement of the ship), a vague, subjunctive mode ('which meant'; 'as if') and a generic pronoun ('you') to simultaneously downplay and highlight its force as an erotic scene. Not only is this scene structured rhythmically as a sexual act, but the sentence also urges us to imagine sexual orientations and encounters that exceed its heterosexual surface.[20]

The corresponding sentence in De Quincey's 'Dream-Fugue' opens part I:

> Lo, it is summer – almighty summer! The everlasting gates of life and summer are thrown open wide; and on the ocean, tranquil and verdant as a savannah, the unknown lady from the dreadful vision and I myself are floating – she upon a fairy pinnace, and I upon an English three-decker.[21]

The preceding section is based on the author's experience of nearly colliding with a young couple as a passenger on a mail coach, and his vision of a woman near death haunts 'Dream-Fugue' in recurring scenes. In complete contrast to Woolf's prelude to her sentence, De Quincey's prelude to part I addresses the subtitle of his literary fugue ('Founded on the Preceding Theme of Sudden Death').[22] 'Dream-Fugue' explores an affective spectrum far removed from that of *Orlando*: moments of stillness generally portend anguish and despair. The scene where De Quincey's war ship meets a lady on a small, light vessel reverberates with 'sweet girlish laughter'[23] – nothing like the lovers' animalistic cry in *Orlando*. Then suddenly, as the ship moves closer, all is quiet and the pinnace is dismantled. The narrator is seized by a gripping fear: has he once again put the young woman in fatal danger through the unstoppable course of his vehicle? After this hushed moment follows an increasingly turbulent prose in part II, where the same woman is seen on a frigate that barely avoids a collision with the ship; here De Quincey builds up 'the roll of the long sentence that sweeps its coils in and out, that piles its summit higher and higher':[24]

There she stood, with hair dishevelled, one hand clutched amongst the tackling – rising, sinking, fluttering, trembling, praying; there for leagues I saw her as she stood, raising at intervals one hand to heaven, amidst the fiery crests of the pursuing waves and the raving of the storm; until at last, upon a sound from afar of malicious laughter and mockery, all was hidden for ever in driving showers; and afterwards, but when I know not, nor how,[25]

This pattern is repeated in part IV: a moment of eerie suspense is followed by the onward movement of a powerful vehicle, which threatens to collide with a girl in a frail carriage. In part III, she is on the run from some danger, and at the narrator's cry of warning, she runs even faster, only to drown in quicksands ahead. In each part, the moment near death forms the textual climax in long, frantically paced sentences like the one cited above.

Woolf's De Quinceyan episode clearly parodies De Quincey's verbosity and obsession with death and anxiety; in the long sentence that outlines in comic detail every gloomy connotation of the name 'Bonthrop', for instance, Orlando is teased for her melancholy tendency, and the transition to the following paragraph – 'After some hours of death, suddenly a jay shrieked "Shelmerdine"' – is playfully vibrant.[26] As Woolf transforms the long De Quinceyan sentence, she reverses the gender politics of 'Dream-Fugue'. While his sentences perform the fugal movement of flight and pursuit, building swift affective transitions through paragraphs 'flowing and following like the waves of the sea',[27] she uses the rhythm of waves to build up a gradual sensual arousal towards an orgasmic climax within a single sentence. This climax is distinctly female: the quivering sails evoke an intense, steady pleasure in a visual correlation with female orgasm. And does the ambiguous 'which meant' refer, innocently, to the name 'Orlando', or to the phrase 'He saw her, and heard her coming'? De Quincey's recurring present participles ('rising, sinking, fluttering, trembling, praying') are syntactically transformed into Orlando's confident movement: 'and rides over the crest of this wave and sinks into the hollow of that one' – words that, when read aloud, enact Orlando's movement towards, or with, Shelmerdine. Woolf does nothing less than hijack De Quincey's three-decker and its male crew, making the female Orlando embody the majestic ship. She also appropriates De Quincey's textual imitation of waves – traditionally 'the very metaphor of pursuit'[28] – to create a scene where Orlando determines the pace and rhythm of the encounter with Shelmerdine, a feminine man in a cockle-boat (a small boat towed behind a larger vessel). Shelmerdine's preoccupation with snail shells also echoes part IV of 'Dream-Fugue', in which the woman, now in the shape of a female child, is playing with 'shells and tropic flowers' as a carriage thunders closer.[29]

It may well be the overt allusion to De Quincey's 'Dream-Fugue' with its familiar maritime motif of female flight and male pursuit that enabled Woolf to get away with her erotically charged sentence and its radical gender politics.[30] A similar theme appears throughout *Orlando* in recurring allusions to the Apollo and Daphne story, as told in Ovid's *Metamorphoses*.[31] Turning this fugal motif on its head, Woolf makes Orlando embody not only the war ship, but also the two other powerful vehicles figuring in 'The English Mail-Coach': the mail coach itself, and the 'triumphal car' on which the narrator rides in part IV, crowned with laurel, both of which carry the news of Napoleon's defeat at Waterloo. In its reversal of the gender roles dictating lyrical works like 'Dream-Fugue', where male triumph requires the pursual of a female figure and her subsequent metamorphosis (into a child – or laurel tree), Woolf's sentence crowns Orlando's victory as she gains possession of her titles and estate. And, in its De Quinceyan temporal expansion – achieved through the many commas, semi-colons and parentheses that stretch its syntactic boundaries – the sentence presents this triumph as an eternal, symbolic gift to Sackville-West. It is, then, through the shape of her sentence that Woolf disrupts an exclusively male line of inheritance; her architectural metaphor for poetic form in *A Room of One's Own* – 'a book is not made of sentences laid end to end, but of sentences built [. . .] into arcades or domes' (*AROO* 100) – also informs her reading, and appropriation, of De Quincey's unsettling temporality: 'Then suddenly the smooth narrative parts asunder, arch opens beyond arch [. . .] and time stands still'.[32]

A similar effect is achieved in the turbulent wedding scene closing the chapter, which is harmonised on the level of the sentence with both the climactic love scene and the triumphal ending of 'Dream-Fugue'. As we have seen, her lyrical episode incorporates the poetic qualities she ascribes to De Quincey's writing: after 'the roll of the long sentence', she notes in 'De Quincey's Autobiography', 'followed a discipline exacted, most drastically, by the fineness of his own ear – the weighing of cadences, the consideration of pauses; the effect of repetitions and consonances and assonances' (*E5* 454). Her own careful use of sound, rhythm, repetition and recurring motifs makes her lyrical sequence at the end of Chapter V recognisably De Quinceyan, although, unlike De Quincey, she does not emulate the strict formal structure of the musical fugue.[33] However, the successive, imitative cries 'Shelmerdine', 'Shelmerdine', 'Orlando', and finally 'Marmaduke Bonthrop Shelmerdine!' followed by 'Orlando!', give this sequence a polyphonic, and arguably contrapuntal, frame. More generally, imitation – a key fugal feature – is a vital strategy in Woolf's appropriation of De Quincey and other canonical writers in *Orlando*.

The wedding scene in particular is imitational, polyphonic as well as carefully measured. It imitates part IV and V of 'Dream-Fugue', and particularly the frantic race of De Quincey's carriage through an immense cathedral and necropolis. In her first essay on De Quincey, Woolf associates his style with 'an organ booming down the vast and intricate spaces of a cathedral': 'the sounds which he delights in most are those that suggest vast dimly lighted places'.[34] This is an apt description of the scene she would write decades later in *Orlando*, where, as in De Quincey's corresponding episode, the sound of organs reverberates with varying strength, and lights flicker and kindle restlessly. The uproar over which the minister's voice can barely be heard echoes the soundscape of De Quincey's cathedral – the horses' thundering hooves, the organ 'muttering' then breaking into 'heart-shattering music', the choristers' endless chanting, and the Dying Trumpeter's blast:[35] 'All was movement and confusion' (O 181). However, that short sentence is deliberately inserted in between two very long ones, the first depicting the chaotic ceremony, and the second Shelmerdine's departure. Paradoxically, then, the sense of tumult is created through Woolf's De Quinceyan 'care in the use of sound; the [. . .] variety of measure; the length of the sentence is varied and its weight shifted'.[36]

Indeed, Woolf's measuring of the wedding scene establishes a formal harmony with regard to the De Quinceyan section as a whole. For all its frantic pacing and urgency that build up like a musical crescendo, both in terms of sound and intensity, the final sentence of the chapter creates a poised, lyrical symmetry:

> And up they rose with the organ booming and the light playing and the rain pouring, and the Lady Orlando, with her ring on her finger, went out into the court in her thin dress and held the swinging stirrup, for the horse was bitted and bridled and the foam was still on his flank, for her husband to mount, which he did with one bound, and the horse leapt forward and Orlando, standing there, cried out Marmaduke Bonthrop Shelmerdine! and he answered her Orlando! and the words went dashing and circling like wild hawks together among the belfries and higher and higher, further and further, faster and faster they circled, till they crashed and fell in a shower of fragments to the ground; and she went in. (O 181)

In a poetic fashion suggestive of counterpoint as well as the harmony closing the musical fugue, this sentence plays over the subject of Shelmerdine's full 'wild, dark-plumed name' and its affective connotations, which initiated the sequence (O 174). It thereby brings together the themes of Shelmerdine's three names and three wild birds – the rook, the jay and the hawk, harmonising them through the polyphonic repetition of the lovers' call and response that triggered the earlier climactic sentence. This formal unity is reinforced through the De Quincey intertext. 'Dream-Fugue' ends with two equally long, yet carefully measured sentences that play over the themes of the young woman near death, the present participles, and the eternal recurrence of the dream visions; however, the emphasis of these sentences is on victory and deliverance. In making the end of her De Quinceyan sequence coincide with the celebratory ending of 'Dream-Fugue', Woolf turns her Gothic wedding scene into a playful celebration of Orlando's secure possession of her estate, which is sealed for herself and her descendants through her marriage.[37]

The end of the sentence closing Chapter V is also stylistically harmonised with the end of the orgasmic sentence. Building up towards a poetic 'rise', both end with a prosaic 'fall' in a wave-like movement such as Woolf ascribes to De Quincey's writing down to the level of individual sentences: 'we are worked upon as if by music [. . .] The rise and fall of the sentence immediately soothes us to a mood and removes us to a distance where the near fades and detail is extinguished'.[38] Woolf's two sentences literally end with a falling motion, followed by a prosaic closure: 'and then, behold, they drop all of a heap on deck – as Orlando dropped now into the grass beside him'; 'till they crashed and fell in a shower of fragments to the ground; and she went in'. The aesthetic pleasure created through this symmetry confirms the capacity of poetic prose, with its autonomous dream visions, to forcefully manipulate the inheritance structures regulating material as well as aesthetic property. Just as De Quincey's 'enemy, the hard fact, became cloud-like and supple under his hands',[39] the hard fact of women's disinheritance becomes deferred and symbolically undone under Woolf's treatment. As this reading illuminates, the pleasures and playfulness of *Orlando* should not lead us to isolate this novel from her other aesthetically challenging works of the 1920s. While she did set out to satirise poetic novel experiments, including her own 'lyrical vein' (*D3* 131), it was ultimately the playful, poetic qualities of her prose that made possible Woolf's writing of this book as a politically and sexually daring gift.

Notes

1. Virginia Woolf, *Orlando: A Biography* [1928] (London: Penguin, 1993), p. 180.
2. Virginia Woolf, 'The New Biography' (1927), *E4*, p. 473.
3. See Victoria Glendinning, *Vita: The Life of V. Sackville-West* (London: Weidenfeld and Nicolson, 1983), pp. 30–5.

4. Thomas Sackville (1536–1608) dictated that the estate he founded 'be handed from "heir male to heir male" in perpetuity', a principle that to this day has left women in the Sackville family disinherited (Robert Sackville-West, *Inheritance: The Story of Knole and the Sackvilles* (London: Bloomsbury Publishing, 2010), p. xix). However, this tradition was temporarily disrupted between 1815 and 1877, when Knole was inherited by women (Vita Sackville-West, *Knole and the Sackvilles* (London: Lindsay Drummond Limited, 1948), pp. 200–19).
5. See Kathryn Simpson's *Gifts, Markets and Economies of Desire in Virginia Woolf* (Basingstoke: Palgrave Macmillan, 2008) on Woolf's gift economies, which encode female sexuality and same-sex desire.
6. I am indebted to Sandra Gilbert for making this point in her notes to the Penguin edition of *Orlando* (O 258).
7. Woolf devoted three essays to De Quincey: 'The English Mail Coach' (1906), '"Impassioned Prose"' (1926), and 'De Quincey's Autobiography' (1932).
8. John Ferguson suggests that Woolf's bond with De Quincey was 'the most private and profound' among those listed in *Orlando*'s Preface ('A Sea Change: Thomas De Quincey and Mr. Carmichael in "To the Lighthouse"', *Journal of Modern Literature*, 14.1 (1987), p. 61).
9. Virginia Woolf, *A Room of One's Own and Three Guineas* [1929/1938] (Oxford: Oxford University Press, 2008), pp. 99–100.
10. Particular attention has been given to Woolf's De Quinceyan experiments with psychological fiction, dream states, the maritime imagery of oceans and waves, and the contraction and expansion of time (Ferguson, 'A Sea Change'; Harvena Richter, *Virginia Woolf: The Inward Voyage* (Princeton: Princeton University Press, 1970), pp. 16–17, 22–4, 54, 90–2, 156–62, 188–9). Richter goes against a tradition of omitting *Orlando* from accounts of Woolf's lyricism (for an example, see Ralph Freedman, *The Lyrical Novel: Studies in Hermann Hesse, André Gide, and Virginia Woolf* (Princeton: Princeton University Press, 1963)).
11. In thus appropriating what is not legitimately hers, Woolf could be said to pirate De Quincey's sentences in Caren Irr's sense of the term. Irr's *Pink Pirates: Contemporary American Writers and Copyright* (Iowa City: University of Iowa Press, 2010) explores a feminist tradition of women writers challenging a history of exclusionary intellectual property; '"woman" continues to signify a pirate's unstable relation to legitimate ownership' (p. 8). The inalienable possession of its female author, *Orlando* nonetheless makes 'a symbolic assault on private [cultural] property' (Ibid. p. 12) by manipulating canonical writers' sentences.
12. Woolf, '"Impassioned Prose"', *E4*, p. 367.
13. Woolf, 'De Quincey's Autobiography', *E5*, p. 457.
14. Ibid. p. 453.
15. See Woolf, '"Impassioned Prose"', pp. 363, 366; 'De Quincey's Autobiography', pp. 453–5.
16. Woolf, 'De Quincey's Autobiography', p. 453.
17. Cf. '[De Quincey's] most perfect passages are not lyrical but descriptive. They are not cries of anguish [. . .] they are descriptions of states of mind' ('"Impassioned Prose"', p. 367). See also Freedman on Woolf's poetic

prose: it 'begins with the self but leads to its *depersonalization*' (*The Lyrical Novel*, p. 188). Freedman's definition of lyric as 'the expression of feelings or themes in musical or pictorial patterns' (p. 1) informs my reading of Woolf's De Quinceyan experiments.
18. This sense of rivalry was one impulse behind *Orlando*; see especially Woolf's letter to Sackville-West from 9 October 1927 (*L3* 428–9).
19. Cf. 'heave, v.', *OED Online*: 'to cause to swell up or bulge out'; 'to utter (a groan, sigh, or sob; *rarely*, words) with effort'; 'to pant, gasp', available at <www.oed.com/view/Entry/85201> (accessed 2 July 2016).
20. Brenda S. Helt notes that Woolf's crocuses in *Mrs Dalloway* and *Orlando* symbolise female same-sex desire ('Passionate Debates on "Odious Subjects": Bisexuality and Woolf's Opposition to Theories of Androgyny and Sexual Identity', *Twentieth Century Literature*, 56.2 (Spring 2010), p. 163).
21. Thomas De Quincey, 'The English Mail-Coach', in *The Collected Writings of Thomas De Quincey*, ed. David Masson, vol. 13 (Edinburgh: Adam and Charles Black, 1890), p. 319.
22. Ibid. p. 318.
23. Ibid. p. 319.
24. Woolf, 'De Quincey's Autobigraphy', p. 454.
25. De Quincey, 'The English Mail-Coach', p. 321 (closing comma in original).
26. Woolf's long sentences and the chattering jay (genus: *Garrulus*) also parody De Quincey's wordiness – a recurrent theme in her essays. Her notes for 'The English Mail-Coach' include the words 'profoundly garrulous' (*E1* 365).
27. Woolf, '"Impassioned Prose"', pp. 366–7. See 'fugue, n.', *OED Online*: '< French *fugue*, < Italian *fuga* lit. 'flight' < Latin *fuga*, related to *fugĕre* to flee', available at <www.oed.com/view/Entry/75270> (accessed 2 July 2016). The noun is also related to the Latin *fugare* ('to put to flight'): 'In music the word denotes a composition in which three or more voices [...] enter imitatively one after the other, each "giving chase" to the preceding voice' (G. M. Tucker and Andrew V. Jones, 'fugue', in *The Oxford Companion to Music. Oxford Music Online*, available at <www.oxfordmusiconline.com/subscriber/article/opr/t114/e2723> (accessed 2 July 2016)).
28. Richter, *Inward Voyage*, p. 91. In 'Dream-Fugue', section II (p. 320), the woman is 'chased by angry sea-birds and by maddening billows'.
29. De Quincey, 'The English Mail-Coach', p. 324.
30. See Emma Sutton on the fugal dynamics of *Mrs Dalloway*: 'If music allows a flight from inflexible [...] conceptions of gender and sexuality, this is in part the result of its prominent part in homoerotic discourse from the nineteenth century: sexual fugues are among many flights from societal norms in *Mrs Dalloway*' (*Virginia Woolf and Classical Music: Politics, Aesthetics, Form* (Edinburgh: Edinburgh University Press, 2013), pp. 92–4, 101). It is compelling to read the De Quinceyan passage in *Orlando* as a form of 'sexual fugue'.
31. A tapestry at Orlando's estate featuring Apollo and Daphne moves in the breeze 'so that it looked as if the huntsmen were riding and Daphne flying' (*O* 76). See Sarah Annes Brown on *Orlando* in *The Metamorphosis of Ovid: From Chaucer to Ted Hughes* (London: Duckworth, 1999), pp. 201–15.

32. Woolf, 'De Quincey's Autobiography', p. 458.
33. For accounts of the fugal qualities of 'Dream-Fugue', see Calvin S. Brown, 'The Musical Structure of De Quincey's "Dream-Fugue"', *The Musical Quarterly*, 24.3 (1938), pp. 341–50; and Werner Wolf, *The Musicalization of Fiction: A Study in the Theory and History of Intermediality* (Amsterdam: Rodopi, 1999), pp. 114–23. See also Elicia Clements, 'Transforming Musical Sounds into Words: Narrative Method in Virginia Woolf's *The Waves*', *Narrative*, 13.2 (2005), pp. 160–81.
34. Woolf, 'The English Mail Coach', p. 367.
35. De Quincey, 'The English Mail-Coach', pp. 323–6.
36. Woolf, 'De Quincey's Autobiography', p. 454.
37. Unlike the lyrical sentence, however, the legal sentence enforces the order of primogeniture: Orlando's marriage only secures her descendants' inheritance if she has a son (O 176).
38. Woolf, 'De Quincey's Autobiography', p. 453. See Werner Wolf's account of 'Dream-Fugue' as 'a relatively isolated "first" in the [romantic-modernist] history of musicalized fiction': the history of 'the close relationship [. . .] between music, the emotions, the psyche and an a-mimetic conception of art' (*Musicalization*, pp. 123, 120).
39. Woolf, '"Impassioned Prose"', p. 365.

Chapter 4

Rhythms of Revision and Revisiting: Unpicking the Past in *Orlando*

Jane de Gay

> Grass, the power seemed to say, going back with a ruler such as governesses use to the beginning, is all right; the hanging cups of fritillaries – admirable; the snaky flower – a thought, strong from a lady's pen, perhaps, but Wordsworth, no doubt, sanctions it; but – girls?[1]

This sentence comes at a point of indecision and uncertainty for Orlando as a poet. Newly married to Shelmerdine and therefore suddenly finding respectability within nineteenth-century society, she seems to be freed to write. But then maybe she is not. She vacillates between daring to write and not daring; being forced to write, but refusing. When she writes, she does so hastily, prevaricating again as she re-reads her work, feels compelled to stop and then, in this sentence, is urged by the 'spirit of the age' to go back and reconsider what she has written. The oscillating rhythm of writing, re-reading and reviewing that shapes this sentence reflects the pattern of the wider episode. However, as this chapter will also contend, this rhythm characterises the structure of the book as a whole and shapes its treatment of literary history.

The sentence functions as a review of the foregoing lines, purportedly from Orlando's poem 'The Oak Tree', but actually a quotation from Vita Sackville-West's work *The Land* (1926):

> And then I came to a field where the springing grass
> Was dulled by the hanging cups of fritillaries,
> Sullen and foreign-looking, the snaky flower,
> Scarfed in dull purple, like Egyptian girls –

My chosen sentence works to reinterpret, erase and rewrite the quotation from *The Land*, through comments in the voice of the spirit of the Victorian age, or, more precisely, a ventriloquised voice projecting Orlando's beliefs about what her culture demands of her as a writer. As Orlando revisits the lines she has written, the sentence forces the reader to move backwards in the text and re-read the quotation too.

It is a selective re-reading, for only the end-word of each line is chosen for comment. The spirit finds 'grass' acceptable and admires 'fritillaries'. It hesitates at 'snaky flower', inadvertently drawing attention to its sexual overtones. The voice forgives Orlando for this image by accepting that the word 'snaky' is also used by Wordsworth, but questions the reference to 'girls'.

While the sentence creates a non-linear pattern of reading by encouraging a re-reading of the preceding quotation, the reader's eye also has to oscillate across the sentence itself, due to multiple disruptions in the syntax. The reader has to piece together the sense of the sentence by a process of re-reading that involves deleting subordinate clauses. The import of the first clause is that 'grass [. . .] is all right', but this becomes clear only when we excise the whole of the subordinate clause ('Grass, ~~the power seemed to say, going back with a ruler such as governesses use to the beginning,~~ is all right'). In turn, the subordinate clause makes better sense when we cut out a further embedded clause to read 'going back [. . .] to the beginning' ('going back ~~with a ruler such as governesses use~~ to the beginning'). In the next phrase, the reader has to add rather than remove words, supplying verbs to replace the dashes ('fritillaries <are> admirable; the snaky flower <is> a thought, strong'). Syntax seems to break down altogether in the next line, through the extensive use of commas and dashes, and this liberates the reader to interpret the sentence in a variety of ways. For example, the word 'thought' can be read as a noun: the 'snaky flower' is too strong a thought for a woman to entertain. Alternatively, by reading through the comma, 'thought' becomes an adverb modifying the word 'strong': the phrase 'snaky flower' is a little strong for a woman to write.[2] Additionally, two qualifiers threaten to cancel one another out: the language is 'perhaps' too strong for a woman, but is 'no doubt' sanctioned by Wordsworth. The latter phrase sends us analeptically back to the first line of the novel, leading us to recall that, just as there was every doubt about Orlando's sex, we should question whether Wordsworth endorses this image.

The process of analepsis or flashback is central to Woolf's aesthetic and here, as elsewhere, it performs the function of an analeptic, or restorative stimulant, by offering a fresh interpretation of a word or phrase. The sentence finally comes to an abrupt halt with an incomplete question ('but girls?'), echoing the sudden curtailment of the quotation. The completion of the idea relies upon the repetitive effect of the anadiplosis in the next sentence: 'but girls? Are girls necessary?' Just as my chosen sentence forces us to look back over the individual lines of the poem, so each clause within it makes us shuttle back and forth across the sentence itself. We read it in a non-linear way, producing multiple meanings in the process. The sentence thereby defuses the force of the objections raised by the censoring power even as it summarises them; while appearing to concede to the power's demands for revision, it is not actually rewritten to a prescription. Woolf's syntactical disruptions put into practice the feminist challenge to the 'man's sentence' that she advocated *A Room of One's Own*, where she admired Jane Austen's ability to find freedom of expression through devising 'a perfectly natural, shapely sentence proper for her own use', succeeding where Charlotte Brontë and George Eliot had failed for trying to use the masculine sentence forms that they had inherited.[3]

We will return to these questions shortly, but first it is important to stress Woolf's argument that the form of a sentence, or even of an entire literary work, should suit the body of the writer: 'The book has somehow to be adapted to the body' (*AROO* 74). Although it has been debated as to how extensively Woolf herself uses the 'woman's sentence', the elasticity of this particular sentence means that it can fruitfully be analysed in terms of *écriture feminine*. Its non-linear, vacillating structure can be compared with Luce Irigaray's analysis of women's writing:

> In her statements – at least when she dares to speak out – woman retouches herself constantly. She just barely separates from herself some chatter, an exclamation, a half-secret, a sentence left in suspense – When she returns to it, it is only to set out again from another point of pleasure or pain. One must listen to her differently in order to hear an 'other meaning' which is constantly in the process of weaving itself, at the same time ceaselessly embracing words and yet casting them off to avoid becoming fixed, immobilized.[4]

My chosen sentence is 'a sentence left in suspense' (in the manner Irigaray both advocates and practises in this quotation). This incompletion challenges the fixity of the conventional sentence and, as in Irigaray's analysis, thereby challenges the force of the law: the (legal) sentence, the opinion or judgement of the spirit of the age, is likewise left in suspense, allowing other meanings to come into play.

While Irigaray, like Woolf in *A Room of One's Own*, is concerned with creating a language that is closer to the female body, she explicitly champions an autoerotic form of writing. Irigaray encourages women to avoid writing that seeks to flatter men or respond to male arousal (even suggesting that women should 'go on strike' in that respect), writing for their own pleasure instead.[5] Hélène Cixous makes a similar point: 'Write! Writing is for you, you are for you; your body is yours, take it'.[6] Woolf's argument is not as explicit, but she does employ sensual terms that favour touch over penetration: 'all the older forms of literature were hardened and set by the time she became a writer. The novel alone was young enough to be soft in her hands' (*AROO* 74). In my chosen sentence, Woolf re-touches herself by revisiting the previous lines in her own novel, a self-pleasuring literary act that savours the shape and sound of her own words. At the same time, it is a lesbian act, for the words she re-touches (revises, reinterprets, mouths, *caresses*) are those of Sackville-West.

There is risk involved here too, for as in Irigaray, the lines threaten to divulge a 'half-secret' but then stop. Woolf's sentence is left in suspense and this incompletion enables the fluid and playful production of other meanings that are political as well as sexual. In playfully re-touching Sackville-West's work, Woolf threatens to expose lesbian meanings both in 'The Oak Tree' and *The Land* and to signal the lesbian undercurrent of the novel. The shocked reaction of the spirit of the age alerts the reader to the exoticism and the hint at orientalist, forbidden desire in the image of Egyptian girls. Writing in the year of the *Well of Loneliness* trial, Woolf could only aim for an oblique discourse in which 'sapphism' would be 'suggested' (*D3* 131); deriding the force of the patriarchal legal sentence, this feminine sentence performs a striptease, whereby the lesbian meaning is momentarily obvious. Suzanne Raitt has argued that there is a cruel streak in Woolf's project, for the novel was partly motivated by her jealousy that Sackville-West had turned her attention to Mary Campbell.[7] As Woolf insinuated to Sackville-West in a letter early in the writing process: 'suppose Orlando turns out to be Vita; and its all about you and the lusts of your flesh and the lure of your mind' (*L3* 428–9); and later, 'if you've given yourself to Campbell, I'll have no more to do with you, and so it shall be written, plainly, for all the world to read in Orlando' (*L3* 431). Woolf threatens to punish Sackville-West with threefold public exposure: that she is a lesbian writer (thereby at risk of an obscenity trial), that she is in a relationship with Mary Campbell, and that Woolf is leaving her.

The threat of exposure appears to be quickly averted: having suggested that it is immoral to write about girls in this way, the spirit of the age retracts the accusation by noting that Orlando is married and therefore, by convention, heterosexual ('you have a husband at the Cape, you say? Ah, well, that'll do' (*O* 253)). The comment draws attention to Orlando's marriage, ostensibly declaring her work acceptable, but also highlighting her subterfuge of passing as heterosexual. The implication, of course, also extends to Sackville-West's own marriage and act of passing. The paragraph as a whole, therefore, lingers over the secret of lesbianism but then occludes it, allowing it to slip back into an 'invisibility' of the kind that Adrienne Rich was still critiquing in the 1980s.[8]

However, typical of the oscillatory movement of this episode, the following paragraph instigates yet another review of what has just occurred. We are told that Orlando has only paid lip-service to the spirit of the age: she has been deferential, she has worn a wedding ring and then found a man to go with it, and she has written in a style that has not offended contemporary critics. The comment is therefore an instance of the process identified by Madelyn Detloff, whereby Woolf does the work of queer theory 'before queer theory had a name', by examining 'the cultural work done by the logic of entailment or presumed inevitability of heteronorms'.[9] As the narrator notes, Orlando has got away with writing about forbidden desire just as someone might successfully smuggle contraband: the spirit of the age has not examined Orlando's mind closely enough and her writing has luckily escaped censure. The tone of this paragraph is slightly different from the previous one: the joke is now on the spirit of the age for its ignorance, and the paragraph celebrates Sackville-West's and Woolf's success in dislocating language in order to articulate their desire. This is a compromise that frees women and lesbians to write: 'Now, therefore, she could write, and write she did. She wrote. She wrote. She wrote' (O 254). With this line, Woolf's prose finally breaks free of the textual vacillation in which it had been caught: the repetition of 'write' and 'wrote' suggests ongoing composition, a break in the cycle of re-reading and revision.

Intertextual readings

The rhythm of my chosen sentence is profoundly and persistently analeptic: the sentence calls for repeated re-reading, notably of the preceding quotation from Orlando's poem, and the phrase 'no doubt' triggers a flashback to the opening of the novel. In all these respects, it breaks up what Irigaray has described as the 'fixed, immobilized' discourse of the patriarchal sentence (both linguistic and legal) to set new meanings in motion. With the reference to Wordsworth, the sentence invokes another retrospective, intertextual reading process that mobilises further meanings, inviting a reconsideration, not only of Sackville-West's lines, but also of Wordsworth's verse.

The word 'snaky' is found in Book III of *The Prelude*, 'Residence at Cambridge', where Wordsworth draws attention to the artificiality of university life (and his tutors) in contrast to his Lakeland home and those more revered elders, the shepherds. University is a rich but fabricated tapestry, rather than something homespun and sincere:

> The surfaces of artificial life
> And manners finely wrought, the delicate race
> Of colours, lurking, gleaming up and down
> Through that state arras woven with silk and gold;
> This wily interchange of *snaky hues*,
> Willingly or unwillingly revealed,
> I neither knew nor cared for; and as such
> Were wanting here, I took what might be found
> Of less elaborate fabric.[10]

Much as the spirit of the age in *Orlando* tries to invoke Wordsworth in order to neutralise the sexual potential of the 'snaky flower', the seductive force of 'wily' and 'snaky' actually reinforces that potential. Indeed, Wordsworth's poem begins to take on a homoerotic subtext, set as it is in an all-male college. Wordsworth's interpretation of the arras, woven with sexual meanings that are 'willingly or unwillingly revealed' invites us to unearth subtexts of same-sex attraction within Sackville-West's poem. The arras is also a recurring motif in *Orlando*, where the constantly moving picture of Apollo and Daphne is frequently invoked in the context of Orlando's love interests to underscore themes of sex and seduction.

The sentence has multiple allusive layers, for Wordsworth's image of a snake in the arras alludes in turn to an episode from Spenser's *The Faerie Queene*, where the queering of seduction is made more prominent by gender ambiguity: it features Britomart, a woman cross-dressed as a knight, who joins the knight Scudamore in his attempt to rescue his lover from the castle of Busyrane. Among the 'spoils' of love they find in the castle is a rich tapestry, woven with gilt that shows itself 'unwillingly; / Like a discoloured Snake, whose hidden snares / Through the greene gras his long bright burnisht backe declares'.[11] In both Wordsworth and Spenser, the snake in the grass is a metaphor for the dangers of sex and riches. Spenser emphasises these implications by setting up an additional intertextual association between this snake and the story of Proserpine being stolen away to the underworld while picking flowers;[12] behind this is Milton, who compares Eden favourably with Enna, where 'Proserpine gathering flowers / Her self a fairer flower by gloomy Dis / Was gathered'.[13]

The allusion to Wordsworth is therefore part of a chain of intertextual references that give greater depth and danger to Sackville-West's pastoral scene by revealing the snake in the grass (or amid the fritillaries). Read in the light of these allusions, the 'girls' of the poem are indeed sexualised, obliquely confirming that Orlando's poem is a lesbian text; Wordsworth, Spenser, Milton and Roman mythology are all drawn upon to help unlock this meaning, not by invoking them as authorities but by shifting the emphasis from the judgemental to a subversive recognition of sexuality with its possibilities and dangers. These intertextual layers therefore enact what Irigaray describes as the 'weaving' of an 'other meaning'. Irigaray notes that 'one would have to dig very deep in order to find, behind the traces of this civilization, this history, the vestiges of a more archaic civilization which could give some indication as to what woman's sexuality is all about'.[14] In this sense, these analeptic, restorative readings of images from the works of male authors uncover traces of female sexuality from within a tradition that had occluded it. My chosen sentence therefore undermines the prudish attempts of the spirit of the age to sanitise the 'snaky flower' by invoking Wordsworth; literary texts are far too lively and unruly to be constrained by a particular trend in criticism.

The allusion to Wordsworth thereby liberates Orlando's poem from the era in which she is writing, overriding Victorian prescriptions of sexual conduct by showing them to be historically and culturally specific. Indeed, 'The Oak Tree' is by no means a Victorian poem because Orlando has worked on it over many centuries, making it the product of a complex interplay of literary-historical processes. Orlando's writing of the poem in short bursts over the centuries takes a vacillatory pattern like the one displayed in my chosen sentence, and as a result it has acquired accretions of the disparate styles of the different ages, including Elizabethan love poetry, martial and heroic verse (which Nick Greene identifies when he detects traces of Addison's *Cato*), and pastoral verse (again noted by Greene in his comparisons with James Thomson's *The Seasons*) (O 267). The same was true of *The Land*: as Ian Blyth points out, this poem was frequently compared with Thomson, but it also closely replicates the pattern of the Classical georgic and indeed, Sackville-West frequently referred to it in these terms.[15] That 'The Oak Tree' comes to fruition in the hands of a woman in the nineteenth century, and that it is finally published and wins a prize in the twentieth (as Sackville-West won the Hawthornden Prize for *The Land*), is both a testimony to Sackville-West's achievement and a marker of her indebtedness. Both 'The Oak Tree' and *The Land* therefore, in their anachronistic forms and accretions of past styles, evade the literary conventions of the nineteenth and early twentieth centuries with their historically restrictive norms of sexuality.

Creative anachronisms

Orlando's success in exempting herself from the strictures of the spirit of the age becomes clearer when we recognise the prevalence of creative anachronisms across the novel as a whole. Our deepening awareness over the course of the text as to how 'The Oak Tree' (like its natural namesake) has grown by accretions over the ages facilitates further analeptical readings across the novel. Thus, the verse that Orlando hastily scripts in the nineteenth century can be seen as a fresh attempt to solve the problem faced by her younger, male self in the sixteenth: the question of how to represent nature when 'green in nature is one thing, green in literature another' (*O* 16). Orlando at this earlier stage displays an anachronistic Romantic desire to represent nature in an unmediated fashion, against conventions of his time that privileged artifice and rhetoric. By contrast, although the nineteenth-century Orlando has Romantic concepts of nature at her disposal, she actually finds the derivative and allusive element of writing enabling: expression becomes possible because conventions have been established.

Creative anachronism is central to Woolf's conception of literary heritage. Woolf had long been aware that texts were not just the accumulation of past writings but also spaces in which such writings remained alive and subject to playful manipulation. In her essay 'Reading' (1919), Woolf represented literary history as a kind of gallery in which past writers were not just physically present but alive and active:

> If I looked down at my book I could see Keats and Pope behind him, and then Dryden and Sir Thomas Browne – hosts of them merging in the mass of Shakespeare, behind whom, if one peered long enough, some shapes of men in pilgrims' dress emerged, Chaucer perhaps, and again – who was it? some uncouth poet scarcely able to syllable his words; and so they died away. (*E3* 142)

Woolf's image of literary history is distinctive and clearly antithetical to Eliot's view that 'you cannot value [the poet] alone; you must set him, for contrast and comparison, among the dead'.[16] Unlike Eliot, Woolf was aware that literary tradition is not a set of 'monuments', but alive and subject to change, and that all texts are intertexts formed from the mass of writing over the ages. She theorised this more fully in *A Room of One's Own*: 'masterpieces are not single and solitary births; they are the outcome of many years of thinking in common, of thinking by the body of the people, so that the experience of the mass is behind the single voice' (*AROO* 63). A focal point for the idea of common culture is the figure of 'Anon': the 'uncouth' (unknown or anonymous) poet who wrote ballads and folk songs and set literary tradition in motion and who, Woolf speculates, may well have been a woman (*AROO* 49). It is no coincidence that *A Room of One's Own* and *Orlando* can be traced to the same period in Woolf's career.

In the first five chapters of the essay, Woolf figures literary heritage in explicitly gendered terms: a woman writer is inhibited by a male literary past and needs to recognise and embrace female precursors in order to write: 'we think back through our mothers if we are women. It is useless to go to the great men writers for help' (*AROO* 72–3). *Orlando*, too, shows the inhibiting effect of a literary tradition that is hardly female at all, for the Orlando who begins the writing process is male, as indeed are most of the writers he, then she, meets or emulates. Orlando's struggles with writing after becoming a woman exemplify the challenges faced by female writers responding to a male tradition (particularly when she encounters the misogyny of the Augustans and is effectively reduced to the status of a patron). Woolf's solution in *Orlando* is less about positing a female history than about using a lesbian sensibility to unsettle the work of male writers, as we have seen. However, Woolf suggested that while male writers are not helpful, we can go to them 'for pleasure' (*AROO* 73): in *Orlando*, her unlocking of lesbian subtexts from within their work is a demonstration of one source of pleasure. The joke of a male writer suddenly becoming female is another.

Woolf's non-linear conception of tradition is essential to her playful, liberating treatment of the literary past. This can be seen in a related form of playing with time evident in both 'Reading' and *Orlando*. In 'Reading', Woolf sets past writers apart spatially but not temporally, and in doing so she envisages the non-linear dynamic that prevails in *Orlando*. Time does not move forward, destroying everything behind it, for the past remains intact and accessible.[17] Indeed, Woolf reprises her image from 'Reading' in the closing pages of *Orlando*, where she describes the gallery of the ancestral home:

> The gallery stretched far away to a point where the light almost failed. It was as a tunnel bored deep into the past. As her eyes peered down it, she could see people laughing and talking; the great men she had known; Dryden, Swift, and Pope [. . .] The long gallery filled itself thus, and still peering further, she thought she could make out at the very end, beyond the Elizabethans and the Tudors, some one older, further, darker, a cowled figure, monastic, severe, a monk, who went with his hands clasped, and a book in them, murmuring –
> (*O* 304–5)

This analeptic moment reprises foregoing scenes and revives characters from earlier in the text, almost in the manner of the grand finale to a play. Dryden, Swift and Pope from Chapter IV make a fresh appearance, as do the Elizabethans from the first chapter. The gallery scene telescopes further into the past with the dour figure of a medieval religious, or even the Greek monk from Woolf's early story 'A Dialogue upon Mount Pentelicus', who brings with him an 'atmosphere' that encompasses the world in a 'girdle of eternity'.[18] The creative anachronism of putting writers from several eras together in the same room celebrates the non-linearity and intertextuality that have been evident throughout the novel. The wider structure of *Orlando*, by which the past is revisited from the standpoint of the present and replayed in present time, therefore exemplifies the rhythm of revision and revisiting in my chosen sentence and its associated analeptic reading process.

Past and present are united even more powerfully in *Orlando*, as they meet in the body of the androgynous protagonist who has lived for over 350 years. This is emphasised in the closing pages as Orlando's memories range randomly over different periods of her life so that episodes lived as 'boy and woman' (*O* 302) are integral to one character. Orlando herself therefore embodies the 'many years of thinking in common, of thinking by the body of the people' that Woolf suggested constitute literary tradition. This common life is a matter of dialogue and multiplicity, for Orlando recognises the importance of dialogic interaction to her success as a prize-winning poet: 'Was not writing poetry a secret transaction, a voice answering a voice?' Importantly, this process has a sexual dimension: it is 'secret', 'slow' and 'like the intercourse of lovers' (*O* 310). Among the voices Orlando has answered is that of the 'garden blowing irises and fritillaries' (*O* 310): a final, oblique echo of Woolf's intimate response to the work of Vita Sackville-West.

Woolf's representation of Orlando's androgyny in a scene that also reprises many earlier scenes from the novel paves the way for the theory of androgyny she sets out in the final chapter of *A Room of One's Own*. Moving beyond her analysis of the inhibiting effects of the male literary tradition, Woolf recognises the importance of openness and dialogue between male and female within the same mind. Continuing the sexualised imagery of creativity from *Orlando*, she notes that 'a woman also must have intercourse with the man in her [. . .] It is when this fusion takes place that the mind is fully fertilized and uses all its faculties' (*AROO* 94). Any heterosexual implications of this metaphor are sublimated into self-pleasuring, for male and female are contained in one mind. But lest this appear too inward-looking, Woolf immediately broadens the definition of androgyny to mean a capacity for openness and receptivity. Re-interpreting Coleridge (as she re-reads Wordsworth in my chosen sentence), and reappraising Shakespeare by claiming him as an androgynous antecedent, she argues that 'he [Coleridge] meant, perhaps, that the androgynous mind is resonant and porous; that it transmits emotion without impediment; that it is naturally creative, incandescent and undivided' (ibid.). This expanded definition represents a stage of development in Woolf's thinking from her suggestion that 'Anon' may be female to her argument in 1940 that 'Anon is sometimes man, sometimes woman' – like Orlando.[19]

Conclusion

The rhythms of revision and revisiting in my chosen sentence ostensibly accede to censorship; however, they actually serve to liberate feminist and lesbian meanings from the text. The novel itself follows a similar rhythm, where we are constantly invited to revisit earlier scenes, to re-read literary works, and to reconsider the relationship between past and present. *Orlando* thereby challenges the censoring ideology that had excluded women and lesbians from literary history. The novel's radical conclusion that vast swathes of literary history can be present in one queer body undercuts male discourses of history, but also paves the way for Woolf's formulations concerning the importance of rewriting history: first in *A Room of One's Own*, and much later in 'Anon'. The moment of impasse that Orlando experiences as she is forced to revisit her verse leads to liberation, and the potentially laborious process of revisiting and rewriting that momentarily traps her becomes one of *jouissance*. The same is true of Woolf's revision of particular past writings and her re-conception of literary history as a whole.

Notes

1. Virginia Woolf, *Orlando: A Biography* [1928] (Oxford: World's Classics, 1992), p. 253.
2. A comparable example of reading across the comma to produce an alternative meaning is found in the dinner scene of *To the Lighthouse* [1927] (Oxford: World's Classics, 1992), where Mrs Ramsay serves *boeuf en daube* to Mr Bankes (p. 142): 'It partook, she felt, carefully helping Mr Bankes to a specially tender piece, of eternity'. Mrs Ramsay is aware that the occasion is so momentous that she and her guests are touching eternity through the meal, but if we ignore the comma and run two phrases together, she is physically giving Mr Bankes a 'piece of eternity', as though the meat had undergone transubstantiation.
3. Virginia Woolf, *A Room of One's Own* [1929] (London: Grafton, 1977), p. 73.
4. Luce Irigaray, 'Ce sexe qui n'en est pas un' ['This Sex which is Not One'], in Elaine Marks and Isabelle de Courtivron (eds), *New French Feminisms: An Anthology* (New York: Schocken Books, 1981), p. 103.
5. Ibid. p. 106.

6. Hélène Cixous, 'The Laugh of the Medusa', in Marks and Courtivron, *New French Feminisms*, p. 246.
7. Suzanne Raitt, *Vita and Virginia: The Work and Friendship of V. Sackville-West and Virginia Woolf* (Oxford: Oxford University Press, 1993), p. 18.
8. Adrienne Rich, 'Compulsory Heterosexuality and Lesbian Existence', *Signs*, 5.4 (1980), pp. 631–60.
9. Madelyn Detloff, 'Woolf and Lesbian Culture: Queering Woolf Queering', in Bryony Randall and Jane Goldman (eds), *Virginia Woolf in Context* (Cambridge: Cambridge University Press, 2012), p. 346.
10. William Wordsworth, *Poetical Works: With Introduction and Notes*, ed. Thomas Hutchinson; new edn, rev. by Ernest de Selincourt (Oxford: Oxford University Press, 1969), *The Prelude*, Book III, 559–66. Emphasis added.
11. Edmund Spenser, *Poetical Works*, ed. J. C. Smith and Ernest de Selincourt (Oxford: Oxford University Press, 1985), *Faerie Queene*, Book III, canto xi, verse 28.
12. Spenser, *Faerie Queene*, Book III, canto xi, verse 1.
13. John Milton, *Paradise Lost*, ed. Alastair Fowler (Harlow: Longman, 1971), Book IV, 269–71.
14. Irigaray, 'Ce sexe', p. 100.
15. Ian Blyth, 'A Sort of English Georgics: Vita Sackville-West's *The Land*', *Forum for Modern Language Studies*, 45.1 (2008), pp. 22–3.
16. T. S. Eliot, 'Tradition and the Individual Talent', in T. S. Eliot, *Selected Essays* (London: Faber and Faber, 1932), p. 15.
17. Lily Briscoe has a similar experience as she works on her painting while recalling Mrs Ramsay: 'as she dipped into the blue paint, she dipped too into the past there' (*TL* 232).
18. Virginia Woolf, 'A Dialogue upon Mount Pentelicus', *CSF*, pp. 67, 68.
19. Brenda R. Silver, '"Anon" and "The Reader": Virginia Woolf's Last Essays', *Twentieth-Century Literature*, 25.3/4 (1979), p. 382.

Chapter 5

'Let us go, then, exploring': Intertextual Conversations on the Meaning of Life

Sanja Bahun

Let us go, then, exploring, this summer morning, when all are adoring the plum blossom and the bee.[1]

Cushioned in a poetic, meta-textual interlude in Chapter VI of *Orlando*, this sentence initiates a significant transformation in the tone and pace of the narration. This change is inextricably related to the nature of the sentence as a complex intertextual statement, referencing and tapping the rhythm of the opening lines of T. S. Eliot's 'The Love Song of J. Alfred Prufrock' (1915): 'Let us go then, you and I / when the evening is spread out against the sky / like a patient etherised upon the table'.[2] The sentence is preceded by a paragraph in which the narrator playfully departs from the not-so-inspiring protagonist in search of life elsewhere, that is, outside the human consciousness trapped in the labours of imagination and cogitation. On the other side, the sentence ushers us into a carefully metered, poetic passage, later also included in Vita Sackville-West's anthology of poetry, *Another World than This*.[3] This passage tracks, indeed rejoices in, the different species of life, including and beyond the human subject, and culminates in the question that punctuates this chapter in *Orlando*: 'What is life?' This inquiry is presented in the text as simultaneously pompous, genuinely urgent, and ultimately unresolvable. The only answer the narrator provides seems to be that of actively 'in-taking' life rather than reflecting on it. Prompted by the suggestion of an intimate investigation in Woolf's (and Eliot's) sentence, my chapter examines this response and the interstices of semantics, poetics and gender that both separate and bind Woolf's and Eliot's narrators and their exploratory gestures.

Woolf's sentence interacts closely, through its syntax, rhythmical arrangement and even lexical choice, with the first three lines of Eliot's poem. The components of Eliot's first line, 'Let us go then, you and I', are replicated and retained in their syntactic source-place, save for the insertion of 'exploring' instead of 'you and I'; the accentual line is watchfully mirrored. This close correspondence is further emphasised through Woolf's strategic placement of the sentence at the beginning of a paragraph. Eliot's second line, 'When the evening is spread out against the sky', is rephrased and repositioned after the Woolfian interlude 'this summer morning'. At the same time, this very clause, when expanded with the subordinate clause 'when all are adoring', rhyming with 'exploring', provides the same number of syllables as Eliot's line, and the temporal clauses signalling 'evening' and 'morning', respectively, are brought into conversation. The third line, 'like a patient etherised upon a table', appears in Woolf's text mimicked in cadence and its referent is re-enunciated in stark opposition as the 'plum blossom and the bee'.

Cautiously crafted as it is, this intertextual edifice is striking because there seems to be nothing in the adoration of 'the plum blossom and the bee', exulted by Woolf's narrator, that would approximate the despair of Eliot's shipwrecked subject as he embarks on his painful examination of the impassable routes of modern subjecthood. Still, the two are interlinked on multiple levels, suggesting a much wider network of intertextual activity. While the category and practice of intertextuality has often been understood as a banal performance (and study) of influence, it is its meaning in Kristevan/Bakhtinian terms that interests me here: that of a necessary 'transposition' of texts, or systems of signs/symbolic orders, into each other, and a creation of a text as a 'mosaic of quotations': that is, a continuous dialogue based on absorption and transformation.[4] On the interior side, the transposition of Eliot's poetry in Woolf's novel dialogises the text from within, animating remarkable inter-genre transfers; outward looking, this move both partakes in and shapes the rich semiosphere that we call modernism. Pursuing both directions at once, the sentence articulates a new dialogised, enunciative and denotative positionality. One such practice, Julia Kristeva claims, transforms all the constituent actors of the text – the writer, the protagonist, the narrator and the reader – into *subjects-in-process*, identifying with the different semantic, syntactic and phonic systems at play in a given text.[5] The creation of just such identities-in-process was Virginia Woolf's lifelong concern.[6]

Before I embark on a closer inspection of Woolf's sentence in its relation to Eliot's poem, though, the immediate personal and intertextual context of this utterance merits illumination. Eliot and Woolf were close friends and professional supporters for more than twenty years; their relationship seems to have been truly intimate, although also guarded and at times competitive.[7] Woolf probably read most of Eliot's poetry produced in her lifetime and discussed it with the poet. Despite their opposite political and religious views, she felt that their aesthetic and existential concerns were commensurable, and that their writings were marked by reciprocal continuities. In 1928 their friendship was at its most precarious height, and, unsurprisingly, the Eliots appear in Woolf's playful acknowledgments in *Orlando*'s Preface. In its textual context, however, Woolf's sentence belongs to a string of covert ventriloquisms of (male) modernist writers in three consecutive paragraphs of Chapter VI. The previous paragraphs, as often noted, host a charged reference to the gamekeeper (as well as to the male novelist who conceives of love as 'slipping off one's petticoat' (O 187–8)) that may well point to D. H. Lawrence and his novel *Lady Chatterley's Lover*, published in 1928 and read by Sackville-West in July of the same year. Most commentators surmise that Woolf must have heard of the novel earlier as these references also appear in the *Orlando* manuscript. Others perceive a reference to another male modernist figure, namely E. M. Forster, and his *Maurice*, published posthumously in 1971, which Woolf had read in manuscript in 1915 (Forster, too, is mentioned in the Preface).[8] Unnoticed so far has been yet another allusion to male modernist writing in the paragraph that follows the 'Let us go, then' section: a gloss on James Joyce's *Ulysses* (1922). Significantly, the last showcases how Woolf's intertextual imagination works. The Joyce reference is mediated and reliant on a multi-plane intersection of textual surfaces: it appears buried in Woolf's invocation of the much debated Homeric epithet for the sea, 'wine-dark', in itself disseminated in Woolf's phrase 'wine-blue purple-dark hill' (O 189) rather than relayed as a calque. The same epithet evocatively opens Joyce's novel in his own game of intertextual transactions. In the first episode of *Ulysses*, we find Buck Mulligan irreverently dissecting the Homeric idiom, finally to exclaim the original phrase in Greek: 'The snotgreen sea. The scrotumtightening sea. *Epi oinopa ponton*. Ah, Dedalus, the Greeks. I must teach you. You must read them in the original'.[9] Woolf, of course, read Greek, and even reflected on the importance of such practice in 'On Not Knowing Greek' (1925). But she also read Joyce, alternatively with enthusiasm and animosity, and understood profoundly Joyce's appetite for deep-history intertextuality and his passion for compound lexemes. So, when Woolf rewrites Homer through Joyce, she does it in such a way that the clamour of compounding is audible, that we are led to *hear* the layers of literary history in it, too. And, like Joyce, she also further dialogises her quasi-Greek expression into a social comment through an ironic nod to the contemporary debate about translating and pronouncing Ancient Greek.

Language in *Orlando*, here and elsewhere, parades its status as a poetic paragram.[10] The effect of such deployment of language is that the novel resembles an exercise in hauntology.[11] Here the narrator's role is one of explorer in a house haunted by the ghosts of other writers for whom a metatextual address to the reader was a norm (a range that spans from Jane Austen to Nikolai Gogol). As a modernist house-text, though, Woolf's novel differentiates not only among the hypotexts but also among the types, levels and uses of them: the *Orlando* edifice is comprised of differently valued and deliberately mixed intertextual material, where quotations, self-quotations, paraphrases, allusions and writerly gestures interact irreverently. They also present a fruitful jumble in terms of both history and literary history. The deep-plane intertextual invocation of Forster, Eliot and Joyce, for example, precedes a surface-level invocation of a series of Victorian writers linked to the diegetic time of the mid-nineteenth century (O 201). Shakespeare, of course, would appear to ghost the entire novel, but in Chapter VI the allusions to Shakespeare are also subject to a double move, as Woolf strives to relay the modernists' (including her own) infatuation with Shakespeare through two-tier ventriloquising. Particular intertextual engagements, like the one with Eliot, are also disseminated across the text so that the reader can reconstruct them only through a careful archaeology. They are subject to further alteration as the reader labours to unveil the guises in which the hypotext is cloaked, aware that some of them will remain impenetrable. Even more disconcertingly, Woolfian intertextual transactions defy an easy division along axiological lines: it is up to the reader to reconstruct their role and their value in the text and for herself. Thus driven by a (constantly frustrated) desire for interpretation, the text gets recreated in each encounter with the reader.

'Let us go, then, exploring' is a case in point. While Woolf's intertextual engagements are often satiric in *Orlando*, that is not the situation here, or, at least, not at the surface level. This stylistic transposition/allusion comes closer to what Fredric Jameson defined as pastiche – namely, 'the wearing of a linguistic mask' that is devoid of 'any of parody's ulterior motives, amputated of the satiric impulse'.[12] At the same time, Woolf's reworking of the signature piece of modernist poetry is not entirely neutral. The sentence, the intertextual context suggests, bespeaks the writer's conscious effort to negotiate her place within and in relation to what, in the late 1920s, presented itself as a swiftly consolidating new canon. In the diegetic world, the same dilemma exasperates the protagonist. While reading *fin-de-siècle* literary scholarship in Chapter VI, Orlando is brought to tears: 'They [critics] made one feel [. . .] that one must always, always write like somebody else' (O 198). Linked to this quandary is the issue of gender, in itself one of the key themes in the novel, and the subject of various intertextual interludes earlier in the narrative. In 'Women and Fiction' (1929), Woolf expounded at length on the gendering of sentences, expressly claiming that a woman cannot and should not write 'like a man': 'the very form of the sentence does not fit her. It is a sentence made by men; too loose, too heavy, too pompous for a woman's use'. She continues to argue that a woman must make for herself a sentence of her own, 'altering and adapting the current sentence until she writes one that takes the natural shape of her thought without crushing or distorting it' (*E5* 32). *Orlando* bears striking witness to this effort to forge a female idiom. As a rule, Woolf's syntax in *Orlando* is rhythmic, convoluted and replete with parataxes; its hallmark is unusual sequencing with the obscured or stalled introduction of the subject position. But, in my chosen sentence, the female thought is challenging itself into an active engagement with a male discourse, starting with an invocation that is grammatically predictable and (already in 1928) canonically recognisable. Within this one sentence, male discourse is being transferred into a female, Woolf's, speech.

Significantly, Woolf's sentence is not a simple borrowing or direct quotation (such abound in *Orlando*, too). Rather, its specific value resides precisely in its seamless move from direct quotation through allusion or literary echo to independence. Woolf exploits the interplay of constraint and freedom that this situation affords her. While the intertextual reverberations and caricature undertones continue as the sentence progresses,[13] the percussive alliteration of bilabials [b] and [p] in 'the plum blossom and the bee' produces a counter-current, and the sentence now hurls to its end as if let loose from the seductive grip of the gestured discourse. The tension of genre transfers contributes to the impression that this literary re-articulation pursues an independent path. Relegating poetry into prose, Woolf manages to reinvent poetry. The most conspicuous trace of Eliot's poem, the first line, unexpectedly becomes the most prosaic part of the new enunciation; it is only when the sentence 'breaks free' that poetic sequencing is marked. Woolf finally 'signs' the sentence with her characteristic use of the present participle – 'the Devil [of poetry writing] himself' (*O* 122) – which in turn helps her forge her own, unashamedly liquid rhyme. More generally, the journey of this sentence mirrors closely the one travelled by Orlando up to this point in the narrative, that is, her coming to a poetic voice of her own.

But the strategic choice of words in the sentence also signals that all these concerns with literary heritage and contemporary canon might be secondary to the inaugurating dilemma of Orlando's vocation as a writer: how – if anyhow – does one represent life? A semantic invariant in Woolf's entire opus, this issue is scrutinised with particular gusto in *Orlando*; and it is this question that connects, most profoundly, Woolf and Eliot. A similar cluster of words appears in the opening pages of the novel, where we find youthful Orlando attempting to write poetry and facing the challenge of abstraction. The Renaissance Orlando is eloquent, but has a problem: much as he tries, he cannot describe nature in all its vivacity. In order to transpose the green of nature into a green of literature, Orlando actually looks at nature, but as soon as one 'look[s] out of a window at bees among flowers, at a yawning dog, at the sun setting [. . .] one drops the pen, takes one's cloak, strides out of the room' (O 13). This is the first time that the dominant motif in *Orlando*, that of looking out of a window, occurs in the narrative and the opposition between nature/life (life-giving outside) and literature/writing (necessary but suffocating inside) is instituted. At this early point in the narrative, Orlando can do nothing but succumb to the drive to go out and explore and therefore leave the whole business of writing behind; and so does the narrator who – attached to the mission of closely tracking his/her human subject – must follow him. When the same trope is revisited in Chapter VI, in which we find Orlando at the end of the nineteenth and the beginning of the twentieth century, something remarkable happens: the chronotope bifurcates into the time-space of the narrator and the time-space of the protagonist. While Orlando stays indoors, writing her poem about nature ('The Oak Tree'), the narrator 'look[s] out of the window' and goes off chasing nature, or, rather, *life* (O 188).[14] Biography, after all, is writing life – *bios* – and life seems to reside outside now. Both the protagonist and the narrator have matured, this move suggests: Orlando has started writing nature, and the narrator has realised that the subject of biography, just like that of fiction, is 'a little other than custom would have us believe it'.[15] When the narrator and the protagonist meet again a few paragraphs down, the narrator confides that s/he has not found the answer to the question of what life is, and Orlando has shaken off the paralysis and has completed her poem.

The question of how one represents life and its meanings is arguably the most significant reason why Woolf ghosts the tone and cadence of 'Prufrock'. Neither Woolf nor Eliot was oblivious to the fact that representation can never attain its object, and the very suggestiveness of their writing relies on an admitted incompleteness of meaning. Like many other modernists, they both make the painful realisation of these representational limits the focal point of their texts. Yet, as they inter- and metatextually explore art and life (and avoid asserting anything final about either), Eliot and Woolf seem to give different answers to this socio-poetic conundrum. Woolf's sentence stands as the centrepiece of this particular dialogue, transporting the reader from the passivity, inertia and deathlike idleness of the writing protagonist and her paralysed consciousness, to the mobile, vibrant life of nature. As such, it establishes both a contrast and a close interaction with the opening of Eliot's poem.

In both texts the enunciating subjects seek an answer to what Eliot describes as 'an overwhelming question' and articulate the belief that the answer can only be found – and figured in writing – through an exploration, as direct as possible, of the pre-figured, 'life' itself (Eliot writes: 'Oh, do not ask, "What is it?" / Let us go and make our visit'[16]). But if their plans for perambulation appear similar, the actual types of activity, settings, and the underlying imagery place them in stark opposition. Semantically, everything after the first line in Woolf's sentence is set up in a relational opposition to Eliot's poem: it is an autumn evening in 'Prufrock'; it is a summer morning in *Orlando*; it is a city through which Eliot's subject would need to traverse; it is nature where Woolf's narrator meanders. While both subjects start by acknowledging that they need to go out to explore life, Eliot's potent image of the evening 'spread out against the sky like a patient etherised upon a table' immediately forces upon the reader an impression of stasis and staying indoors – of delving ever deeper inside; for his is the exploration of the insides of a patient's body. In these first lines we can already intimate: Eliot's hero would not dare to leave his house and make this visit. By contrast, Woolf's narrator goes out to explore the question 'What is life?' by interviewing birds. S/he sighs a relief as s/he starts to produce a slapdash taxonomy of birds – sparrows, starlings, larks, doves and rooks – which expands into an even more haphazard taxonomy of insects – grasshoppers, ants, moths (*O* 188–9).[17] This rambling series is then intercepted by the narrator's concession that it is pointless to ask fish about the meaning of life, and is finally curtailed by her/his admission that, alas, no answer to the 'overwhelming question' has been provided. All this effort seems to have been in vain. Or, has it? Outside, one may say, life has already invaded the pages of Woolf's text, without a sanction: a gregarious starling has already asserted a story of its own, a narrative that installs a jovial, life-giving irresoluteness.

The adventurousness of this narrative move deserves a special note. To facilitate this exit, Woolf deploys a figurative strategy wherein protagonist and narrator are presented as both distinguished – here even physically distanced – and indissolubly interconnected. The former is a human, and, as its counterpart repeatedly highlights, prone to the weaknesses of the human, of which the passion for thinking – or ruminating – is foremost; the latter is a writing act (the instance that narrates) but humanised, with marked character traits, of which the effort to please the public is most ostensible. Still, whereas the chatty narrator, like its many literary predecessors, asserts a personality of its own, his/her and Orlando's lives and writerly fates run parallel, and there is repeated suggestion that the narrator is trapped, or even incarcerated, by Orlando. This love–hate rapport exteriorises on the level of themes and characters the formal struggle between the egoistically controlled narration and the narrative meandering that configures Woolf's text as a whole. This complex relationship of narrative bodies revisits and reshapes Eliot's own bifurcation of the narrative voice in 'Prufrock' into a *you* (a public persona) and an *I* (a thinking self). But Woolf's narrator does escape the solipsism of the indoors and does so genuinely, whereas it is only at his most disingenuous, as a *you*, that the Eliotic subject engages with the outside world. And it is this slippage that illuminates Woolf's complex transpositional procedure. Woolf takes over, verbatim, Eliot's lyric subject and the major key to his poem, namely, the compound, interiorly divided 'you and I', and relegates it to serve her own ends. For all the deliberately gestured similarities, the invitations of Eliot's lyric subject and Woolf's narrator ('let us go, then') are in fact of a different order, and, importantly, they imply a different company. Eliot's 'you and I' solipsistically implode, whereas Woolf's nosism 'us', although ostensibly belonging to *pluralis majestatis*, effectively initiates an intersubjective conspiracy between the narrator and the recipient/reader that functions as a *pluralis modestiae*. The latter collusion is supported by the irreverent act of leaving the biographical subject behind, a move that enables Woolf to further explore one of her career-long formal concerns, namely, the possibility of multi-perspectival, or egoless (while not subjectless) prose. Eliot's egoistic lyric subject does not simply transform but rather disseminates in Woolf's transposition: it becomes a subjectivity-game.

Both Eliot's and Woolf's starting point is the impasse of modern subjecthood – its inertia, its absurd (social, political and psychological) entrapment, existential and ontological loneliness, and its perplexing proclivity to forfeit, or indeed annihilate, itself. The measured poignancy of 'Prufrock', Eliot's most existential poem, draws much of its strength from the poet's decision to stay with the (self-)destructive human subject, since beyond the subject there seems to be no life.[18] Woolf's bold pitching of the image of superior fecundity – 'the plum blossom and the bee' – against Eliot's 'patient etherised upon a table' provides a resonant counterpart to such a vision. And, rather than imagining an abstract or mythically-ritualistically configured fertility, Woolf opts for a specific, vivid, purposeful image, one that may capture, rather than signal, the beat of life. This entry into the world outside the human thus scripts a political and poetic difference from Eliot's poetry while using it. To endorse this message, the dialogue with Eliot is picked up again a few pages later in *Orlando*, where the diegetic circumstance of Orlando giving birth to a baby boy occasions an extensive and profound interaction with Eliot's *The Waste Land* (1922). Re-constellated in Woolf's text, Eliot's 'hyacinth' ceases to operate as a memorial trace of lost fecundity and innocence and becomes alive, bursting with flora that augurs the arrival of the 'kingfisher' (O 203).[19]

Yet, even more than the pitching of fertile life against deadening inertia is at stake in the exit of Woolf's narrator. The ludic paradox of this portion of *Orlando* resides in the fact that, while the protagonist was absent from the narrative, the narrative has written itself; sense-data have been collected. Our sentence both performs and ventriloquises this move from the observable, representable human subject (of biography) to the unobserved. Once she has completed her poem, Orlando is verily surprised that the world had continued all the time that she was writing (O 189): that 'the thing itself went on whatever happened to the artist – in books, in pictures, in building and pots and chairs and tables' (*RF* 242). So this is a question Woolf ponders with Eliot: whether, in the face of the human subject's alarming capacity to efface itself and the inadequacy of human words to embrace experiential meaning, life still persists. It is for this reason that Woolf's narrator also gradually withdraws and hides her/his traces as the sentence progresses. The world unfettered by the observing subject could only be relayed in the language that 'contracts to an unoccupied perspective', Ann Banfield has argued in relation to Woolf's effort to depict the unseen.[20] But unlike *To the Lighthouse*, *The Waves* and *The Years*, all meticulously analysed by Banfield, *Orlando* features few completely 'unoccupied' sentences representing sensibilia only; instead, the text rests on an excessive outpouring of sense-data, suggesting that *bios*, biological life – rather than empty landscape or some other semi-ontologised space – continues even when unobserved. Woolf's use of the bubbly alliterative phrase 'the blossom and the bee' is indicative. While this image conjures easily associations with fertility and lust, it also defies their ontologisation and abstraction. The textual context also suggests that we should understand this image as part of an epistemological and existential quest, where bees seem to possess a life-giving wisdom about interaction, both derived from and orchestrated by pleasure and intuition.[21] Their insight should concern us deeply, Woolf intimates in *Orlando*: life continues in the world without human presence because the world is not created through the subject's observation only.

Nevertheless, this life-world is radically affected by the existence (even *in absentio*) of a consciousness capable of witnessing, that is, sensing, knowing and evaluating the world, and this state of affairs is captured in a truly dialogic representation, as Mikhail Bakhtin hypothesised.[22] Likewise, Woolf knows that while bees may have a life of their own, and this life may involve the evaluation of humans like Orlando, they have life as such independent creatures on the pages of her book because she herself has endowed them with this spectrum of meanings. She is the witness. As the narrator's comically inconclusive expedition in search of an answer to the question 'What is life?' suggests, however, Woolf is a curious witness: one who represents (because *represent* she must, *explore* she must) but abrogates her prerogatives of evaluating and passing judgement on people, or bees.

Woolf knows that she shares with Eliot existential questions, aesthetic demands and ethical conundrums, yet she also finds the scope of his vision limited. From her own enunciating positionality, she responds to these concerns by offering us a glimpse of the world outside the human subject. *En route* she rewrites Eliot's poetry into her own prose-poetry. In *Orlando*, Woolf calls the act of writing poetry 'a secret transaction, a voice answering a voice', an 'intercourse of lovers' (*O* 225). If poetry is a secret conversation, and a transaction of desires, hopes, fears, ideas and symbolic capitals, it is so because writing is by necessity an intentional act, the production of longing utterances oriented towards objects, entities and phenomena whose participation in the dialogue is felt as vital: the voices of nature, the impulses of history and the history of affects, as well as the envisioned reader, apperceived heritage, and, at its most intimate, some undisclosed correspondents. In T. S. Eliot, Woolf found, on more occasion than one, one such perfect secret interlocutor.

Notes

1. Virginia Woolf, *Orlando: A Biography* [1928] (London: Penguin, 1993), p. 188. The sentence appears unaltered, apart from the deletion of one comma, from the earliest drafts of the novel; see *OH*, 232.
2. T. S. Eliot, 'The Love Song of J. Alfred Prufrock', in T. S. Eliot, *Collected Poems 1909–1962* (London: Faber and Faber, 1974), p. 13.
3. Vita Sackville-West and Harold Nicolson, *Another World than This* (London: Michael Joseph, 1945), p. 131.
4. Julia Kristeva, 'Word, Dialogue and Novel', in *The Kristeva Reader*, ed. Toril Moi (New York: Columbia University Press, 1986), p. 37.
5. Julia Kristeva, 'Intertextuality and Literary Interpretation', an interview with Margaret Waller, in *Julia Kristeva Interviews*, trans. Richard Macksey, ed. Ross Mitchell Guberman (New York: Columbia University Press, 1996), p. 190.
6. See Makiko Minow-Pinkney, *Virginia Woolf and the Problem of the Subject* (Brighton: Harvester, 1987).

78 Sanja Bahun

7. The Woolfs met Eliot for the first time in November 1918. They were familiar with his early poems, notably 'The Love Song of J. Alfred Prufrock', and were eager to publish his new poetry. See Leonard Woolf, *Letters of Leonard Woolf*, ed. Frederic Spotts (London: Bloomsbury Publishing, 1990), p. 279. For a biographical sketch of their relationship, see Hermione Lee, *Virginia Woolf* (London: Vintage, 1997), pp. 438–53.
8. For a Lawrence–Woolf link, see Sandra M. Gilbert, 'Notes' (*O* 259); for a Forster–Woolf link, see Michael H. Whitworth, 'Explanatory Notes', in V. Woolf, *Orlando: A Biography* [1928] (Oxford: Oxford University Press, 2015), p. 222.
9. James Joyce, *Ulysses* (Oxford: Oxford University Press, 1993), p. 5. Homer's epithetic phrase 'ἐπὶ οἴνοπα πόντον' ('upon the wine-dark sea') appears recurrently in the *Odyssey* and has been much debated by scholars.
10. On poetic paragram, see Kristeva, 'Word, Dialogue', p. 40.
11. See Erica Johnson, 'Giving Up the Ghost: National and Literary Haunting in *Orlando*', *Modern Fiction Studies*, 50.1 (2004), pp. 110–28.
12. Fredric Jameson, *Postmodernism, or the Cultural Logic of Late Capitalism* (Durham, NC: Duke University Press, 1991), p. 17.
13. Woolf wrote admiringly about Eliot's use of 'caricature', which both of them distinguish from traditional satire (*D2* 68).
14. Many commentators have focused on this portion of the text in light of the novel's status as a (love) letter to Vita Sackville-West, suggesting that the 'life' in the paragraph references Woolf's longing for Vita Sackville-West under the guise of a search for the meaning of life (*vita*); see, for one, Julia Briggs, *Virginia Woolf: An Inner Life* (London: Penguin, 2005), p. 208. Valid as such interpretations might be, they tend to underestimate the writer's creative project, and thin the prose of *Orlando* into a one-layer hypertext. I suggest an alternative, stratified reading of this dynamic, in which Woolf conceals the search for Vita under the question 'What is life?', but also conceals the genuine existential question about life under the reference to Vita.
15. Woolf, 'Modern Fiction' (1925), *E4*, p. 161.
16. Eliot, 'Prufrock', p. 13.
17. Taxonomies of birds abound in Woolf's fiction and diary, usually signalling the search for unity in discord, or dissonant gregariousness. Playful taxonomies of animals more generally also proliferate in Woolf's fiction, frequently questioning the very notion of taxonomy. They often host mongrel species, and surrealistically intersect unrelated series of animate or inanimate objects. Cf. *O* 196: 'Here she was in St. James's Street [. . .] there were pigeons; a mongrel terrier dog; two hansom cabs and a barouche landau. What then, was Life?'
18. In later poems, such as *The Waste Land* and *Four Quartets*, Eliot branches out from the subject. This opening is obtained through mythical or religious impulses, but rarely as a vision of *material* life.
19. Compare *O* 203–4, and Eliot, 'The Waste Land', Part I, *Collected Poems*, especially p. 64.
20. Ann Banfield, *The Phantom Table: Woolf, Fry, Russell and the Epistemology of Modernism* (Cambridge: Cambridge University Press, 2000), p. 316.
21. Bees have a prominent place in Woolf's catalogue of animals: driven by

the force of life itself, they show a capacity to comprehend and an intuitive understanding of humans, while the hive sometimes figures as a surrogate-sign for human interaction. See, for instance, *To the Lighthouse* [1927] (New York: Harcourt, 2005), p. 55.
22. Mikhail Bakhtin, 'Notes Made in 1970–71', in M. Bakhtin, *Speech Genres and Other Late Essays*, trans. Vern W. McGee, ed. Caryl Emerson and Michael Holquist (Austin: University of Texas Press, 1986), p. 137.

Chapter 6

'... and nothing whatever happened': *Orlando*'s Continuous Eruptive Form

Suzanne Bellamy

He saw the beech trees turn golden and the young ferns unfurl; he saw the moon sickle and then circular; he saw – but probably the reader can imagine the passage which should follow and how every tree and plant in the neighbourhood is described first green, then golden; how moons rise and suns set; how spring follows winter and autumn summer; how night succeeds day and day night; how there is first a storm and then fine weather; how things remain much as they are for two or three hundred years or so, except for a little dust and a few cobwebs which one old woman can sweep up in half an hour; a conclusion which, one cannot help feeling, might have been reached more quickly by the simple statement that 'Time passed' (here the exact amount could be indicated in brackets) and nothing whatever happened.[1]

The wondrous whimsy of this sentence shows the hand of a writer so confident in her craft that she can self-mock, choreograph a textual performance with abandon and eight semi-colons, and embody in an act of deconstruction her mastery of the tools she has made from her own ideas. Mixing metaphors, Woolf is a juggler, throwing all the balls in the air, and still holding the pattern of form and order when the sentence settles. In a radical act of textual and literal housekeeping (much like that of the old cleaning woman in the sentence), with a bold clearing of the textual space, Woolf enacts the scrubbing clean of the canvas, the rubbing out of the meanings and the words. She shows not only the brush strokes, but also the rag that wipes them clean, and as she says, mockingly, this clearing work only takes one old woman half an hour. When the change comes, it comes fast. It lets in the air, the light and the colour of a new perception. It breaks the bond between words and old meanings, and enacts the undoing of mimetic representation.

Reminiscent of the radical shift that occurred when Virginia and Vanessa Stephen moved out of the aesthetic entrapment of their parents' Victorian house, or when Woolf threw off the styles of earlier works with her modernist experiments *Monday or Tuesday* (1921) and *Jacob's Room* (1922), and even when she let herself love more openly

Vita Sackville-West in fact and in text, the change in the sentence happens suddenly and completely: everything changes. This creative shift becomes the preliminary to all other acts of story because it is about the tools involved in creative work: the brain, the time and the purpose. In the process, it also honours the writers who have experimented with form, voice and narrative structure – Woolf's forebears, writers such as Laurence Sterne, whose influence forms part of my engagement with this sentence.

The sentence I have chosen has both prefigurative and intertextual links to other Woolf novels. It enfolds village consciousness, vegetative taxonomy, visual perception shifts, earth time and human time, colour theory, eruptive punctuation, sight gags, several forms of comedy, and authorial contestations. It is a very long and daring exercise in linguistic implosion, a high-wire act indeed. The sentence is transitional in the narrative and holds ambiguity. Orlando is still a he, and we are reading his predictable thoughts, what he saw, how he saw, and perhaps what he wrote. The narrator is describing Orlando seeing – ferns and sickles, night and day – with delicious irritation in the commentary, mocking the slow tedium of distorted description and Orlando's clichéd, loaded images. An act of textual interruption breaks the sentence apart: a dash sends it into freefall, and the sentence ends on a note of patronising polite scorn ('one cannot help feeling'), relegating description to so many cobwebs, an editor's red pen and a broom. My exploration of this deceptively light-hearted sentence will examine Woolf's ideas on nature writing, representation, description and cliché, as well as its invocation of her preceding novel *To the Lighthouse* (1927) – particularly the middle section, 'Time Passes'. I will also draw upon the relevant works she was reading at the time of writing *Orlando*, including Sterne's *Tristram Shandy* (1759–66) and Vita Sackville-West's poem *The Land* (1926), with which this sentence creates an intertext. My reading will also consider Woolf's invocation of the reader, Gertrude Stein's work on sentences and meaning in *Composition as Explanation* (1926), and, finally, address how abstraction emerges in this sentence where 'nothing' becomes something new.

The sentence sits in the middle of Chapter II, where Orlando has just read the writer Nick Greene's mocking and hurtful satiric poem, *Visit to a Nobleman in the Country*. Because of this, Orlando destroys all his writings, burning everything (including fifty-seven poetical works), except his magnum opus 'The Oak Tree'. He is left with dogs and nature – things he trusts. 'So feeling quit of a vast mountain of illusion, and very naked in consequence, he called his hounds to him and strode through the Park' (*O* 97). Then for some hundreds of years he goes again and again to the oak tree inspiring his poem, 'day after day, week after week, month after month, year after year' (ibid.). The key sentence occurs at this point, straight after Orlando's shock and withdrawal, so that as he empties out, burning all his books but one, so does the sentence empty of its structure and meanings. The numbness and timelessness depicted in the sentence are traumatic; Orlando is wounded and must go through a long withdrawn time of waiting and repeating. His consciousness finds some comfort in rhythm and clichéd repetition, a kind of recovery period – time out – but this period comes just prior to the big changes in gender, sexuality and place in Chapter III, changes driven by a great shock to the system. Situated after Orlando's wounding experiences with the Russian Princess Sasha and then with Nick Greene, the sentence falls pivotally at a clearing-out point, burning the past. And it is the narrator's boredom with waiting that breaks the spell of rest, withdrawal and thinking.

The context of Woolf's writing and reading as she was composing *Orlando* proves a fruitful source for the many threads and resonances in this sentence. She was writing about Sterne's *Tristram Shandy* during the time of *Orlando*'s composition, her sentences absorbing its anarchic influence. Indeed, the moment of the shift in Orlando's writing crisis under the oak tree, where my sentence sits, closely approximates the time of *Tristram Shandy*'s publication. In her long essay 'Phases of Fiction' (1929), Woolf celebrates Sterne's subtle mind and his sense of elasticity: 'We lose our sense of direction. We go backwards instead of forwards [. . .] we circle; we soar; we turn around' (*E5* 74). Regarding Sterne's method, Woolf focused on the relationship of writer and reader: 'in no other book are the writer and reader so involved together'; 'all the usual conventions are consumed and yet no ruin or catastrophe comes to pass' (*E5* 75). In what might be considered an homage to Sterne, Woolf's essay invokes a jocular, conversational familiarity with the reader. Indeed, *Tristram Shandy*'s disruptive energy also punctuates *Orlando*, especially in my chosen sentence, lending humour and self-mockery, encouraging reader engagement, and displaying the brilliance of Woolf's mind.

As to other creative life contexts, Woolf had visited Knole and her lover Vita Sackville-West in early 1927, prior to Vita leaving for Persia. Soon after, the project of *Orlando* was kindled. In February 1927, Woolf was writing 'Phases of Fiction', and in May *To the Lighthouse* was published. Sackville-West's poem *The Land*, on which Orlando's 'The Oak Tree' is based, won the Hawthornden Prize in June. On 10 November, while Woolf was working on Chapter III of Orlando, Sackville-West revealed her affair with Mary Campbell. In addition to this blow to the heart, Woolf's friend the great classical scholar Jane Harrison died in April 1928. Soon after, *To the Lighthouse* won the Femina Vie Heureuse prize. In July and August, Woolf was finishing articles on Sterne (including her review of *A Sentimental Journey*, published in *New York Herald Tribune* on 23 September 1928) and working again on 'Phases of Fiction', for which she read Henry James.[2] Life's many influences – personal and textual, publishing, honours, losses and rejections – all resonate around the writing of *Orlando* and its twists and turns, layering rich suggestive contexts for the novel and for the threads forming my chosen sentence.

Nature

Concerning Woolf's intense and complex relationship with the writing of nature, Christina Alt has identified her satirising of pedantry and the urge to catalogue in nature study. As Alt demonstrates, nature for Woolf cannot be pinned down; it is irreducible and transient. While the fetish for collecting was a Victorian preoccupation and certainly part of her own childhood experience, Woolf herself 'adopted an observational approach to nature, to living nature, to understanding life processes'; she championed 'a visionary approach to the natural world'.[3] My chosen sentence captures exactly this stance in its parodic, repetitive description of the seasons, and in its evocation of the poetics of naming: it performs Woolf's 'visionary approach' through its unfurling ferns, sickle moons and golden beech trees, while also drawing attention to this poetics as a set of romanticised clichés.

Woolf was, as noted above, also reading Henry James while writing *Orlando*, and in James's work ideas of nature, painting and Englishness recur as a satirical focus. James had remarked in *The Painter's Eye* (1882) that 'English painting interests me chiefly, not as painting, but as English': it is filled, as he saw it, with a great many chairs and tables, windows and doors, green fields and cloudy skies, more anecdotal than visual, all observation and feeling.[4] The idea of the English gaze and its relation to English words and sentences permeates *Orlando*, particularly through Orlando's struggle to see with fresh eyes while living with a Romani community in Chapter III. How, Woolf prompts us to ask, can change be pictured visually, or experienced intellectually and emotionally, with words and visual perception already so heavily laden with old meanings? Depicting the dramatic earth-shifting and life-changing agency of nature becomes a possible new way to break with old ways of seeing, as explored later in Woolf's essay 'Craftsmanship' (1937; *E6*

91–102). Indeed, throughout the whole novel, dramatic shifts and shattering identities burst out of 'nothing'; weather changes and selves fluctuate throughout. An ecology of the self and the culture is ever-present: an exploration of mutability and shift in the visual field, fixity and fluidity, fluid self and fluid earth. Old words thus acquire new meanings, as the 'English disease' identified in Chapter III as 'a love of Nature' (*O* 143) is dissected.

Woolf wrote the natural world as visual composition, much in the way she used techniques of scene-making and still-life perception.[5] Maggie Humm, describing modernist vocabularies of vision, has called *Orlando* multi-media, an image text reframing the visible world.[6] Nature has visual agency, but it is not always compositional in *Orlando*; rather, it is a continuous eruptive presence. Woolf remarked while writing the novel that 'the canvas shows through in a thousand places' (*D3* 176), something that is demonstrated in my sentence through the eruptive syntax, a kind of linguistic sabotage of order. Paradoxically, the sentence has a deliberately rough carelessness: it is tossed about, held up rather like a fly on a pin, or a specimen turned upside down, exposing its lack of meaning and relevance, its predictability and its boredom. It also conveys through this fragmentation the tedium and repetitiveness in the life of Orlando at that moment, and thus triggers Orlando's remarkable and sudden change in identity.

A potential target of these experiments in stylistic mockery is Woolf's wayward lover's poem *The Land*. Indeed, Sackville-West's work as a nature poet sits near the surface of the satire, its form and timing perfectly shaped for mockery, sickle moons and cycles of repetitive seasons being so easy to lampoon. But is this engagement with Sackville-West's poem venomous, mild, gentle or nasty, or perhaps all of these? There are passages from *The Land* in *Orlando*, which form both a direct engagement with and rejection of the mode of nature writing Vita Sackville-West so skilfully produces: her ancestral celebration of the garden, with its cycles of growth and complexity.[7] Fiction and biography, love and criticism merge here, but in the layered complexity of Woolf's satire love endures and even her own hurt feelings about Sackville-West's new lover are balanced with deeper exploration.[8] The self-parody in the sentence, satirising her own 'Time Passes' section from *To the Lighthouse*, reveals Woolf's self-awareness of her love of writing about nature's cycles. Throughout the novel, Orlando's love of nature is certainly portrayed as life-affirming: the oak tree connects him with the spine of the earth (*O* 12), turbulent forces break through surfaces, rivers gain their freedom (*O* 43), while frosts and floods change whole cultures, even the chambers of the brain (*O* 46). Nature can smother a writer alive (*O* 65), expose the discrepancy of time on the clock and time in the mind (O 69), and urge the poet to ask if the sky is blue and the grass is green (O 71).

Time passes

In her overt allusion to the middle section of *To the Lighthouse*, with its square brackets and unsettling temporality, Woolf changes the tense – 'Time passed' – but in the sentence's occurrence during a crucial interim period, time passes indeed. The sentence marks a gap between Orlando's life as a man and his move to Constantinople, where he becomes a woman. It thus also becomes the space between, where everything is unhooked, unhinged and dismembered of orderly textual meaning. The passing of time here is not only about cycles in nature, but about the story arc itself: the narrative interlude between man and woman. In that sense, it functions as the point of change much as the 'Time Passes' section does in *To the Lighthouse*. Straight after this sentence, the space is opened for a passage exploring ideas about 'time on the clock and time in the mind', where we are told that once Orlando turns thirty, the time of thinking is long, the time of acting is short (O 98). Woolf's self-mocking reference to her earlier novel and its devices for change is therefore underpinned by a serious temporal function as it signals the development of the novel as well as the protagonist.

The following, long sentence from the 'Time Passes' section of *To the Lighthouse* invites comparison with my chosen sentence, so much its opposite in dynamism and mood. Here, night and day, month and year 'ran shapelessly together', with amorphous bulks and 'idiot games', lunging and plunging; all is movement, uncertainty and chaos. Nature here is all without reason, the patterns of sameness in my sentence obliterated. Woolf's intensity of focus here is of the moment:

> Night after night, summer and winter, the torment of storms, the arrow-like stillness of fine weather held their court without interference. Listening (had there been any one to listen) from the upper rooms of the empty house only gigantic chaos streaked with lightning could have been heard tumbling and tossing, as the winds and waves disported themselves like the amorphous bulks of leviathans whose brows are pierced by no light of reason, and mounted one on top of another, and lunged and plunged in the darkness or the daylight (for night and day, month and year ran shapelessly together) in idiot games, until it seemed as if the universe were battling and tumbling, in brute confusion and wanton lust aimlessly by itself.[9]

In the *Orlando* sentence, the image of the old woman (though written as a light aside) is perhaps the most powerful, with its clear allusion to the two women who clean the Ramsay house in the 'Time Passes' section of *To the Lighthouse*, Mrs McNab and Mrs Bast. Taking on far more than just 'a little dust and a few cobwebs which one old woman can sweep up in half an hour', the old women in *To the Lighthouse* work hard to re-establish order, while Orlando, as a rich young male, inhabits a world where servants are invisible, their work trivialised even, their labour of no particular consequence. In *To the Lighthouse*, by contrast, the old women's labour is real, hard and deeply meaningful:

> Mrs McNab groaned; Mrs Bast creaked. They were old; they were stiff; their legs ached. They came with their brooms and pails at last [. . .] Slowly and painfully, with broom and pail, mopping, scouring, Mrs McNab, Mrs Bast, stayed the corruption and the rot; rescued from the pool of Time that was fast closing over them now a basin, now a cupboard. (*TL* 215)

John Mepham cites my chosen sentence and its accompanying paragraph, claiming that Woolf is mocking 'her own solemn and mystical style of writing. She makes fun of "Time Passes"'.[10] There is indeed self-mockery, but Woolf also creates intertextual echoes which deepen and add layers to both texts.

The reader

The reader is a prime mover in my sentence, an actively invoked participant asked to bring imagination and engagement to take over, fill in gaps and make adjustments. This invitation is openly stated: 'the reader can imagine the passage'. Woolf establishes an exciting conspiracy here, a conversation with the reader to take apart the sentence, to live inside it and critique it, to join the laughter, and perhaps even dissolve the text. An old narrative contract with the reader here breaks open. The reader is asked to enter the discussion; the silent bond has been exposed. The sentence breaks apart or opens out, thereby breaking the illusion of time: the passage of time is shown to run adrift, while language itself is shown to be filled with new potential. In this respect, Woolf's work on her essay 'Phases of Fiction' gives further resonance to the sentence in *Orlando*. This essay explores the way interactive reading engages with the idea of solidity, facts, and what the reader brings to the fluidity of a text. Reading, for Woolf, can 'reassure us of stability in real life [. . .] until we seem wedged among solid objects in a solid universe' (*E4* 43), whereas eruptive texts can dissolve and yet exist in a solid space of ideas. In *Orlando*, which was much influenced by Sterne, the reader is asked to be a creator in that space, a co-conspirator: 'the reader can imagine the passage which should follow' (*O* 97). *Orlando* is thus a text about modernist creativity and the nature of the space within, breaking, as it does, the frame and the idea of representation. Like the painters of her circle, Woolf was freeing herself from the accepted representation and meanings of things.

Stein and sentences

Woolf had met Gertrude Stein through a connection with the writer Edith Sitwell, who introduced them.[11] The Hogarth Press considered publishing Stein's book *The Making of Americans* (1925), but declined it on the grounds of length. Whether Woolf read much of the larger text is questionable, but Hogarth did publish Stein's *Composition as Explanation* in 1926 as a Hogarth Essay.[12] It began as a much-debated Cambridge lecture, one of the more accessible explanations of Stein's theory of writing, and known among Bloomsbury writers and artists. Rachel Blau DuPlessis has argued that Stein influenced Woolf's writing of *The Waves*,[13] but we can also trace some resonances in *Orlando* from *Composition as Explanation*. Not so much a Steinian influence as a conversation engaging related ideas, Woolf's experiments with sentence structure in *Orlando* explore similar territory to Stein's, but with differing form and outcomes. Experiments with the sentence were happening at around the same time in both Stein's and Woolf's writing, but they were different, even if there are resonant elements such as comparable ideas of space and time, and their breaking up traditional narrative sequencing and patterning.

In a recent update of her original 'Woolfenstein' essay from 1989,[14] 'Woolfenstein, the Sequel' (2014), Rachel Blau DuPlessis argues that Stein uses Laurence Sterne's 'Tristram Shandyan' techniques to create interruption and avoid sequencing as a part of her resistance to 'established norms of writing and thinking'.[15] We can see that Woolf, too, was employing many of Sterne's techniques in producing sentence implosions, addressing the reader, and creating contextual and narrative unpredictability. As DuPlessis shows, both Woolf and Stein address the issue of sequencing, with different results. While Woolf breaks with sequence, consistency and message, Stein 'interrupts and negates contracts with the reader'.[16] So much of this exploration is also clearly happening in my chosen sentence, as it opens out the sequencing of predictable narrative and description, inviting the reader to unpick and comment, undermining outcome, creating 'nothing'. Indeed, the phrase 'a little dust and a few cobwebs' implies decay in the house and in the life of the inhabitants, caused by sameness and lack of renewal: dust has gathered, vitality has gone. There is no 'there' there, the past is past, and all that remains are cobwebs clinging to old forms. The reason perhaps why transformation is then possible is that a change has already happened; the space needed maintenance, a dusting by an old cleaner – an old goddess perhaps – some core energy of renewal. The implication here is that change builds up, bursts through uncontrollably. Can writing capture this process of transformation?

DuPlessis points to a clear difference between Stein's and Woolf's sentence experiments as they each address these matters of change, meaning and sequence: Stein's tactic is dispersive, while Woolf's is unifying.[17] Without definitive proof that Woolf read Stein's essay in depth, except insofar as she was her publisher, DuPlessis concludes nonetheless that Woolf was challenged by the 'formal designs, the repetitions, the grids, the critique of the centre, the radical resistance to sequencing in the work of Gertrude Stein'.[18] Woolf was, like Stein, and much like the Post-Impressionist and modernist painters in both writers' circles, increasingly drawn to ideas about visual and textual abstraction, to its subversive layering under story and its mapping of the space inside the frame. The textual space is conceived as something in itself, untethered from representation. Stein's *Composition as Explanation* resonates with my *Orlando* sentence in this sense. Examples abound in Stein's essay that echo the deeper meaning of Woolf's sentence: 'composition is the difference which makes each and all of them then different from other generations':[19]

> The only thing that is different from one time to another is what is seen and what is seen depends upon how everybody is doing everything. This makes the thing we are looking at very different and this makes what those who describe it make of it, it makes a composition, it confuses, it shows, it is, it looks, it likes it as it is, and this makes what is seen as it is seen. Nothing changes from generation to generation except the thing seen and that makes a composition.[20]

The *Orlando* sentence echoes this intent to remake, break with certainty, and make new order. Their methods differ, but as modernist writers Woolf and Stein sensed the beckoning new space. What indeed makes a composition? What makes what is seen? How do words acquire new meanings? What is a sentence? What is a sentence for?

On the matter of length, the *Orlando* sentence reads like a paragraph; it is very long, complex and twisting. When is a sentence a sentence? When it has eight semi-colons? Stein noted that the English invented the sentence and that the Americans needed to invent the paragraph:

that paragraphs relate to a sense of space and the land for Americans, and sentences to 'daily island life' for the English.[21] In 'What is English Literature' (1934) from Stein's *Lectures in America* (1935), and earlier in *How to Write* (1927), Stein further suggested that paragraphs are emotional and sentences are not: 'emotional paragraphs are made up of unemotional sentences'.[22] For Stein, disconnection and breaking down the paragraph was one method for changing the dynamic of her writing, and she interrupted the sentence as a self-conscious outsider. Woolf's method – writing the inside-out of the sentence – proved as fruitful a strategy for challenging staleness while keeping the sentence, exposing predictability and cliché while celebrating the inside of the English sentence. Stein writes that when change comes 'the rapidity of the change is always startling',[23] and 'beginning again and again and again explaining composition and time is a natural thing'.[24] This explanation of how meaning is created in composition is also what Woolf performs in the *Orlando* sentence: she unpacks and starts the sentence again in time and space. What is seen is challenged as hollow; intervention is sought from the active reader. A new composition is envisaged but not created, in a space and time where nothing happens but everything becomes possible.

Stein and Woolf both seek some new modernist interaction between what is written and how it is read, dissolving the space between, and yet maintaining a whole new textual rigour. For Stein, 'composition is not there, it is going to be there, and we are here': 'everything is the same except composition and time, composition and the time of the composition and the time in the composition'.[25] There and here, the line between writer and reader blurs, and the question looms: what is composition, and where does it settle – in the act of reading or in the mind after the interaction? In the *Orlando* sentence there is a list, a bracket for a random number, a broom, an expression of doubt, a touch of exaggeration, and the simple statement that 'nothing whatever happened'. Woolf's technique of opening up the layers and the space between the words, both literally and textually, becomes dynamically possible, once this clearing away of predictable patterning has been achieved. In the context of the whole novel, the jump to 'the present moment' through a long temporal tunnel can only happen because of the prior clearing of space in Orlando's life and the text, as in this later passage: 'the immensely long tunnel in which she seemed to have been travelling for hundreds of years widened; the light poured in; her thoughts became mysteriously tightened [. . .] It was 1928. It was the present moment' (*O* 218–19).

Visual and textual abstraction: nothing happens

Beyond the aerobatics performed by Woolf in my *Orlando* sentence, there are tempting themes to be teased out about her attraction to abstraction, encouraged by the Post-Impressionist painters as well as writers like Stein. What is left inside the space when the clutter dissolves? What is the 'nothing' that remains? What happens when nothing happens? Something is left – an endless visual possibility. The critical tools remain, and a lightness of textual spirit. A painterly space emerges, that which exists inside the space and remains there to be drawn out: the blank canvas, text and image. The great breakthrough of the modernists, to wipe clean and open up that space, is all about remaining attentive to what happens inside it. Many sentences in the novel perform this clearance. It is also particularly characteristic of the feminist Woolf that she equates this clearance of old meanings with women's work, with housekeeping and clearing out the cobwebs: the old dusty associations and meanings. It is part of a woman's energy to see what is clogging things up and sweep it away. With words, Woolf does what the modernist painters did: she opens up and frees the space from the past and its clichés, its slavishness to representation, making new lines of aesthetic connection.[26]

This sentence from *Orlando* is above all about the meaning of description and representation, how words work, and the variability of time. It engages deeply with ideas in space and time. 'Nothing whatever happens', we are told, but in fact so much happens inside the sentence. There are huge shifts, and a bold arresting of certainties. Language and its meanings are challenged, and made to be denuded of permanence. As a whole, the novel is a vibrant Post-Impressionist experiment, consistent with the larger development of Woolf's *oeuvre*. In the example of this specific sentence, through abstraction – forms twisting in space – the sentence becomes a kind of painting; a movie collage; an empty beginning. Before the creation of new content, the more radical act is the wiping clear of the past, in the process of which the new tools are sharpened and ready for use. Clearing the ground utterly of meaning by reducing the sentence literally to 'nothing', via the agency of time, Woolf opens the door to marvellous new purposefulness.

Notes

1. Virginia Woolf, *Orlando* (New York: Crosby Gage, 1928), pp. 97–8.
2. Edward Bishop, *A Virginia Woolf Chronology* (Boston: Macmillan, 1989), pp. 101–15.

3. Christina Alt, *Virginia Woolf and the Study of Nature* (Cambridge: Cambridge University Press, 2010), pp. 93, 85, 71.
4. Henry James, 'London Pictures', in H. James, *The Painter's Eye: Notes and Essays on the Pictorial Arts* (Madison: Wisconsin University Press, 1956), p. 202.
5. See Diane F. Gillespie, *The Sisters' Arts: The Writing and Painting of Virginia Woolf and Vanessa Bell* (New York: Syracuse University Press, 1991).
6. Maggie Humm, *Modernist Women and Visual Culture* (New Brunswick, NJ: Rutgers University Press, 2003), pp. 1–2.
7. See Mark Hussey, *Virginia Woolf A–Z* (Oxford: Oxford University Press, 1995), p. 202. Vita Sackville-West's poem *The Land* (lines from the Spring section) is quoted in Chapter VI of *Orlando* (pp. 47–8).
8. For critical discussion of the personal and textual relationship with Vita Sackville-West, and its impact on *Orlando*, see Louise DeSalvo and Mitchell Leaska (eds), *The Letters of Vita Sackville-West to Virginia Woolf* (London: Virago Press, 1984), pp. 31–2; Hermione Lee, *Virginia Woolf* (London: Chatto and Windus, 1996), pp. 519–23; and Hussey, *Virginia Woolf*, pp. 200–3.
9. Virginia Woolf, *To the Lighthouse* (London: Hogarth Press, 1927), p. 208.
10. John Mepham, *Virginia Woolf: A Literary Life* (London: Macmillan, 1991), p. 128.
11. Edith Sitwell campaigned to promote Stein in England, reviewing her writing, and introducing her to Leonard and Virginia Woolf. See Ulla E. Dydo, *Gertrude Stein: The Language That Rises. 1923–1934* (Evanston: Northwestern University Press, 2003), pp. 79–81.
12. Gertrude Stein, *Composition as Explanation* (London: Hogarth Press, 1926).
13. Rachel Blau DuPlessis, 'Woolfenstein', in Ellen G. Friedman and Miriam Fuchs (eds), *Breaking the Sequence: Women's Experimental Fiction* (Princeton: Princeton University Press, 1989), pp. 99–114.
14. Rachel Blau DuPlessis, 'Woolfenstein, the Sequel', in Janet Boyd and Sharon J. Kirsch (eds), *Primary Stein: Returning to the Writing of Gertrude Stein* (Plymouth: Lexington Books, 2014), pp. 37–55.
15. Ibid. p. 37.
16. Ibid. p. 38.
17. Ibid. p. 40.
18. Ibid. p. 44.
19. Stein, *Composition*, p. 5.
20. Ibid. p. 6.
21. Gertrude Stein, *How to Write* (New York: Dover Publications, 1975).
22. Ibid. p. xxi.
23. Ibid. p. 10.
24. Ibid. p. 12.
25. Ibid. pp. 14, 23.
26. Jane Goldman, *The Feminist Aesthetics of Virginia Woolf: Modernism, Post-Impressionism and the Politics of the Visual* (Cambridge: Cambridge University Press, 1998), pp. 110–11.

Chapter 7

Orlando, Greece and the Impossible Landscape

Vassiliki Kolocotroni

So she was thinking, one fine morning on the slopes of Mount Athos, when minding her goats.[1]

Orlando's Greek pastoral idyll is a brief but crucial stage of her travels and travails homeward and into the present day. In transit between identities and divested of her title and cultural position, she finds herself the guest of a nomadic tribe, who tend but do not own the ancient land that accommodates them. Her passage through Northern Greece is significantly located: setting one of Orlando's transformative epiphanies against the backdrop of Mount Athos, a site of gender exclusion, Woolf casts Orlando in the role of an unwitting interloper, trespassing on time and tradition, once again, and formatively, out of place. The episode hones Orlando's poetic disposition but also homes in on the ambivalent effects of one of its tested tropes – on the Greek mountain, Orlando both embodies and deploys the allegorical mode. As a woman (hidden among the 'gipsies' and under her 'light burnous'), she is at once the emblem of an impossibility, a female creature on a sacred, forbidding all-male space, and of the very possibility of trespassing that space, on her way home. At the same time, as a pastoral poet, exercising the licence that allegory affords, she claims her own patrimony in a vision of renewed ownership, transformed by the passing of time and gender privilege. This chapter glosses the effect and provenance of this allegorical trope through a brief account of Woolf's Harrisonian Hellenism and her own passage through the Greek landscape, considered here in the light of Denis E. Cosgrove's foundational definition: 'landscape represents a way of seeing – a way in which some Europeans have represented to themselves and to others the world about them and their relationships with it, and through which they have commented on social relations'.[2]

The unseen

'The unseen is always haunting me, surging up behind the visible', Jane Ellen Harrison writes in 'Alpha and Omega' (1915), her defence of atheism, or the 'free idea' as expression of the belief in the sacramental, mystical vitality of human experience.[3] As ever, she turns to Greece to illustrate her point:

> I had often wondered why the Olympians – Apollo, Athena, even Zeus, always vaguely irritated me, and why the mystery gods, their shapes and ritual, Demeter, Dionysus, the cosmic Eros, drew and drew me. I see it now. It is just that these mystery gods represent the supreme golden moment achieved by the Greek, and the Greek only, in his incomparable way. The mystery gods *are* eikonic, caught in lovely human shapes; but they are life-spirits barely held; they shift and change.[4]

Harrison's passionate and partisan Hellenism influenced a generation of modernist writers, willing experimenters with 'shifting and changing' form. Woolf is perhaps the closest in her concerns to Harrison, as her carefully calibrated use of allegory sets ancient shades loose from the limits of classical Greek light. Informed by her copious reading of classical texts, reinforced by visits to Greece in 1906 and 1932, Woolf's engagement with Greek inflects all of her work in subtle but sure ways.[5] Though not formally taught by Harrison, Woolf read and published her work, and famously monumentalised her as a shadowy figure that still haunted College grounds, in a passing valedictory reference in *A Room of One's Own*. This polemical lecture on women's writing rights was given at Cambridge in October 1928, six months after Harrison's death and in the same year as the publication of *Orlando*:

> The windows of the building, curved like ships' windows among generous waves of red brick, changed from lemon to silver under the flight of the quick spring clouds. Somebody was in a hammock, somebody, but in this light they were phantoms only, half guessed, half seen, raced across the grass – would no one stop her? – and then on the terrace, as if popping out to breathe the air, to glance at the garden, came a bent figure, formidable yet humble, with her great forehead and her shabby dress – could it be the famous scholar, could it be J—— H—— herself? All was dim, yet intense too, as if the scarf which the dusk had flung over the garden were torn asunder by star or sword – the gash of some terrible reality leaping, as its way is, out of the heart of the spring.[6]

Not unlike one of Harrison's insatiable life spirits, a changeable yet unstoppable *daimon*, the figure is barely visible 'in this light', 'half guessed, half seen', which is of course always the best look in Harrison's and Woolf's books; as Woolf put it in an early story, 'figures are slippery things!',[7] or in a later, more Harrisonian formulation in *Orlando*: 'One can only believe entirely, perhaps, in what one cannot see' (*O* 123).

The seen

At once her most visual and 'slippery' of novels, *Orlando* is a fantastic, parodic extravaganza or, to ground it in terms of the other important Hellenising influence in Woolf's formation, a Paterian 'imaginary portrait'.[8] The young aristocrat whose imaginary life this portrait draws is of course Vita Sackville-West, dedicatee of the book and at the time an intimate friend. Through shape-changing, gender-bending escapades and dashing derring-do (and don'ts), *Orlando* manages to contain references to Sackville-West's extremely colourful personal and public life, as famous heiress, establishment wife and writer of considerable reputation. Her long narrative poem *The Land* (1926), a 2,500-line four-part Georgic work describing the agricultural activities of the Kentish weald, had won her the prestigious Hawthornden Prize in 1927, and provided the pre-text for *Orlando*'s treatment of the pastoral mode. The main character's magnum opus 'The Oak Tree', written during the novel despite the interruptions of gender and generational change, is evidence of ambition but also of the arch, self-conscious and at times pathetic, if not pathological, Virgilian sensibility of its author. The poem's good fortune, like that of aristocratic Orlando herself, is cheekily treated by the narrator:

> (Here she turned into the High Street of her native town, which was crowded, for it was market day, with farmers, and shepherds, and old women with hens in baskets.) I like peasants. I understand crops. But (here another self came skipping over the top of her mind like the beam from a lighthouse). Fame! (She laughed.) Fame! Seven editions. A prize. Photographs in the evening papers (here she alluded to the 'Oak Tree' and 'The Burdett Coutts' Memorial Prize which she had won [. . .]) [. . .] Fame! she repeated. A poet – a charlatan; both every morning as regularly as the post comes in. (*O* 194–5)

Woolf exposes here the self-absorbed Orlando's lyrical thought processes as she drives her motorcar poetically down the busy street. It is only when faced with the very unpoetic subject of carpenter Joe Stubbs and his deformed thumb that Orlando is shaken out of herself: 'The sight was so repulsive that she felt faint for a moment, but in that moment's darkness, when her eyelids flickered, she was relieved of the pressure of the present' (*O* 201). The matter is resolved with Orlando burying her poem under the old oak tree that in a way bore it, and asking for once the right question of herself: 'What has praise and fame to do with poetry?' (O 203). The concreteness of the image that bespeaks real manual labour, in other words, forces the reflex of relegating the patrician imaginings to the place of invisibility, or the symbolic source which generated them. At once a humbled and redeeming gesture, this return of the poem to its roots makes literal what the pastoral mode can only allegorise or elide.

Orlando/Sackville-West's chastisement by Woolf may be read politically as an instance of the latter's deep ambivalence about the kind of hereditary entitlement that licenses the poem's proprietorial pastoral vision. That is a vision which Woolf cannot countenance, least of all when it is offered by a male persona – and it is in the male voice that *The Land* is written (this may be another reason why Vita had to be un-manned in *Orlando*) – but also when it presumes to fix and define those shapes that 'shift and change'. The very character of Orlando may embody a double identity, but once fixed as a 'man' or 'woman', as s/he must necessarily be, s/he inhabits a space or spaces (however exotic or homely) that necessarily, by virtue of (sexual) difference, (spatial) distance and (social) distinction, enforce exclusivity. Appropriately, then, Orlando has a series of visions that always 'place' him or her.[9] Tellingly, however, of the many panoramas available to Orlando in her journey from the past to the present, of the many 'hauntings' that shade her vision,[10] there is one which reveals at least the possibility of an 'other' composition, an allegorical scene, which Woolf sets in Greece.

The scene

Having woken one morning in Constantinople as a woman, Orlando sheds his ambassadorial robes and flees the city in the company of a gipsy tribe. The setting for that twist in the plot has been read by many as appropriate for its evocation of 'Sapphic love', as well as the licence for cross-dressing 'passings' that the Orient traditionally affords the traveller. David Roessel, for instance, argues that Constantinople for Woolf was a 'multivalent symbol encompassing three of the most significant forces in her life, Sapphic love, death, and war',[11] and similarly for Krystyna Colburn, 'Constantinople conjures sapphism and domes'.[12] In Susan Bazargan's reading, Woolf's choice of setting here corresponds with 'what Marjorie Garber, in her discussion of transvestism, has called a "third" space, a "space of possibility" in which gender indeterminacy becomes viable'. According to Bazargan:

For Woolf this was the Orient as constructed by the Western imagination, a space of fantasy in which binary notions of gender identity can become blurred. Drawing on the power of the cliché, the magic of the orient and all its one-thousand-and-one-nights aura, Woolf could make Orlando's amazing transformation believable.[13]

The gipsy entourage also throws up an oblique reference to Sackville-West's first 'Greek love': her youthful, scandalous escapade with Violet Trefusis.[14] But it is also as an Arnoldian 'scholar-gipsy' that Orlando appears in that section of the book; like the persona of Matthew Arnold's eponymous 1853 poem, the impoverished Oxford student who, 'tired of knocking at preferment's door', abandons his studies and joins a band of gipsies, from whom he learns lessons in life and the unfettered imagination, Orlando appears in this section of the novel ever ready to 'listen with enchanted ears', or see the world anew 'on some mild pastoral slope':[15]

> She compared the flowers to enamel and the turf to Turkey rugs worn thin. Trees were withered hags, and sheep were grey boulders. Everything, in fact, was something else. She found the tarn on the mountain-top and almost threw herself in to seek the wisdom she thought lay hid there; and when, from the mountain-top, she beheld far off, across the Sea of Marmara, the plains of Greece, and made out (her eyes were admirable) the Acropolis with a white streak or two, which must, she thought, be the Parthenon, her soul expanded with her eyeballs, and she prayed that she might share the majesty of the hills, know the serenity of the plains, etc. etc., as all such believers do. (O 89–90)

Her lyrical disposition, her 'hauntings' seem hackneyed here, and, though innocent of the Grand Tourist clichés themselves, the gipsies soon begin to grow weary of Orlando's allegorical ways:

> She need not even look at them, and yet they felt, here is someone who doubts; (we make a rough-and-ready translation from the gipsy language) here is someone who does not do the thing for the sake of doing; nor looks for looking's sake; here is someone who believes neither in sheep-skin nor basket; but sees (here they looked apprehensively about the tent) something else. (O 91)

Though free of her ambassadorial duties and her maleness, and for all the fraternising with free spirits, Orlando is still bound by the wrong kind of yearning, that sensibility which turns land into landscape and living space into a still life with figures, or the scene of a modern Georgic poem, in the manner of Sackville-West's *The Land*.

A sudden transformation does occur, however, in a strange place:

> What was to be done, Orlando could not think. To leave the gipsies and become once more an Ambassador seemed to her intolerable. But it was equally impossible to remain for ever where there was neither ink nor writing paper, neither reverence for the Talbots nor respect for a multiplicity of bedrooms. *So she was thinking, one fine morning on the slopes of Mount Athos, when minding her goats.* And then Nature, in whom she trusted, either played her a trick or worked a miracle – again, opinions differ too much for it to be possible to say which. (O 93–4; my emphasis)

This is a magical moment, such as could only be possible in a place which her presence as a woman makes *im*possible – that is, Mount Athos, the Northern Greek mountain and peninsula occupied by the Autonomous Monastic State of the Holy Mountain, which prohibits the entry into its territory of women or female animals. Woolf would have surely registered the existence of that historical and theological anachronism through reading Harrison's pointed account of it in her *Reminiscences of a Student's Life*, which the Hogarth Press published in 1925: 'Long after, I visited Mount Athos. Of course, as a woman I could not set foot on the sacred promontory [. . .] We mere women were left behind on the yacht disconsolate'.[16] Years before that recollection, in April 1912, Harrison had written to her mentor, classical scholar Gilbert Murray, with an equally poignant reflection on the inaccessibility of a site of such resonance for those keen to trace remnants of a once potent matriarchal presence:

> Mt Athos is extraordinarily beautiful: the monasteries hang like birds' nests all round the rocks – have you been? I got some letter-paper from a monastery with a picture of the Holy Mountain and just near the peak an apocalypse of your Holy Mother. As the legend was in Russian it had to go to Rosalind, but it has just occurred to me that it is really a survival of the *Mêtêr Oreia* (mountain mother). All these peaks had either a mother or else as on Olympos they had Zeus Helios and then the old patriarch Elias took them over, and isn't it a splendid triumph of patriarchy that though the Panaghia [Holy Mother] is still worshipped no woman may set her foot on the Holy Mountain? How things do last on.[17]

And in October 1935, most likely on Ethel Smyth's recommendation, the Hogarth Press was to publish an illustrated travelogue, *The 6,000 Beards of Mount Athos*, by Ralph H. Brewster, grandson of Smyth's friend H. B. Brewster. Smyth provided an introduction and Woolf some grudging entertainment for the author, whom she registered as having 'large hands, hanging: only just neat enough to have tea. A sudden amused kindling in the gooseberry eyes; & the profuse storytelling of those who have lived with savages' (*D4* 323).

Seeing other

As Joel Fineman argues, 'allegory seems regularly to surface in critical or polemical atmospheres, when for political or metaphysical reasons there is something that cannot be said'.[18] It is appropriate, then, that Orlando, herself 'otherised' or excluded here 'sees (as) other', for once at home in the space of allegory, or in another sense, a true utopia:

> Orlando was gazing rather disconsolately at the steep hill-side in front of her. It was now midsummer, and if we must compare the landscape to anything, it would have been to a dry bone; to a sheep's skeleton; to a gigantic skull picked white by a thousand vultures. The heat was intense, and the little fig tree under which Orlando lay only served to print patterns of fig-leaves upon her light burnous.
>
> Suddenly a shadow, though there was nothing to cast a shadow, appeared on the bald mountain-side opposite. It deepened quickly and soon a green hollow showed where there had been barren rock before. As she looked, the hollow deepened and widened, and a great park-like space opened in the flank of the hill. Within, she could see an undulating and grassy lawn; she could see oak trees dotted here and there; she could see the thrushes hopping among the branches. She could see the deer stepping delicately from shade to shade, and could even hear the hum of insects and the gentle sighs and shivers of a summer's day in England. After she had gazed entranced for some time, snow began falling; soon the whole landscape was covered and marked with violet shades instead of yellow sunlight. Now she saw heavy carts coming along the roads, laden with tree trunks, which they were taking, she knew, to be sawn for firewood; and then appeared the roofs and belfries and towers and courtyards of her own home. The snow was falling steadily, and she could now hear the slither and flop which it made as it slid down the roof and fell to the ground. The smoke went up from a thousand chimneys. All was so clear and minute that she could see a daw pecking for worms in the snow. Then, gradually, the violet shadows deepened and closed over the carts and the lawns and the great house itself. All was swallowed up. Now there was nothing left of the grassy hollow, and instead of the green lawns was only the blazing hill-side which a thousand vultures seemed to have picked bare. At this, she burst into a passion of tears, and striding back to the gipsies' camp, told them that she must sail for England the very next day. (O 93–5)

On one level, with this vision, Orlando seems, like the speaker in Andrew Marvell's 'The Garden', to be 'Annihilating all that's made / To a green thought in a green shade';[19] but there's more than scholarly allusion going on in this passage. Read through a utopian allegorical lens, what unfolds in front of Orlando's eyes (or her mind's eye) is both an eclipse (of the 'yellow sunlight') and a transfiguration, a new coloration, or indeed, if we take it that Woolf's palette is precise, the green, white and violet tricolour of the Suffragettes.[20] Here is a polemical landscape, then, defiantly uncanny in its estrangement of or from a 'home' as known or previously experienced, as well as an instructive one, at least for those who can see. In this sense, it could be seen to fit Elizabeth Helsinger's definition of landscape as 'also at once an epistemology – a mode of explanation – and a practice – a mode of participation, a site of agency'.[21] Its Greek setting adds a most important nuance to its intelligibility, as it collapses the past and the present in one mystical, exclusive continuum, within which women are always abstracted, deducted, distinguished by their absence or invisibility.[22]

This corner of Woolf's Greece signifies, interestingly enough, another absence: that of modern Greece itself in the scholarly treatment of the book.[23] As is the case with all allegorical elision, this absence 'hold[s] something else in reserve', as Helsinger puts it.[24] Indeed, one could trace this effect of sudden, epiphanic defamiliarisation in Woolf's persistently allegorical use of Greek vistas elsewhere in her writing. Diary entries during the second visit to Greece in 1932 record again the tropes she so artfully deconstructs in *Orlando*. The 'hauntings' are always there, as a familiar gesture:

> Yes, but what can I say about the Parthenon – that my own ghost met me, the girl of 23, with all her life to come: that; & then, this is more compact & splendid than I remembered. The yellow pillars – how shall I say? Gathered, grouped, radiating there on the rock, against the most violent sky, with staring ice blue, & then cinder black; crowds flying as if suppliants (really Greek schoolchildren). (*D4* 90)

The allegorical prerogative that can transform modern Greek schoolchildren into ancient suppliants is exercised here by Woolf as cliché from the traveller's repertoire, and perhaps with the same (though self-directed in this case) irony that inflects the representation of Orlando's precocious tendency always to see 'something else' (*O* 91). The effect relies on the trick of collapsing the space and time of the now into a primitive pastoral idyll: 'How strange the patiently amenable flat land is, set with biblical trees, grazed by long woolled sheep, & not a house to be seen. This is England in the time of Chaucer' (*D4* 92). The simultaneity of the vision tallies with what Johannes Fabian has defined as the 'allochrony' of the traveller's and anthropologist's perspective,[25] but it also resonates with the melancholy, Harrisonian, allegorical vision of a land where, paradoxically, the eclipse of solar, patriarchal dominance (in all its resonances and effects) is still possible:

> Greece then, so to return to Greece, is a land so ancient that it is like wandering in the fields of the moon. Life is receding (in spite of that donkey). The living, these worn down, for ever travelling the roads Greeks, cannot master

Greece any longer. It is too bare too stony, precipitous for them [...] Such solitude as they must know, under the sun, under the snow, such dependence on themselves to clothe & feed themselves through the splendid summer days is unthinkable in England. The centuries have left no trace. There is no 18th 16th, 15th century all in layers as in England – nothing between them & 300 B.C. 300 B.C. somehow conquered Greece & still holds it. So it is the country of the moon; I mean, lit by a dead sun. (*D4* 94)

Woolf exercises the right of the cultivated traveller to Greece to arrest time, landscape it, and mythologise. In this 'cenotaphic signification',[26] the Greeks worth writing home about are fleeting shadows; as Woolf put it in a letter to Sackville-West on 8 May 1932: 'The sea gets in everywhere [...] And snow mountains beyond, and bays as they were when Eve – no it should be Persephone – bathed there.'[27] Like Orlando surveying the impossible landscape on Mount Athos, Woolf visualises another epiphanic scene:

Then I had the vision, in Aegina, of an uncivilized, hot new season to be brought into our lives – how yearly we shall come here, with a tent, escaping England, & sloughing the respectable skin; & all the tightness & formality of London; fame, & wealth; & go back & become irresponsible, livers, existing on bread yaot [*sic*], butter, eggs, say in Crete. This is to some extent a genuine impulse, I thought, coming down the hill with easy strides; London is not enough, nor Sussex either. One wants to be sunbaked, & taken back to these loquacious friendly people, simply to live, to talk, not to read & write. And then I looked up & saw the mountains across the bay, knife shaped, coloured, & the sea, brimming smooth; & felt as if a knife had scraped some incrusted organ in me, for I could not find anything lacking in that agile, athletic beauty, steeped in colour, so that it was not cold, perfectly free from vulgarity, yet old in human life, so that every inch has its wild flower that might grow in an English garden, & the peasants are gentle people; & their clothes, worn & burnt, are subtly coloured, though coarse. (*D4* 97)

This vision may be closer to the personal than the political outlook of *Orlando*'s allegorical transformations, but it shares with them a conviction in and desire for the freedom of 'seeing other' as a strategy for living, simply, the unfettered human life. The landscape is infused with a pastoral temporality that both elides the real time of the scene ('old in human life'), and encapsulates it in the desire, so familiar to allegory, to seize and project it onto an eternal coevality and coexistence ('so that every inch has its wild flower that might grow in an English garden'). As Jean-Luc Nancy puts it:

A landscape is always a landscape of time, and doubly so: it is a time of year [...] and a time of day [...] as well as a kind of weather [...] In the presentation of this time, which unfolds with every image, the present of representation can do nothing other than render infinitely sensible the passing of time, the fleeting instability of what is shown.[28]

Like Orlando's, Woolf's vision of and in Greece creates impossible, unstable landscapes, populated by the seen and unseen, animated by the desire for equality and transformation.

Notes

1. Virginia Woolf, *Orlando: A Biography* [1928] (London: Grafton Books, 1977), p. 94.
2. Denis E. Cosgrove, 'Introduction to *Social Formation and Symbolic Landscape*', in Rachel Ziady DeLu and James Elkins (eds), *Landscape Theory* (New York and London: Routledge, 2008), p. 20.
3. Jane Ellen Harrison, 'Alpha and Omega', in J. E. Harrison, *Alpha and Omega* (London: Sidgwick & Son, Ltd, 1915), p. 206.
4. Harrison, 'Alpha and Omega', pp. 204–5.
5. See for instance, Rowena Fowler, 'Moments and Metamorphoses: Virginia Woolf's Greece', *Comparative Literature*, 51.3 (Summer 1999), pp. 217–42; Vassiliki Kolocotroni, '"This Curious Silent Unrepresented Life": Greek Lessons in Virginia Woolf's Early Fiction', *Modern Language Review*, 100.2 (April 2005), pp. 313–22; Vassiliki Kolocotroni, 'Strange Cries and Ancient Songs: Woolf's Greek and the Politics of Intelligibility', in Bryony Randall and Jane Goldman (eds), *Virginia Woolf in Context* (Cambridge: Cambridge University Press, 2013), pp. 23–38; Theodore Koulouris, *Hellenism and Loss in the Work of Virginia Woolf* (Farnham, Surrey: Ashgate, 2011); Angeliki Spiropoulou, '"On Not Knowing Greek": Virginia Woolf's Spatial Critique of Authority', *Interdisciplinary Literary Studies*, 4.1 (2002), pp. 1–19.
6. Virginia Woolf, *A Room of One's Own/Three Guineas* [1929/1938], ed. Michèle Barrett (Harmondsworth: Penguin Books, 1993), p. 15.
7. Virginia Woolf, 'The Journal of Mistress Joan Martyn' (1906), in V. Woolf, *The Complete Short Fiction*, ed. Susan Dick (London: Triad Grafton Books, 1991), p. 57.
8. Walter Pater is acknowledged in Woolf's Preface as one of the 'many friends [who] have helped me in writing this book' (*O* 7). For the most thorough account of Woolf's debt to Pater, see Perry Meisel, *The Absent Father: Virginia Woolf and Walter Pater* (New Haven, CT, and London: Yale University Press, 1980).
9. As Erica L. Johnson puts it in 'Giving Up the Ghost: National and Literary Haunting in *Orlando*': 'By substantiating the continuity in Orlando's transhistorical, transgender character through national identity, though, Woolf shows Englishness to be composed of exclusions as well as inclusions, revealing the extent to which national identity is haunted by what she might have called "invisible presences", which inhabit national space not as subjects and citizens, but as ghosts' (*Modern Fiction Studies*, 50.1 (Spring 2004), p. 113).

10. Ibid. p. 110.
11. David Roessel, 'The Significance of Constantinople in *Orlando*', *Papers on Language and Literature*, 28 (1992), p. 398.
12. Krystyna Colburn, 'Spires of London: Domes of Istanbul', in Beth Rigel Daugherty and Eileen Barrett (eds), *Virginia Woolf: Texts and Contexts – Selected Papers from the Fifth Annual Conference on Virginia Woolf* (New York: Pace University Press, 1996), p. 252.
13. Susan Bazargan, 'The Uses of the Land: Vita Sackville-West's Pastoral Writings and Virginia Woolf's *Orlando*', *Woolf Studies Annual*, 5 (1999), pp. 49–50.
14. According to Kirstie Blair, who has commented on the episode, 'in the two novels [Sackville-West] wrote during their involvement, *Challenge* (written in 1918 but unpublished in Britain) and *Heritage* (1919), the gypsy is a potent presence. *Challenge*, a loosely disguised fictional study of her relationship with Trefusis, centers on the turbulent romance between Julian, the upper-class hero, who is dedicated to the cause of an independence movement on a fictional Greek island, and Eve, who is uninterested in his politics and seeks to prioritize their love at the cost of all else. Sackville-West represents Eve as the type of the seductive, ultra feminine gypsy woman, a suitable foil to her masculine Julian' ('Gypsies and Lesbian Desire', *Twentieth Century Literature*, 50.2 (Summer 2004), p. 105). Vita, whose paternal grandmother was a Spanish gipsy dancer (and who also makes a cameo appearance in *Orlando*'s Sultan Court as Rosina Pepita), communicated with Violet in gipsy code, and would cross-dress as a man called 'Julian' when out with Violet during their brief elopement in Paris.
15. Matthew Arnold, 'The Scholar Gipsy', in Helen Gardner (ed.), *The New Oxford Book of English Verse 1250–1950* (Oxford and New York: Oxford University Press, 1972), p. 693.
16. Jane Ellen Harrison, *Reminiscences of a Student's Life* (London: Hogarth Press, 1925), p. 69.
17. Cited in Jessie Stewart, *Jane Ellen Harrison: A Portrait from Letters* (London: Merlin Press, 1959), p. 134.
18. Joel Fineman, 'The Structure of Allegorical Desire', in Stephen J. Greenblatt (ed.), *Allegory and Representation* (Baltimore, MD, and London: Johns Hopkins University Press, 1981), p. 28.
19. Andrew Marvell, 'The Garden', in Gardner, *The New Oxford Book of English Verse*, p. 336.
20. For a reading of Woolf's colourism and an elaboration of the eclipse trope in the context of her aesthetics and politics, see Jane Goldman, *The Feminist Aesthetics of Virginia Woolf: Modernism, Post-Impressionism and the Politics of the Visual* (Cambridge: Cambridge University Press, 1998).
21. Elizabeth Helsinger, 'Blindness and Insights', in Rachel Ziady DeLue and James Elkins (eds), *Landscape Theory* (New York and London: Routledge, 2008), p. 323.
22. On the 'mode of perceiving Greece and the Greeks [...] as a "discourse of ab-sense"', see Vangelis Calotychos, *Modern Greece: A Cultural Poetics* (Oxford and New York: Berg, 2003), p. 47.
23. One notable exception to the absence of modern Greece in the scholarship on *Orlando* is Rowena Fowler, who notices but does not elaborate on the

particular setting of Orlando's epiphany ('Moments and Metamorphoses', pp. 217–42; 235).
24. Helsinger, 'Blindness and Insights', p. 323.
25. Johannes Fabian, *Time and the Other: How Anthropology Makes Its Object* (New York: Columbia University Press, 2002). Briefly, 'allochrony' denotes the (anthropological) concept which allows for the consideration of two worlds that exist contemporaneously to be seen as occupying different eras.
26. See Calotychos, *Modern Greece*, p. 47.
27. Cited in Jan Morris (ed.), *Travels with Virginia Woolf* (London: Pimlico, 1997), p. 221.
28. Jean-Luc Nancy, 'Uncanny Landscape', in J.-L. Nancy, *The Ground of the Image*, trans. Jeff Fort (New York: Fordham University Press, 2005), p. 61.

Chapter 8

Orlando *Famoso*: Obscurity, Fame and History in *Orlando*

Angeliki Spiropoulou

> The pith of his phrases was that while fame impedes and constricts, obscurity wraps about a man like a mist; obscurity is dark, ample, and free; obscurity lets the mind take its way unimpeded.[1]

The above sentence from *Orlando* serves as the starting point for some reflections on the dialectics of obscurity, fame and history in one of Virginia Woolf's most famous novels. While a concern with these concepts is recurrent in Woolf's *oeuvre*, the issue of fame lies at the heart of *Orlando*'s pseudo-bio/historiographical narrative, intertwined with questions of gender and time, aesthetics and ethics. Typical of Woolf's poetics, the sentence is rich with tropes of antithesis, rhetorical repetition, personification of abstract notions, and analogies. It also epitomises much of her thinking about the historical conditions and goals of writing in their relation to subjectivity. In many ways, then, this sentence points to the possibility of reading *Orlando* as a comment on a genetics of writing, in its constitutional imbrication with a politics of the self in time.

As a mock-biography in the form of a novel, *Orlando* ironically points to biography's generic function of immortalising its subject. It foregrounds the fact that biographies give their subject a name and singular identity, and are thus inextricably bound with fame in at least two seemingly antithetical ways. On the one hand, biographies are consequent on fame, precisely because it is for already famous people that the writing of *bios* is typically reserved; and, on the other, a biography arguably confers fame on its subject by singling out a person's life as worthy of recording for posterity. It has become a commonplace to point out Woolf's understanding of the political significance of biography, and her subversion of the standard biographical bias for 'great men', great deeds and teleological narratives. In a 1927 letter, she described the conception of *Orlando* in terms of her desire to 'revolutionise biography in one night' (*L3* 429). The text explicitly satirises the stale conventions of the genre, which, as Woolf notes in 'The New Biography' (1927; *E4* 474), were established at the onset of Western modernity:

> Happy the mother who bears, happier still the biographer who records the life of such a one! [...] From deed to deed, from glory to glory, from office to office he must go, his scribe following after, till they reach whatever seat it may be that is the height of their desire. (*O* 12)

Taking the stress off great men and actions, *Orlando* points to the presumptions and omissions defining standard biographical narratives.[2] In doing so, the text also interrogates the cult of the individual and the desire for fame as the premises of artistic creation and historical tradition.

As we are informed early in the novel, noble Orlando of Elizabethan times was 'afflicted with a love of literature' generated by a 'germ said to be bred of the pollen of the asphodel and to be blown out of Greece and Italy' (*O* 57). On a first reading, Woolf's mention of a 'germ', transmitted from ancient sites and times, seems to allude simply to the passion for reading and writing. A few pages down, however, that germ is claimed to be capable of making a rich man 'give every penny he has [...] to write one little book and become famous' (*O* 59). Thus, it indeed proves 'deadly' (*O* 57), insofar as it refers to the desire for (writing for) *fame*, which puts one's life at risk. Fame was in fact a dominant and literally 'deadly' drive in ancient times, revived by the Renaissance. The paradigm of this is found in the Homeric *Iliad*, where Achilles, the archetypal hero, declares that he is willing to die so as to be immortalised by song.[3] *Kleos*, the Greek term for fame, was the unique goal of the epic hero, while *epos*, the ancient equivalent for biography, served as the medium of celebrity construction in the cult of the Greek hero. It is revealing that, as Gregory Nagy remarks, the word *kleos* was 'used in Homeric poetry to refer to both the medium and the message of the glory of heroes': that is, both to the fame of the subject and the song itself as agent of fame.[4] Literature, then, was concomitant with reputation building, 'a constructor and preserver of glory', as *kleos* was both 'the words to be heard (from the Muses/poet) and the fame or glory that such a song confers on the subjects of the song'.[5] The hero was ensured 'immortal fame' through the song of the poet whose fame, in turn, increased in direct analogy to that of his subject.

Although poets were duly honoured in ancient Greece, it was in Renaissance Italy that the cult of the poet virtually replaced that of the classical hero. In his foundational study *The Civilization of the Renaissance in Italy* (1860), Jacob Burckhardt describes how artists became a vehicle for fame and influence for the fourteenth-century Italian despot. He also identifies a moment in the fifteenth century when writers claimed glory for themselves, no longer restraining themselves to singing the praise of heroes, as in Homeric epics. This development marks a break with the medieval communal spirit as it is linked with the rise of individualism and the pursuit of a 'sort of outward distinction – the modern form of glory', which revived some of the imperial Roman spirit in early Western modernity.[6] While in what Burckhardt calls the 'Northern countries' poetical fame remained a matter of a class or guild, Renaissance Italy paved the way for the modern cult of the artist/critic – the poet laureate and public intellectual who was put on a par with saints and stately heroes and placed in the (literary) Pantheon, which comprises tradition.

These figures were the precursors of later critics and reviewers, impersonated in *Orlando* by the poet and critic Nick Greene, much admired by Orlando, who thinks of the poet's as 'the highest office of all' (*O* 133). Greene reappears at different historical epochs, each time proffering the exact same indictment of his contemporaneous literature in the name of traditional authors. He praises the ancients in Elizabethan times and the Elizabethans in Victorian times. With Shakespeare, Marlowe, Browne, Donne and Jonson still writing, Mr Greene nevertheless insists that 'the great age of literature was the Greek; the Elizabethan age was inferior in every respect to the Greek. In such ages men cherished a divine ambition which he might call La Gloire' (*O* 69). When he re-emerges in the nineteenth century, now 'the most influential critic of the Victorian age' (*O* 222), he contradicts his previous assessment, while keeping to his axiom that it is always the dead poets who are worthy of admiration:

> 'ah! my dear lady, the great days of literature are over. Marlowe, Shakespeare, Ben Jonson – those were the giants. Dryden, Pope, Addison – those were the heroes. All, all are dead now. And whom have they left us? Tennyson, Browning, Carlyle!' – he threw an immense amount of scorn into his voice. 'The truth of it is [...] that all our young writers are in the pay of the booksellers'. (*O* 212)

Beyond the obvious irony in the critical banality of cherishing what has already been canonised and is therefore beyond judgement, what is striking in this passage is that literary antiquity is evoked as superior to the present not for its intrinsic aesthetic quality, but because of its loyal quest for fame – 'La Gloire' – over material gain. Fame is thus revealed to be the axis along which the mechanics of literary creation/reception and the making of tradition are based.

Woolf's diary entries at the time of the creation and publication of *Orlando* – which proved an exceptional best-seller running into several editions – also manifest a marked preoccupation with fame. On 7 November 1928, Woolf notes how she had 'become one and a half inch higher in the public view' due to the book's unexpected acclaim, and adds (not without complacency): 'I think I may say that I am now among the well known writers' (D3 201). While she complained that her increased fame was obstructing the writing of what was to become *The Waves* (D3 209), she nevertheless rejoices at the 1929 review of *Orlando* in the *Manchester Guardian*, where, she boasts, the novel was 'recognized for the masterpiece that it is' (D3 217). The sensation *Orlando* caused in literary circles was equally reflected in the sarcastic remark made by her perennial rival, Arnold Bennett, that 'you cannot keep your end up at a London dinner party these weeks unless you have read Mrs Virginia Woolf's *Orlando*', which was used in turn by the Hogarth Press to advertise the novel.[7] In other words, what was initially planned as an 'escapade', a piece of fun and fantasy (D3 131), became a turning point in Woolf's own literary fame.

The novel's title strategically connects Woolf's *Orlando* to its famous blueprint, Ludovico Ariosto's epic *Orlando Furioso* (1532), itself inspired by Matteo Matia Boiardo's *Orlando Inamorato* (1495), with which it shares the (disappointed) love theme here modelled on Woolf's infatuation with Vita Sackville-West *qua* Orlando. However, the novel has also been perceived as a masterful piece of satirical criticism, bringing together, as Rachel Bowlby observes, fun and seriousness, work and love, despite their standard conception as antithetical.[8] The strange porosity of the latter binary – work and love – becomes most apparent, perhaps, in the novel's transformation of erotic desire into desire for fame. While Sackville-West's own literary ambition may have been the obvious prototype for Orlando's inclination to authoring, when Orlando's literary passion is first revealed, it is presented as a remedy for love treachery. Upon venturing to write, he has a vision of the face of the unfaithful Russian princess superimposed by the face of a poet, 'as one lantern slide is half seen through the next' (O 62). No sooner has Orlando been disappointed in love than he is conquered by 'Ambition the harridan, and Poetry, the witch and Desire of Fame, the strumpet' (O 63). Overcome by that desire, 'he vowed that he would be the first poet of his race and bring immortal lustre upon his name' (ibid.).

This transposition of love into ambition, involved in Orlando's turn from one idealised Other (the princess) to another (the poet), points to these concepts' common matrix as demands; the act of writing appears to be not a gift but a demand for love at risk of being misguided by 'strumpets'. Orlando's quest for love or fame evokes the Hegelian doctrine of recognition by the other as the basis of subjectivity itself, as indicated in the following formulation: 'Self-consciousness exists in itself and for itself, in that, and by the fact that it exists for another self-consciousness; that is to say, it *is* only by being acknowledged or "recognized"'.[9] Once Orlando's desire for recognition is frustrated, first by Sasha's infidelity and then by Mr Greene's ruthless satire, he disavows the pursuit of both love and fame: 'Love and ambition, women and poets were all equally vain. Literature was a farce' (O 75). Fame, he concludes, 'is like [. . .] a braided coat which hampers the limbs; a jacket of silver which curbs the heart; a painted shield which covers scarecrow', and he swears to write no longer to 'please Nick Greene or the Muse', but in order 'to please [him]self' (O 80). Nevertheless, the impossibility of keeping to such a resolution is revealed later, in the nineteenth century, when his only surviving and much revised creation 'The Oak Tree, A Poem', openly demands to be read: 'The manuscript which reposed above her heart began shuffling and beating as if it were a living thing [. . .] It must be read' (O 208). This striving for recognition at the heart of writing resonates with Woolf's pondering on the matter in her diary entry of 7 November 1928, nearly a month after *Orlando*'s publication:

> And this shall be written for my own pleasure, –
> But that phrase inhibits me: for if one writes only for one's own pleasure, – I dont [sic] know what it is that happens. I suppose the convention of writing is destroyed; therefore one does not write at all. (D3 201)

To return to Orlando's ambivalence towards fame or the desire for recognition, it may for the most part be attributed to his feelings of rejection. However, it is at the same time related to fame's own ambiguous status, associated as it is with two conventionally contrary ideas at once. On the one hand, fame is related with material success (in modernity), and, on the other, with the spirit and immortality (in antiquity). Nick Greene's recycled lament about the present state of literature encapsulates this tension. He repeats twice his complaint that 'now all young writers were in the pay of the booksellers and poured out any trash that would sell' (O 69, 212), and counsels that 'we must make the best of it, cherish the past and honour those writers [. . .] *who take antiquity for their model and write, not for pay but for Glawr*' (O 70; my emphasis). Such linking of fame with excellence and a contempt for material goods was indeed forged by the Greeks, as is evidenced by the pre-Socratic philosopher Heraclitus's laconic thought fragment: 'The best of men choose one thing in preference to all else, immortal glory in preference to mortal goods'.[10] However, Woolf shows up the irony of making this claim in modern times by complicating the putative heroism of poets, since Greene himself does not appear to be beyond material interests or free of hypocrisy. While, in Elizabethan times, he states that 'Glawr [. . .] is the spur of noble minds', he nevertheless begs for some material gain: 'Had I a pension of three hundred pounds a year paid quarterly, I would live for Glawr alone' (O 70).

The materialist motives underlying Greene's conditional proposition seem to serve Woolf's satiric demystification of poetic genius, also attempted at later points in the novel where the flaws of celebrated wits, such as Alexander Pope, are sarcastically exposed and literary fame is presented as a matter of acquaintances, coteries and petty favours. When Mr Greene agrees to publish 'The Oak Tree' in the nineteenth century, ironically because it contains 'no trace [. . .] of the modern spirit' (O 214), he names the standard publicity tactics thus:

> As for the reviewers, he would himself write a line to Mr –, who was the most influential; then a compliment – say a little puff of her own poems – addressed to the wife of the editor of the – never did any harm. He would call –. So he ran on. (O 214)

Paradoxically, however, Greene's indirect request for material support in the Elizabethan age as well as his public relations persona in Victorian times are also resonant with Woolf's emphasis on the material conditions of 'spiritual' creation, paradigmatically demonstrated by her famously setting a room and a steady income as the prerequisites for writing in *A Room of One's Own*. The link between money and culture is further brought into relief by the proud mention of the amount that goes with the literary award Orlando receives in the twentieth century, while the fame coming with the prize is downplayed – 'two hundred guineas are not to be sniffed at', the biographer remarks (O 241). Woolf implies here that art is labour and takes part in a modern monetary economy that translates spiritual value into quantifiable reward.

Woolf's own involvement in the sphere of book publishing, reviewing and concomitant activities of marketing and (self-)promotion further complicate her attitude toward the relation between art, publicity and money.[11] Nevertheless, 'true art' – a recurrent concern in *Orlando* as a spoof *Künstlerroman* – is more often defined as opposed to both materialist goals and the personal vanity entailed in achieving fame. It is instead connected with some secret communication, as in a passage following the success of 'The Oak Tree':

> What has praise and fame to do with poetry? What has seven editions (the book had already gone into no less) got to do with the value of it? Was not writing poetry a secret transaction, a voice answering a voice? So that all this chatter and praise and blame and meeting people who admired one [...] was as ill suited as could be to the thing itself – a voice answering a voice. (O 247)

The irrelevance of praise and fame to 'the thing itself' of poetry may be compared with the contentious state of ambition in Plato's thinking, which broke with the Homeric and, more generally, the Pre-Socratic tradition of pursuing fame as the highest value and ultimate form of distinction. In *The Republic*, Plato relegated ambition to the *thymikon*, or the 'spirited' part of the psyche that lies between the *logistikon* (the rational) and the *epithymiton* (the desiring) elements of his tripartite cartography of the soul, anticipating the Freudian second topography of the mind.[12] The aim for profit and for material, carnal pleasure belongs to the appetitive aspect of the soul while the desire for reputation, power and victory belong to the *thymikon*, which, as it is positioned in the middle, can be either carried away by lowly desires or harnessed to the interests of lofty Reason.[13]

The ambiguous status of fame, which is consonant with the Platonic schema but lost in the Renaissance revival of poetic glory as ideal, is also emphasised in those passages of *Orlando* where glory is linked with ill emotions, such as egotism and envy, which are not supposed to belong with art and artists. Here, as in her late works, Woolf seems to place a higher value on obscurity than ambition. Obscurity emerges as the precondition of great art and an attribute of all great poets in the following passage, picturing Orlando thinking:

> how obscurity rids the mind of the irk of envy and spite; how it sets running in the veins the free waters of generosity and magnanimity; and allows giving and taking without thanks offered or praise given; which must have been the way of all great poets [...] for, he thought, Shakespeare must have written like that, and the church builders built like that, anonymously, needing no thanking or naming. (O 81)

Woolf's apparent ambivalence over fame is also associated with women's complicated relation to tradition, defined as crystallised reputation. Orlando becomes a published and awarded poet only after she turns into a woman, but precisely because she is a woman she appears indifferent to fame. Her aesthetic forges a link between obscurity, art and gender which has important political and ethical implications. Orlando may scorn fame, but the narrator also observes that, as Orlando walks through the crowds in the market, 'no one noticed her. A porpoise in a fishmonger's shop attracted far more attention than a lady who had won a prize' (O 238). In *A Room of One's Own* (1929), Woolf characteristically attributes women's conspicuous absence from (literary) history to the obstruction of their creativity and the ability of 'making a name' for themselves, even 'ventur[ing] to guess that Anon, who wrote so many poems without signing them, was often a woman'.[14] By reviewing history through the perspective and the prospects of the woman writer in *Orlando*, Woolf seems to reinstate the feminine in (literary) history while demonstrating that what is passed on as tradition is ineluctably gendered.

Exclusion is, however, paired with freedom. Against the canonical notion of tradition consisting of great (men's) names, proposed by T. S. Eliot, for example,[15] Woolf values anonymity for the artist at the same time as she criticises its standard imposition on women's creations across history. Orlando stresses the 'delight of having no name' (O 81), which is typically afforded to women, and the gendered dialectical image of the anonymous artist appears even more forcefully in her last works. *Between the Acts* notably features Miss La Trobe, the woman director of a village pageant, wishing for anonymity and 'darkness in the mud', instead of visibility and fame.[16] By choosing obscurity, she both remains freer as an artist and reinstates art for and by the community. This attitude evokes Woolf's vindication of obscurity for artists and the ordinary for art, insofar as 'masterpieces are not single and solitary births; they are the outcome of many years of thinking in common, of thinking by the body of the people, so that the experience of the mass is behind the single voice' (*AROO* 68). While Orlando speaks of the 'anonymous work of creation' (O 182), 'Anon' was the starting point of Woolf's sketches of a 'Common History' which was to follow her *Common Reader* series and mark the course of her ideas from a common to communal art.[17]

The redemption of the obscure for art from pre-modern times could be seen as a reaction against the modern pressures of publicity and the cult of celebrity which she associates with selling out. In *Three Guineas*, for example, Woolf explicitly extorts that 'we must extinguish the coarse glare of advertisement and publicity' (*TG* 322). Such an injunction accords with the stance she shares with other modernists of negativity towards the commercial as well as individualist culture of modernity. However, the gender inflection of Orlando's contempt for fame is significant:

> Fame! Seven editions. A prize. Photographs in the evening papers (here she alluded to the 'Oak Tree' and 'The Burdett Coutts' Memorial Prize which she had won; and we must snatch space to remark how discomposing it is for her biographer that this culmination to which the whole book moved,

this peroration with which the book was to end, should be dashed from us on a laugh casually like this; but the truth is that when we write of a woman, everything is out of place – culminations and perorations; the accent never falls where it does with a man). (O 238)

Shifting between the protagonist's and the putative biographer's viewpoints, the self-reflexiveness of the narrative destabilises received attitudes toward subjectivity and biography *apropos* the issue of fame. On one level, there is an obvious allusion to Sackville-West being awarded the Hawthornden prize for her poem *The Land* (1926). However, there is also a warning that while achieving fame is supposed to be the *telos* of any subject worthy of biography, women's stories defy 'culminations and perorations', as the 'big event' here is mentioned in passing and placed within brackets. It is no accident, moreover, that both the achievement and the questioning of fame take place not only when Orlando is a woman, but also immediately after her reflections on the possibility of 'two thousand and fifty-two' selves 'having lodgment' in 'the human spirit' (O 235). The category of the 'I', which Woolf typically associated with masculinity, is undermined by the obscurity and multiple selves championed by the female artist. Orlando's multiplicity of selves experienced in the present as well as his/her exceptional longevity do not allow for the closure of identity which both fame and biography traditionally impose. As Hannah Arendt has argued in *The Human Condition*, 'immortal fame' is reserved for (male) heroes dying a premature death that stabilises their identity and allows one story to be told of them.[18] Orlando's exceptionality as a biographical subject is not owing to deeds, but to his/her ambiguous ontological status: his/her androgyny, multiplicity and survival through time. Orlando's claim to immortality relies not on his/her fame as a writer but rather on his/her multiple subjectivity, forever at odds with his/her times and hence with a fame premised on death and a unitary concept of the subject.

The Portuguese author Fernando Pessoa, whose numerous 'heteronyms' (or alternative authorial personae) virtually illustrate the theory of multiple selves heralded in *Orlando*, also separates fame from immortality, against the ancient tradition.[19] In his posthumously published *Erostratus: The Search for Immortality*, written circa 1929, he reflects on literary genius and fame across history, drawing inspiration from Erostratus, who in 356 BC set fire to the Temple of Diana in Ephesus, one of the ancient wonders, in order to achieve eternal fame. Pessoa links immortality to genius and fame to convention, concurring with Woolf's depiction of the fallacies of critics epitomised by Mr Greene's conservatism and petty politics. He, too, expresses a modernist sense of the futility of the quest for perfection and permanence in modernity when he writes that while 'the Greeks lusted for fame in [. . .] everything; we lust for fame in sports and hobbies because we can lust for fame in nothing else',[20] least of all in poetry and thinking. This resonates with Woolf's verdict on the ephemerality and incompleteness of the modern artwork in 'How It Strikes a Contemporary' (1923):

> If we make a century our test, and ask how much of the work produced in these days in England will be in existence then, we shall have to answer not merely that we cannot agree upon the same book, but that we are more than doubtful whether such a book there is. It is an age of fragments. (*E3* 355)

Fame is associated here with the historical rather than the eternal; as in *Orlando*, inversely, historical epochs are defined by the varying reception of the artwork. This confirms Walter Benjamin's idea that in 'the analysis of fame' lies 'the foundation of history'. In Benjamin's own words:

> Historical 'understanding' is to be grasped, in principle, as an afterlife of that which is understood; and what has been recognized in the analysis of the 'afterlife of works', in the analysis of 'fame', is therefore to be considered the foundation of history in general. [21]

Woolf's novel historicises fame and tradition, and thus problematises them by putting into question their naturalised permanence. Orlando makes explicit the link between fame, tradition and historical temporality when he remarks that 'there is no such thing as [eternal] fame and glory. Ages to come will never cast a thought on [her] or on Mr Pope either', and asks: 'What's an "age", indeed? What are "we"?' (*O* 157).

It is Orlando's distance from his/her contemporaneity, as she confronts 'the spirit of the age' through her multiple selves haunted by memories of the past, that both enables and is ensured by her immortality, against the ephemerality of fame, which is too tied to the historical present. However, while seeming out of place, a stranger to her home, her land and her epoch, Orlando may be deemed to be truly contemporary, for as Giorgio Agamben argues, contemporariness is 'a singular relationship with one's time, which adheres to it and, at the same time, keeps a distance from it'.[22] The contemporary is he who 'holds his gaze on his own time so as to perceive not its light, but rather its darkness', the obscure. He also experiences his age as a 'too soon' that is also 'too late', an 'already' that is also a 'not yet'.[23] Similarly being at odds with his/her time by embodying different temporalities at any one time and opting for obscurity, immortal Orlando offers a historical understanding of every present, connecting it to the past while gesturing to futurity.

And further, insofar as contemporaneity is a speculation on what it means to be in time, it is not just the basis of historical thinking, but also the foundation of the satiric writing which *Orlando* epitomises by making a case for being at once inside and outside what one's time defines as the limit of recognition.

Notes

1. Virginia Woolf, *Orlando: A Biography* [1928] (London: Grafton Books, 1977), pp. 80–1.
2. Cf. Virginia Woolf, 'The Art of Biography' (1939), *E*6, pp. 181–9. See also Laura Marcus, *Auto/Biographical Discourses: Theory, Criticism, Practice* (Manchester: Manchester University Press, 1994), pp. 90–134.
3. Homer, *The Iliad*, trans. A. T. Murray (Cambridge, MA: Harvard University Press, 1924), Book 9, ll. 410–15.
4. Gregory Nagy, *The Ancient Greek Hero in 24 Hours* (Cambridge, MA: Harvard University Press, 2013), pp. 26–7.
5. Simon Goldhill, *Essays on Poetics and Greek Culture* (Cambridge: Cambridge University Press, 1991), p. 70.
6. See Jacob Burckhardt, *The Civilization of the Renaissance in Italy*, trans. S. G. C. Middlemore (London: Penguin, 1990), pp. 104–10.
7. Arnold Bennett, 'A Woman's High-Brow Lark', *Evening Standard*, 8 November 1928, p. 7; John K. Young, '"Murdering an Aunt of Two": Textual Practice and Narrative Form in Virginia Woolf's Metropolitan Market', in Jeanne Dubino (ed.), *Virginia Woolf and the Literary Marketplace* (New York: Palgrave Macmillan, 2010), p. 187.
8. See Rachel Bowlby, 'Orlando: An Introduction', in R. Bowlby, *Feminist Destinations and Further Essays on Virginia Woolf* (Edinburgh: Edinburgh University Press, 1997), p. 156.
9. Georg W. G. Hegel, *Phenomenology of the Spirit*, trans. A. V. Miller (Oxford: Clarendon Press, 1977), p. 229.
10. Heraclitus, *Fragments*, trans. T. M. Robinson (Toronto: University of Toronto Press, 1987), §B29.
11. On this matter, see Alice Staveley, 'Marketing Virginia Woolf: Women, War, and Public Relations in *Three Guineas*', *Book History*, 12 (2009), pp. 295–339.
12. Plato, *The Republic*, ed. G. R. F. Ferrari, trans. Tom Griffith (Cambridge: Cambridge University Press, 2000), §441a, p. 137. See also Sigmund Freud, 'The Ego and the Id' and 'The Dissection of the Psychical Personality', in *The Standard Edition of the Complete Psychological Works of Sigmund Freud*, vols 19 and 22, trans. and ed. James Strachey (London: Hogarth Press, 1961 and 1964), pp. 56 and 72 respectively.
13. See Plato, *The Republic*, §§581a–b, pp. 297–8.
14. Virginia Woolf, *A Room of One's Own and Three Guineas* [1929/1938], ed. Morag Shiach (Oxford and New York: Oxford University Press, 1992), p. 63.

15. See T. S. Eliot, 'Tradition and Individual Talent', in T. S. Eliot, *Selected Essays: 1917–1932* (London: Faber and Faber, 1932), p.16.
16. Virginia Woolf, *Between the Acts* [1941] (London: Hogarth Press, 1947), pp. 227, 237.
17. See Brenda Silver (ed.), '"Anon and 'The Reader": Virginia Woolf's Last Essays', *Twentieth Century Literature*, 25.3–4 (1979), pp. 356–441. For a discussion of obscurity, community and history in Woolf's work, see Angeliki Spiropoulou, *Virginia Woolf, Modernity and History: Constellations with Walter Benjamin* (London and New York: Palgrave Macmillan, 2010), especially Chapters 6–8. It is noteworthy that Woolf placed at the centre of the first volume of the *Common Reader* (1925) her essay 'The Lives of the Obscure', which aims to both rescue the marginalised lives of the obscure for history and restore obscure writers for literary history.
18. Hannah Arendt, *The Human Condition* (Chicago: University of Chicago Press, 1998), pp. 193–4.
19. See Fernando Pessoa, *The Selected Prose of Fernando Pessoa*, trans. and ed. Richard Zenith (New York: Grove Press, 2001), p. 392.
20. Ibid. p. 427.
21. Benjamin, *The Arcades Project*, trans. Howard Eiland and Kevin McLaughlin, ed. Rolf Tiedemann (Cambridge, MA: Harvard University Press, 1999), N2.3, p. 460.
22. Giorgio Agamben, 'What is the Contemporary?', in G. Agamben, *What is an Apparatus? and Other Essays* (Stanford: Stanford University Press, 2009), p. 44.
23. Ibid. pp. 44, 47.

Chapter 9

Bibliographic Parturition in *Orlando*: Books, Babies, Freedom and Fame

Alice Staveley

So here then we are at Kew, and I will show you to-day (the second of March) under the plum tree, a grape hyacinth, and a crocus, and a bud, too, on the almond tree; so that to walk there is to be thinking of bulbs, hairy and red, thrust into the earth in October; flowering now; and to be dreaming of more than can rightly be said, and to be taking from its case a cigarette or cigar even, and to be flinging a cloak under (as the rhyme requires) an oak, and there to sit, waiting the kingfisher, which, it is said, was seen once to cross in the evening from bank to bank.[1]

Situated in the culminating pages of *Orlando*, this sentence, bursting with biographical evasion, coy euphemism, faux calm and literal legerdemain depicts the risky, high-stakes ventures of women who labour. The biographer's hand, like a doctor screening a woman's erogenous and procreative zone, conjures the cloak to obscure from view the birth of Orlando's son. Distraction is privileged over attraction. 'Look! Look!' the narrator-biographer seems to urge the reader; take in the view of Kew – 'Kew will do' – at whose entry gates two lions, we learn just before this sentence, stand 'couchant' (O 215) as if to avert attention from the crowning head. Topographical entrances (the gates of Kew) and morphological exits (the birth canal) exchange furtive glances just before the cloak is, gauntlet-like, flung under the oak tree in flamboyant obscurantism. The rhyming play (kew/do; cloak/oak) conjures delay and delight; it soothes and lulls like a nursery rhyme while the kingfisher's flickage from 'bank to bank' rhythms uterine pulsations. Yet, on a deeper, more chthonic level, the playful language engages with what Gillian Beer calls the 'anarchic neatness of rhyme [that] pins together the unlike':[2] in this instance, the uneasy, metaphorically commonplace, but, for the woman writer, paradoxical pairing of book and baby. Orlando's poem, 'The Oak Tree', and her son here have simultaneous, analogous births. The controlled anarchy of their doubling interrogates the tensile interrelationships between life and art for a transhistorical, transgendered woman who dares to joyously have it all. The material-historical and ideological paradoxes at the heart of the book/baby metaphor alter reader reception of this parturition scene, unprecedented in Woolf's oeuvre.[3] They raise complicated interpretative stakes for what Susan Stanford Friedman describes as a woman writer's 'double birthing potential':[4]

> The paradox of the childbirth metaphor is that its contextual resonance is fundamentally at odds with the very comparison it makes. While the metaphor draws together mind and body, word and womb, it also evokes the sexual division of labour upon which Western patriarchy is founded. The vehicle of the metaphor (procreation) acts in opposition to the tenor it serves (creation) because it inevitably reminds the reader of the historical realities that contradict the comparison being made. Facing constant challenges to their creativity, women writers often find their dilemma expressed in terms of the oppositions between books and babies [. . .] Male paternity of texts has not precluded their paternity of children. But for both material and ideological reasons, maternity and creativity have appeared to be mutually exclusive to women writers [. . .] The metaphor's literal falsehood remains the same [in a female-authored text] as it does in a male comparison. Babies are never books. But the reader's awareness that the metaphor features a woman changes how the biological and historical resonances work.[5]

This chapter contextualises the paradoxical construction of this metaphor, given the material history of Woolf's role as a self-publisher, at a juncture of her writing life when *Orlando*'s composition and production marked the ten-year anniversary of the founding of the Hogarth Press. Woolf believed that the passage of a decade always forces a reckoning on time, progress and art, as she wrote to Gerald Brenan on Christmas Day 1922:

> Every ten years brings [. . .] one of those private orientations which match the vast one which is, to my mind, general now in the race. I mean, life has to be sloughed: has to be faced: to be rejected; then accepted on new terms with rapture. (*L2* 598–9)

Orlando is a rapturous text whose depiction of a woman writer's negotiations with, and fantastical transformations of, the material impediments to the simultaneous production of books and babies makes it so much more than a 'joke', and so prescient of a feminist modernity deserving of extensive, multifaceted excavation.

At the gates of Kew Gardens, both Orlando's son and her poem, 'The Oak Tree,' emerge into a defiantly anti-Eliotic paradise, where survival, suffrage, and sublimity telegraph in colour-coded semaphore. April may be the cruellest month, but birth pangs in March bring untrammelled and pre-emptive double joy. The tripartite green (Kew), purple (plum tree/

hyacinth), and white (almond bud) suggest a veritable suffrage banner in the year that British women will finally gain enfranchisement equal to men: a delayed-by-a-decade second act that Woolf's doubling invokes and collapses.[6] The boundlessness of generative possibilities now open for women are a sign of the changing times where synchrony and simultaneity triumph over chronology and ever-deferred telos. Biological reproduction and cultural production appear as one: Orlando's son emerges safely to continue the family line while the lines of 'The Oak Tree' flourish likewise, the book running to 'seven editions' (O 238). Productivity and profligacy, uneasy bedmates for Woolf at other times, are here celebrated as co-conspirators and lucky twins borne of a writer, Orlando, no longer afraid of their multiple but not irreconcilable contradictions. One might argue that after surviving 400 years, evading mortality in a series of twilight sleeps, and undergoing a change of sex to make it happen, Orlando well deserves this double bounty.[7] Four centuries of gestation, capped by a two-and-a-half-week labour, are marked by innumerable politically and sexually coded delays – 'Wait! Wait! The kingfisher comes; the kingfisher comes not' (O 215). Orlando has surely endured one of the longest arrested labours in history.

As Orlando becomes a mother, she transitions from being a centuries-long struggling writer to published author, a maternal authorial function that mitigates, or perhaps equalises, the patrilineal privilege represented by the first-born son.[8] Yet for all the celebration of double life and mutual transformation the sentence encodes, it also speaks to deeply held taboos surrounding biographical depictions of parturition. These taboos intersect broader cultural suspicions of a woman writer's relationship to the book she births, which are further intensified in a narrative about a woman who was once a man. Phallogocentric censorship parries with gendered perspectivalism, and the problems of universalising witness: is Orlando, in early parturition, attended behind the arras by a cigar-smoking father-in-waiting? Or is that biographer/narrator a woman writer, dragging phenomenologically on her cigarette/cigar, rather like the narrator of 'The Mark on the Wall' (1917), who defers epistemic knowledge in favour of the mind's stationary wandering? Just how close can either get to the experience of the subject who births, whether book or baby, from the outside or spectatorial viewpoint? Might not the subject herself find a language to bear witness to such a profound metamorphosis and (self)transformation?

Much is at stake, bibliographically speaking, in this particular representation of the book/baby paradox since authorial self-reflexivity abounds. Woolf's own compositional chronology is carefully woven into Orlando's progress. For Julia Briggs, the transgendered and transhistorical plot parlays an allegorical history of Woolf's genealogical relationship to books and reading:

> For if Orlando is Vita, she is also many other things – the English language, perhaps, or even Virginia herself, growing up, moving in slow motion from her own prepubertal readings of literature as if she were a boy, passing from the male world of the Elizabethan lumber room [. . .] to a reluctant puberty, and the onset of menstruation that defines the adolescent body as female, into her twenties, a Victorian age in which preoccupation with marriage leads her to the altar with a man who, like Shel, is a pilgrim and a stranger, to a birth that is not that of Vita's sons [. . .] but rather that of the book itself.[9]

How then might we read the chronological 'birth narrative' of this scene of parturition as Woolf plants clues within the text itself? In the published text, the narrator takes us to the gates of Kew Gardens on 2 March, where Orlando's labour begins; finally, on 20 March, Orlando is delivered of a son – three days after Woolf records the completion of the holograph draft of the *Orlando* manuscript on 17 March 1928 (due dates for manuscripts and babies are notoriously inexact). In this reading, the novel itself might indeed be the self-same manuscript that was 'thrust into the earth in October [1927]', written at the fastest speed of any of Woolf's works – 'I write so quick I can't get it typed before lunch. This I suppose is the main backbone of my autumn – Orlando' (*D3* 164) – and thus found 'flowering' five months later in March 1928.

Speed, surprise, urgency and interruptive fecundity animate almost all of Woolf's diarised commentary on the novel's progress. In December 1927, she even records the genesis of *Orlando* the previous March in terms analogous to an unexpected pregnancy: 'extraordinarily unwilled by me but potent in its own right [. . .] as if it shoved everything aside to come into existence' (*D3* 168). Observing this alacrity in her diary, she then flips the pages back to March 1927, delighted to have confirmed the integrity in 'spirit if not in fact' (ibid.) of the original compositional impulse (and a Cinderella-inspired timestamp that will return in the last line of the published novel):

> Suddenly between twelve & one I conceived a whole fantasy to be called 'The Jessamy Brides' [. . .] Two women, poor, solitary at the top of a house. One can see anything (for this is all fantasy) the Tower Bridge, clouds, aeroplanes [. . .] No attempt is to be made to realise character. Sapphism is to be suggested. Satire is to be the main note – satire & wildness. (*D3* 131)

Remembering in December the March 'conception' date, Woolf anticipates an ambitious, calendrically congruent publication date for *Orlando* in spring 1928. Revved up, she hopes in vain for a rapid transformation from manuscript to typescript to proof to publication in just two months

(*D3* 167), perhaps anticipating in her mind the scene of Orlando's double delivery with the Hogarth Press's aspirational publication date of *Orlando*.

Revised throughout the summer, Woolf readied her novel for target publication on 11 October 1928, a date proleptically added to the final typescript to chime with the last line of the last sentence of the first edition (to live, presumably, in print perpetuity in all subsequent editions). Conflating the temporal fantasies inscribed in its origin story with its set-in-stone publication date, the last line of *Orlando* declares: 'And the twelfth stroke of midnight sounded; the twelfth stroke of midnight, Thursday, the eleventh of October, Nineteen Hundred and Twenty Eight' (*O* 241). On the one hand, embedding this particular time, day and month of publication may have been Woolf's Plan B. On the other, apropos of the seasonal inversions and non-linear timescales in the fauxbiography itself, it playfully gestures to the book trade markets where books are regularly positioned for autumn 'arrival' in the lead-up to the Christmas selling season. Nature's seasonal cycles (a georgic feature of Vita Sackville-West's poem *The Land*, which is one model for 'The Oak Tree') and book production cycles are not always aligned. As both a publisher and the daughter of a former academic surrounded in her youth by brothers and male friends whose yearly academic cycles always began in the autumn, Woolf was well acquainted with this ever-present rhythm of the bookish life in the northern hemisphere. It was, and is, a rhythm deeply inured. As such, we might overlook the ironic piquancy a woman writer marginalised from those institutions of higher learning might bring to her interpretation of a season that births a counterintuitive return to the book. 'For academics, autumn is the beginning,' writes Elaine Showalter, so 'novelists play on the ironic ambiguities of that autumnal start'.[10]

When it came to sales of *Orlando*, however, Woolf feared that she might have gone unintentionally one ironic inversion too far. By adding a subtitle, *A Biography*, she worried that booksellers would refuse to buy it in bulk and choose to position it erroneously among the 'real' biographies: 'I doubt therefore that we shall do more than cover expenses – a high price to pay for the fun of calling it a biography' (*D3* 198). The betwixt-and-between nature of the book's hybrid generic form, including its self-reflexive manipulation of conception and arrival schedules implicated in the book/baby paradox, also extended to the problem of pricing. Pegged at 9s, *Orlando* was slightly more expensive than a novel (7s 6d) but slightly less than a standard biography (12s), 'an in-between pricing', Claire Battershill argues, 'that places the book immediately in the grey area between the genres [of fiction and biography]'.[11] If Orlando's narrative identity was deliberately hard to pin down, so too was *Orlando*'s bibliographic identity once it was published – a problem that Suzanne Raitt notes subsequent editions would skirt by dropping the subtitle altogether.[12] Woolf's fears proved unrealised. *Orlando* became Woolf's first bestseller, and earned the Hogarth Press more income in 1928 than in any previous year. For the Hogarth Press and Woolf's own negotiations with her authorial identity and her relationship to a large public readership, it proved a tipping point.

Woolf was known to play with numbers when it came to their semiotic within her publisher's imaginary, not just fiscally and not always parodically.[13] Just one year before *Orlando*'s publication, she had elevated maternal privilege above paternal signification with the publication date of *To the Lighthouse*: 5 May 1927, the thirty-second anniversary of her mother's death. A feminist book-historical interpretation would note that a novel begun compositionally, and ending narratologically, with the de-mystified vision of 'The Old Man' (*D2* 317) asserts on its publication day the ontological force of the mother's loss, turning a datapoint of bibliographic interest into heftier 'bibliographic code' that intensifies the novel's elegiac affect.[14] Where *Orlando* would come to celebrate the 'birth' of the artist-as-mother, *To the Lighthouse* allowed Woolf to experiment with the artist-daughter's freedom to mark that maternal/material presence through the radical formal reinvention of a novel predicated on access to the levers (literal and metaphoric) of the printing press. Benjamin Harvey and Laura Marcus have both cited this novel as having been influenced by Woolf's access to print technologies. Extrapolating from their arguments, we might imagine how, for instance, the hieroglyphic Woolf sketched in her writing notebooks visualising the form of *To the Lighthouse* as 'two blocks joined by a corridor' may have been inspired by the composing stick, an H-like printer's tool Woolf used frequently in the Press's early years to set stories and poems into type.[15] It also evokes the first letters of the home, Hogarth House, which gave the Press its name: domesticity wed to a creative ambition and intentionality as powerful as procreative drive, a theme Woolf would often wittingly, and wittily, incorporate into her descriptions of the Press's dominant presence in her marital life.[16]

Founded in 1917, the Hogarth Press also inaugurated Woolf's experiments in modernist form, its ethos of self-ownership defiantly feminist: 'I am the only woman in England free to write what I like', Woolf declared in 1925, 'the others must be thinking of series and editors' (*D3* 43). In practical terms, she meant liberation from editorial oversight, but in psychological terms, she was envisioning the crucial freedom to establish her own institutional and professional identity as a self-made author. Her ownership of the means of self-production and publication at the

Hogarth Press ensured that she circumvented the external oversight or control she knew could compromise creative integrity, particularly for women artists. Lily, the artist figure in *To the Lighthouse*, struggles to achieve an autonomy of vision, assailed from all sides by naysayers: '"Women can't write, women can't paint . . ."' intones Charles Tansley,[17] the dangling ellipsis evocative of any number of parallel denunciations, including 'women can't print'. Woolf learned to typeset at home from a manual; she and Leonard had tried to learn compositing from St Bride's printing school, but were refused, a rejection Leonard recalls in his memoirs as stemming from ageism and classism – 'we learned that the social engine and machinery made it impossible to teach the art of printing to two middle-aged, middle-class persons'[18] – but which was also certainly compounded by the fact that compositors' guilds were notoriously sexist.[19]

Calling literature in her 'Professions for Women' speech the 'freest of all professions for women', Woolf alludes in public to what we might call her private emancipation declaration ('I am the only woman free to write what I like'), but leavens it with gentle irony: there were stories about women's experiences not just as bodies but as embodied by institutional structures (pregnancy, birth, maternity and the book/baby double bind one crucial matrix) that were, in the late 1920s, still occluded and still far from democratically realisable. For Woolf, however, the Hogarth Press had broken the hold of a variety of formal constraints to allow her to begin experimenting with new forms for new fictions, offering her hands-on tools for remaking and reconfiguring the terms of her creative world. As I have argued elsewhere, form, function and feminism came together for Woolf after she learned to set type in 1917.[20] And perhaps nowhere was that triumvirate consolidated more powerfully than in her first freestanding self-published short story, 'Kew Gardens'. Inspired by and formally replicative of her conversations and epistolary exchanges with Katherine Mansfield in the summer of 1917, 'Kew Gardens' appeared as a hand-printed, handsewn booklet in May 1919, publication No. 3 of the neophyte Hogarth Press.[21] It was her first autonomous book publication from the Press, and would presage the appearance of all her subsequent novels under her own imprint.

> 'Oh yes, it is Kew! Well, Kew will do. So here then we are at Kew . . .'

This line from the parturition paragraph in *Orlando*, ushering us into Kew Gardens (O 215), signals an authorial (re)turn to the origins of

Woolf's own aesthetic modernism borne of her liberating access to the print technologies and creative affordances of the Hogarth Press. The quick, exclamatory inspiration of breath affirms a coy surprise and delight at this arrival-as-return ('Oh yes, it is Kew!'). The scaling descant exhale in the couplet rejoinder – 'Well, Kew will do' – acts as a calculated deflation to throw off the scent and censure – 'So here *we* are at Kew' (emphasis added) – of those for whom a woman's too obvious delight at her creative (not to mention procreative) breakthroughs might prove not just unseemly, but a target for take-down (even today the root animus of the 'having it all' epithet resides in antipathy to women's double empowerment to bear children and to pursue public achievement).

Only in private did Woolf claim an autonomous freedom from her own press; in public, she modulated her words with a communal impulse intended to bind young women to the struggle, but also to cultivate multifarious, cooperative, multi-gendered freedoms. Woolf knew or intuited, moreover, what contemporary social theory has the data to back up: that a woman's personal ambitions are best fulfilled when couched in communal language.[22] The 'Kew/do' rhyme operates as discussed earlier, to 'pin together the unlike', but also, given this specific self-referential intertext, helps to further attenuate the paradoxical book/baby pairing. There are, in short, rather more books than babies in this scene. For if this is an allusive bibliographic return to 'Kew Gardens' for Woolf, to that early hand-printed inaugural modernist production, it is also a more immediate intertextual reference to the recent republication of that story in an elaborate and lushly illustrated new edition.[23] We could argue that this third edition of 'Kew Gardens', published in November 1927, was not so much 'thrust into the earth' in October as luxuriant in its visibility and appeal while Woolf was writing *Orlando*, the novel she described as the 'backbone of [her 1927] autumn'. The writing of *Orlando* and the re-emergence of 'Kew Gardens' were a double act. For Orlando's parturition scene, Woolf deliberatively chose the form of that specific book-object to turn a narratological modernist motif of closure-as-return into a materialist tribute, a new edition that reanimates an old story (not unlike children extending the lives of their parents). She paid tribute to the story's groundbreaking significance in her writing life, and to the debt she owed the Hogarth Press in bringing it into the world.

This book's bibliographic code – large print face, lavish illustrations by Vanessa Bell on every page, hardbacked, paperboard covers, and high price point (15s) – signalled a different sort of arrival for Woolf than had the first edition, whose readers (until a highly favourable *Times* review compelled a quick second edition) were a coterie of Hogarth

Press subscribers. Reaching out both to the luxury book market, and to a popular readership alongside *Orlando* itself, the 1927 edition of 'Kew Gardens' shows Woolf attempting to reconcile competing claims on her authorial identity, not unlike those between mother and writer: as both popular and highbrow modernist, categories always already gendered;[24] as a woman writer in florid if not in fact extravagantly 'floral' control of her own means of creative production (one of Woolf's most under-examined books, the 1927 edition of 'Kew Gardens' gives full reign to Bell's curlicue decorations);[25] and as a woman navigating fame as a variation on the theme of the 'offspring' of creative success. Woolf, in 1927, even before the idiom was coined, was invested in upping while maintaining control over her own 'Q rating'.[26] Indeed, Woolf's navigation of the popular and luxury markets was something *Orlando* itself parlayed. Amy Elkins notes that while the conventional history dates the first edition of *Orlando* as appearing on 11 October 1928, there was, in fact, an earlier 'pre-emptive' first edition for luxury acquisition.[27] On 2 October 1928, the New York publisher Crosby Gage printed 800 copies of *Orlando* on special Whitmanian green pages signed by Woolf herself, an edition that boasted different chapter titles than either the British or American 'first' editions,[28] a sign that Woolf's own editorial practices were in constant motion. Similarly, the 1927 edition of 'Kew Gardens' was also a signed text, containing both Virginia Woolf's and Vanessa Bell's signatures as part of its privileged appeal and high price point.

This double signature returns us to the concluding scenes of *Orlando*, where Woolf's authorial self-reflexivity intensifies, as she works to balance the visibility of fame with anonymity and privacy. This negotiation is made manifest in a telling postpartum transformation of the book/baby paradox into a reclamatory metaphor rooted literally in the open book. Leaving the geospatial arena of Kew Gardens behind, Orlando moves seamlessly forward in possession of both her completed poem 'The Oak Tree' (burst from her bosom in comic response, perhaps, to the partially censored parturition at Kew) and a new child. She is whisked along a fast-track transportation system into the heart of the city, historical and technological progress transmogrifying carriage to steam train to motor car. Time accelerates, and as it moves Orlando ever closer to an epistemological centre that materialises the public and published text, it deposits her at the foot of the oak tree to dialogue with the value of fame and its influence on the writing process. There readers find Orlando attempting, enigmatically, to bury a copy of her poem 'signed by author and artist' at the base of the inspirational oak (O 238). Often taken to mean Vita's Hawthornden Prize-winning poem, *The Land*, which was published with illustrations by George Plank and, indeed, signed by both author and artist, 'The Oak Tree' might just as well refer to the 1927 'Kew Gardens' which was *also* signed by author and artist and marketed as such.[29] *Orlando* itself is often read as Woolf's symbolic 'return' to Vita/Orlando of her beloved Knole (a bookish substitution of ownership rights filched by laws of patrilineal inheritance), and the novel moves toward its final act with a scene that pivots from occlusion and burial to surface elevation, if not revelation: the book Orlando attempts to bury is not submerged beneath the soil but instead left 'unburied and dishevelled on the ground' (O 238), its pages well-exposed to the elements, or the critics, or the eyes of whomever should care to look.

The open book which comes to lie on open ground, exposed and dishevelled but inviolable, is a hybrid text commingling *The Land*, 'Kew Gardens', and *Orlando*. Its bibliographic symbolism resides in its comfortable visibility, its unflappable openness to a public readership and an authorial comfort with 'letting go' of its critical destiny. Signalling Woolf's transformation as a Hogarth 'product' or brand, a transition ratified by the elaborately illustrated double-signed 1927 'Kew Gardens', its meaning does not, however, signify only the generic transition from manuscript to published text, from writer to reader; in this particular context, the site of the open book resolves the conceit between sleep (as death/burial) and wakefulness (as birth/life) that has defined every major transition in Orlando's life. For it is rarely observed that the parturition scene narrated at Kew Gardens proceeds from an almost evolutionary struggle with a species of death-as-sleep recurrent throughout the novel, which, just before the arrival at Kew, notably puns on maternal demise, the ever-present threat of maternal mortality in birth-giving presaging the ontological extinction of the mother-as-writer:

> sleep, sleep, so deep that all shapes are ground to dust of infinite softness, water of dimness inscrutable, and there, folded, shrouded, like a *mummy*, like a moth, prone let us lie on the sand at the bottom of sleep.
> But wait! but wait! we are not going, this time, visiting the blind land. Blue, like a match struck right in the ball of the innermost eye, he flies, burns, bursts the seal of sleep; the kingfisher [. . .] (O 216; my emphasis)

To refuse to visit the blind land is to see with the inner- and outermost eyes that Kew Gardens – the place, the book(s), and the Press that cultivated it – has become a site of awakened pilgrimage for Woolf. Where the other two twilight sleeps in *Orlando* had registered grief and a brand of denial that traffics in blindness (Orlando's depressive sleep on the loss of Sasha, followed by her sex change that occurs while deep in the clutches of sleep), the scene of bibliographic and morphological parturition in *Orlando* refuses those earlier occlusions, kicking fiercely against their hidden cultural prohibitions that silence any number of uncomfortable truths about the body, including, not least, the assumption that 'maternity and creativity [...] be mutually exclusive for women writers',[30] and privileging in their stead an alert, in control, and declaratively female author/creator ('I am the only woman') joyously at the top of her game, controlling her own press.

Rapture, indeed.

Notes

1. Virginia Woolf, *Orlando: A Biography* [1928] (New York: Harcourt Brace, 2006), p. 215.
2. Gillian Beer, *Virginia Woolf: The Common Ground* (Edinburgh: Edinburgh University Press, 1996), p. 133.
3. Marylu Hill rightly notes that Orlando's parturition scene is 'sadly underrated'; see her *Mothering Modernity: Feminism, Modernism and the Maternal Muse* (New York: Garland, 1999), pp. 203–5.
4. Susan Stanford Friedman, 'Creativity and the Childbirth Metaphor', in Robyn R. Warhol and Diane Herndl (eds), *Feminisms: An Anthology of Literary Theory and Criticism* (New Brunswick, NJ: Rutgers University Press, 1991), p. 377.
5. Ibid. 373–7.
6. Only property-owning women over the age of 30 won suffrage in 1918. In 1928, women's suffrage was lowered to age 21, the same age as men's. On feminist colour coding, see Jane Goldman, *The Feminist Aesthetics of Virginia Woolf: Modernism, Post-Impressionism and the Politics of the Visual* (Cambridge: Cambridge University Press, 1998).
7. The *OED Online* defines twilight sleep as 'a state of amnesia and partial analgesia induced by the administration of morphine and scopolamine (hyoscine), esp. to lessen the pains of childbirth'. Available at <www.oed.com/view/Entry/208059> (accessed 2 May 2017).
8. The *Orlando* movie starring Tilda Swindon (1992) changed the sex of the child from boy to girl in a second-wave feminist rebranding.
9. Julia Briggs, 'Editing Woolf for the Nineties', *The South Carolina Review*, 29.1 (1996), p. 75.
10. Elaine Showalter, *Faculty Towers: The Academic Novel and Its Discontents* (Oxford: Oxford University Press, 2005), p. 13.
11. Claire Battershill, 'No One Wants Biography: The Hogarth Press Classifies *Orlando*', in Ann Martin and Kathryn Holland (eds), *Interdisciplinary/Multidisciplinary Woolf: Selected Papers from the Twenty-Second Annual International Conference on Virginia Woolf* (Clemson, SC: Clemson University Digital Press, 2013), p. 244.
12. Suzanne Raitt, *Vita and Virginia: The Work and Friendship of V. Sackville-West and Virginia Woolf* (Oxford: Oxford University Press, 1993), p. 18.
13. Julia Briggs, *Reading Virginia Woolf* (Edinburgh: Edinburgh University Press, 2006), pp. 96–112.

14. George Bornstein, *Material Modernism: The Politics of the Page* (Cambridge: Cambridge University Press 2001), p. 6.
15. Benjamin Harvey, 'Bloomsbury's Books and Blocks', in Nancy E. Green (ed.), *A Room of Their Own: Bloomsbury Artists in American Collections* (Ithaca: Cornell University Press, 2008), pp. 88–115. Laura Marcus, 'Virginia Woolf and the Hogarth Press', in Ian Willison, Warwick Gould and Warren Chernaik (eds), *Modernist Writers and the Marketplace* (London: Macmillan, 1996), pp. 124–51.
16. Catherine W. Hollis, 'Virginia Woolf's Double Signature', in Karen V. Kukil (ed.), *Woolf in the Real World: Selected Papers from the Thirteenth Annual Conference on Virginia Woolf* (Clemson, SC: Clemson University Digital Press, 2005), pp. 18–23.
17. Virginia Woolf, *To the Lighthouse* [1927] (New York: Harcourt Brace, 2005), p. 51.
18. Leonard Woolf, *Beginning Again: An Autobiography of the Years 1911–1918* (New York and London: Harcourt Brace Jovanovich, 1963), p. 233.
19. Sian Reynolds, *Britannica's Typesetters: Women Compositors in Edwardian Edinburgh* (Edinburgh: Edinburgh University Press, 1989).
20. Alice Staveley, 'Conversations at Kew: Feminist Narratology in "Kew Gardens"', in Kathryn N. Benzel and Ruth Hoberman (eds), *Trespassing Boundaries: Virginia Woolf's Short Fiction* (New York: Palgrave, 2004), pp. 39–62.
21. Alice Staveley, 'Reconfiguring "Kew Gardens": Virginia Woolf's *Monday or Tuesday* Years' (DPhil thesis: University of Oxford, 2001), pp. 80–112.
22. Sheryl Sandberg, *Lean In: Women, Work, and the Will to Lead* (New York: Alfred A. Knopf, 2013), p. 47.
23. My arguments here theorise a feminist-materialist bibliographic critique for the scene of double birth; see Alice Staveley, '"Kew will do": Cultivating Fictions of Kew Gardens', in Diane F. Gillespie and Leslie Hankins (eds), *Virginia Woolf and the Arts: Selected Papers from the Sixth Annual Conference on Virginia Woolf* (New York: Pace University Press, 1997), pp. 57–66.
24. Woolf, fearing the booksellers' misshelving, makes a revealing confession that she had expected *Orlando* to be her 'one popular book' (*D3* 198).
25. For commentaries on the physical lay-out of the 1927 'Kew Gardens', see Diane Gillespie, *The Sisters' Arts: The Writing and Painting of Virginia Woolf and Vanessa Bell* (New York: Syracuse University Press, 1988) and Harvey, 'Bloomsbury's Books'.
26. The *OED Online* glosses 'Q' rating, noting its American etymology and giving its first reported usage in 1958: '*N. Amer. Marketing.* A measurement of the popularity of a public figure, television programme, etc., based on survey data recording whether respondents are familiar with, and have a favourable opinion of, the subject under consideration'. Available at: <www.oed.com/view/Entry/155604> (accessed 2 May 2017).
27. Amy E. Elkins, 'Old Pages and New Readings in Virginia Woolf's *Orlando*', *Tulsa Studies in Women's Literature* 29.1 (Spring 2010), pp. 131–6.
28. Elkins, 'Old Pages', p. 133.
29. Staveley, *Reconfiguring Kew Gardens*, p. 252.
30. Friedman, 'Creativity and the Childbirth Metaphor', p. 373.

Chapter 10

The Day of *Orlando*

Bryony Randall

Once more Orlando stood at the window, but let the reader take courage; nothing of the same sort is going to happen to-day, which is not, by any means, the same day.[1]

This sentence inaugurates the frantic acceleration into modernity that is the final section of the final chapter of *Orlando*: the section that brings us to 'the eleventh of October [. . .] 1928 [. . .] the present moment' (*O* 206). It is because we conclude with this extended narrative of a single day that, according to James Hafley (in one of the earliest monographs on Woolf's work), 11th October 1928 can be seen as nothing less than *the* day of Orlando: 'in a sense, *Orlando* occupies only the one day in 1928, and from it are projected back into space the three hundred years of its first five chapters'.[2] Hafley's explicitly Bergsonian reading, emphasising the perpetual presence of the past, disrupts the conventional characterisation of the novel as a capacious, sweeping, and specifically historical epic by drawing our attention to the importance, even primacy, of its final day.

Orlando has, of course, a complex relationship with the very notion of history. On the one hand, it is a deeply historical text, reaching back centuries into the past and including numerous historical personae. Many of its earliest reviewers explicitly praised it as a new history of England, and specifically of English literature (albeit an unconventional one).[3] In characteristically Woolfian style, there are aspects of the novel which celebrate conventional historical narratives even while the text as a whole parodies the historical panorama it surveys. On the other hand, arguably its most important aim is rewriting history: not just producing a new version of it, but fundamentally challenging the discourses and paradigms through which history is constructed. As Angeliki Spiropoulou puts it in her work on Woolf's engagement with the concept of history, in this novel 'Woolf extends her critique of traditional notions of subjectivity through biography [...] not so much in order to write history as to upset the terms and assumptions of history writing concerning method and truth'.[4] Spiropoulou later specifies that Woolf's text 'mocks the conventional method of concentrating on major events or deeds of great men in history writing, by undermining any credibility in the exactitude of chronological demarcation of historical time'.[5] Indeed, Orlando herself and her biographer agree that 'it is not articles by Nick Greene on John Donne nor eight-hour bills nor covenants nor factory acts that matter; it's something useless, sudden, violent; something that costs a life; red, blue, purple; a spirit; a splash' (O 199). So when Sandra Gilbert asserts that 'Orlando *is* history'[6] she both reinforces the centrality of the concept to the text (in some ways, *Orlando* is history too, a history of sorts), and insists on its complete revision in the novel, so that history is no longer a discourse imposed on individuals and constructed from a distance but instead a dynamic expression of corporeal life.

Orlando does not, then, appear to express quite the extent of the 'revulsion toward history' that Steven G. Kellman, in company with many other critics, identifies in major modernist writers – Proust, Kafka, Joyce and so on (likewise, neither does Woolf reject entirely the importance of legal reforms, 'eight hour bills' and their ilk).[7] But Kellman goes on to associate this 'revulsion' with the expression of a 'rejection of the symbiosis of story and history',[8] a narrative gesture which we can surely agree is characteristic of Woolf's novel perhaps more than any other. In the argument that follows, Kellman proposes that the one-day narrative may be one particularly apt means of expressing this rejection. This proposition supports my reading of *Orlando*'s final resolution into a concentrated, extended description of a single day as a key part of the text's undoing of traditional history; a history whose focus on 'eight-hour bills [...] covenants [...] factory acts' would presumably not permit detailed investigation of the sensations of just one among the many days it would purport to summarise (O 199).

Temporal limitation – to the scope of a day, for example – need not, of course, imply limited scope or ambition, as *Mrs Dalloway* (1925) and James Joyce's *Ulysses* (1922) (among others) show us. Indeed, the reverse might well be the case: Robert Weninger has observed that 'the expansion of time through the reduction of time, is surely one of the prime characteristics of the modernist novel';[9] Steven Connor similarly argues that:

> Many a modernist work contrived to be less and more at once: less than the world in its concentration and condensation (the events of a single day in

Joyce's *Ulysses* and Woolf's *Mrs Dalloway*) and yet containing more than the world in its accumulation of allusion and interconnection.[10]

Orlando, of course, contrives (and the word is apt) to be much more than the world as we know it, but it also displays those qualities of concentration and condensation particularly intensely in the final part of the novel, which does indeed cover just one day in 1928. So while we may not want to go so far as Hafley, we might nevertheless take up the challenge implicit in his statement to investigate the extent of *Orlando*'s daily qualities – in particular, its engagement with the temporality of the day.

A close sequential reading will provide an initial indication of how features of daily temporality operate in my chosen sentence. We note, first, that this sentence begins a new section, normally signalling a break with what has gone before – most usually the passing of time, or some other shift, perhaps in perspective or location. The very possibility of a break with what has gone before is, however, a key concern of the sentence itself. The sentence opens by asserting that Orlando is doing something again – 'Once more Orlando stood at the window'. Our attention is drawn in this phrase both to previous instances of this standing, and to this particular instance. The word 'once' evokes singularity, uniqueness; the word 'more' addition, accumulation. This tension between sameness and difference is at the heart of the temporality of dailiness.[11] It is also the basis of one of *Orlando*'s key narrative effects: the repetition of various figures, objects and tropes across the centuries it spans, including 'The Oak Tree', Orlando's ancestral home, Sasha, Harriet/Harry, Nick/Sir Nicholas Greene, and of course Orlando him/herself. By replaying these characters in entirely different historical contexts, Woolf's fantasia emphasises that repetition of any kind always involves change, even where the person or object is supposedly the same, just as each day is always necessarily different from any other. This tension – 'once' yet also 'more' – is echoed in Orlando's physical location at this moment. She is standing by a window and thus in a liminal position: inside, looking out, and also in principle available to be looked at from the outside in.

The reader is now asked to 'take courage', as if this posture of Orlando's is one which might cause us alarm or anxiety. The possible cause of this alarm is alluded to in the next clause (after a semi-colon, as if allowing for a fortifying intake of breath): that is, the possibility that something 'of the same sort' might be about to happen. What this might be, we understand, is childbirth, because the previous sentence, which also ends a section, has described the delivery of Orlando's son. Sure enough, this process apparently began with Orlando 'looking out

The Day of Orlando   131

of the window' some paragraphs earlier (O 202). So the biographer is seeking here to reassure the reader that he or she is not going to be confronted with further instances of childbirth, as if this is something both biographer and reader can agree would be, if not necessarily undesirable as such, then at least inopportune. But the biographer does not say, for example, 'the same *thing* is not going to happen to-day'. Instead, we are left to puzzle out what might be of 'the same sort' as childbirth. One might suppose childbirth to be *sui generis* – what can possibly compare with the experience of producing another human being from one's own body? But childbirth is in fact the vehicle for countless familiar metaphors, and thus understood to be of the 'same sort' as various other experiences, the most significant for our purposes being that of producing an artwork. Indeed, just a few pages previously, Orlando has finally (after several centuries) divested herself of her epic poem 'The Oak Tree', leaving it in the hands of the now respectable Sir Nicholas Greene, and leaving 'a bare place in her breast where she had been used to carry it' (O 202).

   Then, for the second time in this part of the sentence, the biographer opts for a qualifying expression: today is not 'by any means' the same day. This might simply have been a clarifying deictic phrase, emphasising that the narrative has moved on to a day after that on which Orlando gave birth. It is worth noting that although it would also in principle be possible to have moved back in time to an earlier day – and although this narrative is far from averse to playing fast and loose with conventional temporality – the narrative is strikingly orthodox in its temporal direction, moving always forward in time on the surface at least. But the biographer adds the phrase 'by any means' – again by way of emphasising that we are not going to be faced with more parturition, but also leading us to wonder by what 'means' this might, in fact, be the same day. In summary, the sentence worries at various key issues in the temporality of the novel as a whole when viewed through the lens of the temporality of dailiness: primarily, the dynamic of and tension between sameness and difference; cognate questions of the status of the present ('to-day'); and the connected concepts of uniqueness, engendering and originality as embodied here in the notion of childbirth.[12] So when a few sentences – though 'some days' – later the final day of *Orlando* begins, it has been introduced via a somewhat anxious evocation, with its tension between insistence and qualification, of what a day might be, how unique it might (or might not) be, and what kind of engendering it might contain or constitute.

   It is worth dwelling on the slippage between the 'to-day' of my chosen sentence here and the 'to-day' of 'the present moment' – of 11th October 1928. An inattentive reader (such as myself, the first few times I read this sentence) might easily come away with the impression that the 'to-day' when 'once more Orlando stood at the window' is indeed 11th October 1928. The narrator has insisted on our mutual inhabiting of 'to-day', and repeatedly reminded us that it is a new and different day from that which has just been described, which might lead one to assume that it is therefore a significant day, one on which we are going to dwell. Instead, rather like the 'vanishing bird' who 'darts of a sudden from bank to bank' (O 204), the narrative here alights only very briefly on 'to-day'; three sentences later, we move ahead 'some days' to what is probably the day before 11th October 1928. Orlando then observes evening falling, surveys the lamplit night-time streets, and 'returns at mid-day'; finally, at the end of this paragraph, we are told that 'in fact it was ten o'clock in the morning. It was the eleventh of October. It was 1928. It was the present moment' (O 206). It is of course entirely congruent with the temporal slippages of the narrative as a whole that we are teasingly presented with what appears to be a firm temporal location – 'to-day' – only to have this pulled out from underneath us.

The narrative has, to this point, started to be increasingly insistent about its temporal location. The final chapter specifies various dates: '(the second of March)' (O 203), and then 'March the 20th' (the date of the birth of Orlando's son – her first as a woman) (O 204); and then, three times, the 11th October 1928 (although this is the first instance where the year is mentioned). This final day also becomes increasingly marked by clock time – echoing *Mrs Dalloway*'s chiming Big Ben, the hour strikes out throughout the day until we reach midnight. And yet, as in that novel, this apparent tethering to public time is in tension with the fluidity and depth of the experience narrated. Certainly, it is possible to describe what appears to actually happen on this day: Orlando motors through London, visits a department store, drives out to the country, visits her ancestral home, and finally climbs a hill to meet her husband – who arrives by aeroplane – under the oak tree. But this far from fully expresses Orlando's experience of the day, which is replete with challenges to her sense of self, visitations by figures from her past, visions of her centuries-long life, and the collapse of landscapes into each other. *Orlando*'s evocation of 11th October 1928 vividly expresses the quality of the day as haecceity, as itself, as 'this'. Gilles Deleuze and Félix Guattari write:

> A season, a winter, a summer, an hour, a date have a perfect individuality lacking nothing, even though this individuality is different from that of a thing or subject. They are haecceities in the sense that they consist entirely of relations of movement and rest between molecules or particles, capacities to affect and be affected.[13]

The 11th October 1928 is indeed here characterised by its energetic movement, whether literal (in the speeding motorcar), psychic or affective. Its haecceity – or thisness – is investigated and evoked intensely and sustainedly.

The fugitive, ceaselessly transitioning qualities of this day – 'to-day' – are, however, set at odds with one of its necessary temporal qualities: presentness. Rather than celebrating and revelling in the inhabiting of the present which a deep engagement with 'to-day' might be assumed to entail, the present is presented as, primarily, terrifying and shocking: 'For what more terrifying revelation can there be than that it is the present moment? That we survive the shock at all is only possible because the past shelters us on one side and the future on another' (O 206). This articulation of the sensation of experiencing the present in an unmediated way implies that the present offers a traumatic repleteness of meaning, even a full authenticity, albeit one which is at odds with the relational and mobile model of existence that Woolf proposes in the novel, and in this day as haecceity. As Gabrielle McIntire comments on this part of the text: 'The present means too forcefully, leaving insufficient room for the multiple and endlessly proliferating turnings of memory that Woolf wants to celebrate'.[14] There are, however, various other ways in which the present is reflected upon in this part of the text. In the department store, the shop assistants 'chose to let down the impervious screen of the present' to obscure the fact that they had descended 'even from such depths of the past as [Orlando] did' (O 210). Here, the present appears not as a realm of intensity and terror, but instead is figured as a protective covering, reminiscent perhaps of Freud's model of the protective covering which our mind, or brain (variously articulated) requires in order to operate from day to day; or Bergson's recognition that for practical purposes only a small amount of the memory that we carry with us can be present to our consciousness at any one time.

Screening and the concealment it implies are, however, anathema to this novel's aesthetics and gender politics, insofar as a scene of failed screening is at the very heart of the text. At the crucial moment when Orlando's change of sex is revealed, the sisters Purity, Chastity and Modesty 'make as if to cover Orlando with their draperies' (O 96) but are ultimately powerless in the face of the 'THE TRUTH!' (O 97) – that Orlando is now a woman, which fact Orlando recognises by composedly looking at his [sic] transformed naked body 'up and down in a looking-glass' (O 98). The sisters' failed attempt to cover – to screen – Orlando's nakedly gendered, and indeed sexy, body forms part of Woolf's dwelling on sensual pleasure and corporeality in this book: her insistence that we inhabit sexual bodies, and that the feelings yielded by our bodies (and our contact with others' bodies) are central to our experience of being human. Their powerlessnes in the face of the 'Truth' also reinforces Woolf's resistance to normative categories of sex and gender, failing to screen the existence of more than one gender in a body which is (a few minor changes aside, presumably) more or less the same. So while this scene does not involve a 'screen of the present' as such, it reinforces the text's critique of the gesture of screening as concealment. In summary, then, the final part of the novel on the one hand valorises yet fears the present as a realm of excessive intensity, and on the other regards it as functioning as a screen from the fullness of existence.

The question of 'existence', no less, recurs a few pages later, where we find that:

> the process of motoring far out of London so much resembles the chopping up small of identity which precedes unconsciousness and perhaps death itself that it is an open question in what sense Orlando can be said to have existed at the present moment. (O 212)

Here, we are perhaps initially inclined to read this dissolution as negative, associated as it is with what precedes death. But existing at the present moment has already been articulated as intensely painful, even unbearable, so that becoming a 'person entirely disassembled' (O 212) might appear (temporarily) as an appealing alternative. There is throughout Woolf's oeuvre, and her own life, a tension between the terror of dissolution and of loss of identity, and a yearning for it, undeniably expressed, of course, in her own suicide. Rhoda in *The Waves* is perhaps the most eloquent expression of this tension in a single character; a tension that that novel as a whole also formally expresses. 'Exist[ing] at the present moment' is again far from being a simple matter.

Despite the apparent dissolution that is held out as a possibility in this part of the text, there is an attempt to include the reader in its own present moment, insofar as this is possible in a written narrative. Partly this is achieved by the detailed and intense evocation of the progress of the day – one would say from hour to hour except that the tolling of the hour is only one of the many temporalities at work in the final section, which ceaselessly plunges us into Orlando's excessively multifarious past. It does this both by evoking the material reality of modernity and by rejecting some of its most potent ideologies. So, for example, Orlando leaves the department store 'without the sardines, the bath salts, or the boots' (O 211) she went in for (though she does manage to acquire some sheets for the royal bed) – she largely eschews the act of purchasing by which few days in modernity are unmarked, but comes away instead with a vision of her erstwhile lover Sasha, a recollection of the frozen Thames, the sensation that now, in her middle age, 'nothing is any longer one thing,' and gets 'into her motor-car with her eyes full of tears and visions of Persian mountains' (O 210). These and not the commodities for sale are the intangible yet richly rewarding fruits of Orlando's visit to the department store; it is they that mark Orlando's day of absolute modernity – 'the present moment'.

The other obvious way in which the reader is interpellated as coexisting with the text's moment is in its insistence on its now-ness – 11th October 1928. It is only in this chapter that the narrator has started to refer to 'to-day', a temporal location that purports to include the narrator, characters and reader. My chosen sentence, of the day which is 'by no means' the same day, has, as I have argued, intensified our focus on what it means to inhabit a particular day, what a day might comprise, and how it might be the same as or different from another. But the reader is aware that they will always come to this day belatedly; there is necessarily a time lag, infinitesimal though it might be, between the moment when something is written and the moment when it is read. In addition, there is a paradox in the fact that this insistence on the present as 11th October 1928 becomes almost immediately anachronistic. There was only one period of twenty-four hours in which that was indeed 'the present', 'to-day', and that period is now (today) long past. The significance of this date is intensified when we remember that this is also the date on which Woolf presented the text to Vita Sackville-West, Woolf's erstwhile lover and the model for Orlando, and Sackville-West read the novel in – as one might imagine – a heightened emotional state: she wrote to her husband in a letter dated 11 October 1928 that in anticipation of reading the book 'I scarcely slept with excitement all night, and woke up feeling as though it were my birthday, or wedding day, or something unique'.[15] McIntire summarises the unique temporal qualities of that single day where she says that:

> Woolf thus again creates a double temporality: one that will forever remain frozen as the present historic of the novel's tense, and one in which two October elevenths, and two Vitas, co-existed for a single day more than three-quarters of a century ago. By the end of the novel, that is, the novel's temporality has caught up with the time of writing, so that Orlando, Woolf and Sackville-West share a synchronous temporality in the final pages.[16]

McIntire's identification of a double temporality in this text in fact constitutes a further complication to the already multiple temporality of any narrative,[17] but it is an additional complication brought about specifically by the text's insistence on its existence in the present moment.

This observation that by the end of the novel there is a 'synchronous temporality' speaks to Kellman's suggestion of a particular affinity between the one-day novel and the autogenous text – the text that emerges from itself, or where the text whose emergence is heralded more or less explicitly at its close is in fact the one we have just read (as in, for example, Marcel Proust's *À la recherche du temps perdu* or Dorothy Richardson's *Pilgrimage*). Kellman observes that 'the one-day novel does describe the same pattern of circularity and self-containment as the autogenous text, for which the reading experience becomes a kind of Mobbius [sic] strip'.[18] Leaving aside for the moment Kellman's focus on one particular aspect of daily temporality, we might ask whether, if *Orlando* can be read as a kind of one-day novel, it can also be read as an autogenous one. McIntire's discussion of the language of the maternal in *Orlando* and the way that Woolf's biographer-narrator figures their subject reinforces, and specifies, this text's particular concern with its own genesis: 'as both lover and mother [the biographer] androgynously desires and bears Orlando as his son, daughter, lover, and historical subject'.[19] The subject of this text is produced by it. This is, of course, in some ways true of any text. But in this case, the language of maternity and engendering used by the biographer draws particular attention to the way in which a biographer brings his (or her) subject into being, a key facet of Woolf's intervention in the genre of biography.[20] In the traditional mode, the biographical subject has a discrete existence prior to and separate from his or her biography, and it is the biographer's job simply to record this as accurately as possible, whereas Woolf's own position emphasises the way in which any biography necessarily sculpts and shapes the biographical subject as it proceeds. But we can move beyond this general observation to argue that the structure of the novel, *per* Hafley, encourages us to view the *text* as a whole as having been produced by one day, by 11th October 1928. One response to Hafley's suggestion that the novel can be seen as a one-day text is indeed to turn back to the beginning (literally or metaphorically) and read this chronicle of the past as having been released only by the temporal intensities of that single day. It is the day on which Orlando literally becomes *Orlando*; the text that has gone before it would not have been possible without that date and its momentary coming together of literary and historical time. Specifying that this day is '11th October 1928' gives it an intense sense of presentness, of vitality, which would not be achieved simply by insisting on it being 'now' – now always, necessarily, being a moving deictic marker, gone as soon as the word is uttered. The further question then raised is whether the *Orlando* of – that is, released by, engendered on – 10th, or 12th October 1928, or 11th November 1928, or 11th October

1927, or any other date, would be a different *Orlando*? This is certainly the case if we follow the logic of Spiropoulou's Benjaminian reading of Orlando, that the novel 'emphasises the need to rewrite history from the point of view of the present'.[21] If 'the present' of this text, the day on which it becomes itself, were different, then Orlando would, necessarily, be different – and surely *Orlando* would be too.

In the same way, my version of *Orlando* is a product of its day. Kellman emphasises the 'circularity and self-containment' which, no doubt, are evoked by the one-day novel. But such texts also, necessarily, always gesture onward to the next day. While the words 'The End' do appear at the end of the text of Orlando (after its index), nevertheless, as Chiara Briganti argues, in life 'a day will be followed by another day; one does not write the word "end" at the end of the day'.[22] This recurrence of the daily is paradoxically reinforced by the novel's insistence on 11th October 1928. We know, as Woolf must have known, that in fact 11th October 1928 is not 'to-day'; there have been many more 'to-days' after it, in some ways the same, in most ways different, up to the present day of our reading it – and the present day of my writing about it, on Wednesday, the nineteenth of April, Two thousand and Seventeen.

Notes

1. Virginia Woolf, *Orlando: A Biography* [1928] (London: Penguin, 1993), p. 205.
2. James Hafley, *The Glass Roof: Virginia Woolf as Novelist* (Berkeley and Los Angeles: University of California Press, 1954), p. 98.
3. For example, one such review of *Orlando* called it 'perhaps the first readable history of our literature' (Henry Seidel Canby, '*Orlando*, a Biography', *The Saturday Review of Literature*, 3 November 1928, p. 313; repr. in Eleanor McNees (ed.), *Virginia Woolf: Critical Assessments* (Robertsbridge: Helm Information, 1994), pp. 416–21).
4. Angeliki Spiropoulou, *Virginia Woolf, Modernity and History: Constellations with Walter Benjamin* (London and New York: Palgrave Macmillan, 2010), p. 75.
5. Spiropoulou, *Virginia Woolf*, p. 87.
6. Sandra M. Gilbert and Susan Gubar, *No Man's Land: The Place of the Woman Writer in the Twentieth Century, Volume 3: Letters from the Front* (New Haven: Yale University Press, 1994), p. 40.
7. Steven G. Kellman, 'Circadia in Paris: The One-Day Novel and the French', *Stanford Literature Review*, 2.2 (Fall 1985), p. 211.
8. Ibid.
9. Robert Weninger, 'Days of our Lives: The One-Day Novel as Homage à Joyce', in Morris Beja and Anne Fogarty (eds), *Bloomsday 100: Essays on Ulysses* (Gainesville: University Press of Florida, 2009), pp. 192–3.

10. Steven Connor, 'Postmodernism and Literature' in S. Connor (ed.), *The Cambridge Companion to Postmodernism* (Cambridge: Cambridge University Press, 2004), p. 68.
11. For discussion of the temporality of dailiness, see Bryony Randall, *Modernism, Daily Time and Everyday Life* (Cambridge: Cambridge University Press, 2007), pp. 22, 30.
12. The term 'engendering' is particularly resonant in Orlando, and can be read as alluding to further layers that might be added to this discussion through specific consideration of Orlando's gender.
13. Gilles Deleuze and Félix Guattari, *A Thousand Plateaus*, trans. Brian Massumi (Minneapolis: University of Minnesota Press, 1987), p. 261.
14. Gabrielle McIntire, *Modernism, Memory and Desire* (Cambridge: Cambridge University Press, 2008), p. 136.
15. Nigel Nicolson (ed.), *Vita and Harold: The Letters of Vita Sackville-West and Harold Nicolson* (New York: Putnam, 1992), pp. 205–6.
16. McIntire, *Modernism*, pp. 134–5.
17. On the complex temporalities of narrative fiction see, for example, Mark Currie, *About Time: Narrative, Fiction and the Philosophy of Time* (Edinburgh: Edinburgh University Press, 2007); and M. Currie, *The Unexpected: Narrative Temporality and the Philosophy of Surprise* (Edinburgh: Edinburgh University Press, 2013).
18. Kellman, 'Circadia in Paris', p. 222.
19. McIntire, *Modernism*, p. 122.
20. For a discussion of the interlocking language of maternity, desire and (life) writing in the novel, and the way in which this intersects with the relationship between Woolf and Vita Sackville-West, see McIntire, *Modernism*, pp. 119–23.
21. Spiropoulou, *Virginia Woolf*, p. 74.
22. Chiara Briganti, 'Giving the Mundane its Due: One (Fine) Day in the Life of the Everyday', *ESC: English Studies in Canada*, 39.2–3 (June/September 2013), p. 162.

Chapter 11

Satzdenken, Indeterminacy and the Polyvalent Audience

Steven Putzel

> Rough though the staging was, the actors running up and down a pair of steps and sometimes tripping, and the crowd stamping their feet and whistling, or when they were bored, tossing a piece of orange peel at the actors which a dog would scramble for, still the astonishing, sinuous melody of the words stirred Orlando like music.[1]

This intricate and elusive sentence places readers, along with Orlando, in the heart of an impromptu Jacobean audience who have gathered around a makeshift stage (perhaps a pageant wagon or trestle stage) out on the thick ice of the Thames during King James's Great Frost celebration. We, along with the rest of the audience, are just in time to catch Desdemona's death scene from *Othello*. The sentence describes a performance, is itself a performance, and requires reading as performance. Here the medium is indeed the message; the sentence is what it says and does. Content and form are inseparable. It is syntactically chaotic, describing a chaotic scene, yet the syntax comes to equilibrium just as the scene resolves itself within Orlando himself. Woolf offers readers concrete, active visual images (the actors 'running' and 'tripping'), but switches our attention away from the actors, first to the crowd-turned-audience, and finally to the 'point' of the sentence – Orlando's reception. Therefore, there are multiple subjects, objects, and a three-level audience to do the receiving and to make meaning: the Jacobean crowd, Orlando, and us – the readers. We note that the first-level audience is active; they are 'stamping' and 'whistling', and their (re)actions when 'bored' are interactive, even aggressive. Even the dog intervenes, interrupting both syntax and whatever is taking place on stage. In contrast to this active first-level audience, Orlando passively takes in the entire scene, telescoping from stage to audience but certainly not understanding what is going on, until the end of the sentence when the music of the words 'stirs' him. We readers, the third-level audience, take in the action on stage, the actions of the Jacobean audience, and we see that Orlando is 'stirred', but the sentence acts on us, just as it does on Orlando, creating impressions and suggestions more than meaning.

My first step in examining the sentence was to send it to a few grammarians. Reading one of the responses, I realised I had neglected to reveal that Woolf was the author. I was firmly told: 'I suggest you rewrite the sentence'. Another was equally unimpressed:

> My comment on this construction is that grammatically, the gerundives (if that's the word) following 'the staging was' should modify 'staging' or 'rough', but in fact what the audience does and the dogs do is not part of the staging. So the thought (about distractions) does not match the structure (about staging). What the writer wanted to say was something like 'Notwithstanding the rough staging and the distractions offered by the crowds and the dogs, the melody still stirred Orlando'. Whatever 'stirred Orlando' may mean.[2]

Our attempt to tease out word and sentence meaning, to understand syntactic patterns, is to move into what Roman Ingarden calls the 'flow of thinking the sentence' (*satzdenken*). As we settle into this flow 'we are prepared, after having completed the thought of one sentence, to think its "continuation" in the form of another sentence'. The multiple phrases and clauses constituting Woolf's sentence as well as the arrangement of preceding and anteceding sentences do not 'flow' as grammatical and syntactic rules lead us to expect. According to Ingarden, when 'the flow of thought is checked [. . .] a more or less vivid surprise or vexation is associated with the resulting hiatus. The block must be overcome if we are to renew the flow of our reading'.[3] We overcome this 'block' by practising what Ingarden calls 'active' reading. The passive or merely receptive reader reads sentence by sentence, while the active reader 'perform[s] the signitive acts' – 'a series of often complicated and interconnected acts'[4] – and in so doing becomes 'the cocreator of the literary work of art'.[5] The sentence, like *Orlando* itself, forces readers to shift and readjust their horizon of expectations.

So what is it about this sentence that perplexes or dismays grammarians? What compels us to become active readers? The sentence is filled with dependent clauses without being 'compound' or 'complex'. The gerundives – the running and stamping of the actors and the stamping of the crowd – shift agency, leading to some confusion in focus. Even within the sentence, the *satzdenken* or horizon of expectation is repeatedly interrupted, and closure – which shifts yet again to a third agency in Orlando – is significantly postponed. The subject and predicate, where some content-focused readers might locate meaning or 'the point', come at the very end of the structure, not at the beginning. English readers, unlike, for example, readers of German or Latin, have come to expect pointed, balanced, cumulative compound sentences. Woolf's periodic formulation defeats such expectations and forces readers to work for meaning, to select meaning from a pallet of possibilities. Transitive past-tense verbs such as 'was' and 'stirred', placed near the beginning and the end of the sentence, make us search the verbiage for their objects. The introductory dependent clause 'Rough though the staging was', which the reader understands as 'although the staging was rough', encourages us to expect the subject to be immediately forthcoming. We also expect that the delayed subject will contrast with the rough staging. Instead, Woolf provides not the subject but a digression, an example to illustrate the rough staging: actors running and tripping, incidentally adding bodies to the scene.

Then the coordinating conjunction 'and' ironically takes us still further away from the rough stage and from the subject, moving our attention to the crowd, and still more bodies in the chaotic mass. Or, to explore a different horizon, does the conflation of actors and crowd in the same dependent clause suggest that syntactically actors and crowd (and later the dog) are all actually part of the rough staging, for the play or for the reader? Actors, stage and audience are all becoming one. Just when the syntax threatens to crack and break, to slip into the incomprehensibility of subordinate clause fragment, to shift the whole mood with 'when they were bored', and just as the reader almost forgets that the subject and predicate have not yet arrived, all clauses are brought to suspension with the unexpected coordinating conjunction 'still'. Suddenly we have a totally unexpected resolution; we finally have our subject, the 'melody', the predicate verb, 'stirred', and the direct object 'Orlando', all three unforeseen by the start of the sentence. But do we have meaning?

Of course *satzdenken* and cognition depend on more than syntax. Meaning derives from both *Gestalt* and *Gehalt*, form and content (with the implication of a pay-off in the German).[6] Ingarden also recognises that words and sentences have both a 'phonetic stratum' and 'meaning content'[7], or, put more basically, sound and sense. In this case, the sentence's syntax or form and its phonetic stratum or sounds contribute to the sense or meaning. The postponement of closure, the jumble of clauses and prepositional phrases, constitutes a syntactic chaos that not only complements but also helps create the chaos described. Put another way, both the words and the syntax are onomatopoeic. Woolf creates both action and confusion with her use of onomatopoeic present participles: 'running', 'tripping', 'stamping', 'whistling', 'tossing'. Even nouns are made active. The 'stage' was not rough – the 'staging' was. The participle also becomes adjectival: the 'melody of the words' does not 'astonish'; it is ongoing, active – 'astonishing'.

These verbal forms are then also modified, made more chaotic, more active. Actors are not just running; they are 'running up and down a pair of steps', which suggests that the steps form makeshift stage-left and stage-right entry and exit points. This up-and-down movement becomes more chaotic with the information that these rushing actors are 'sometimes tripping'. The comma after 'tripping', together with the coordinating 'and', barely allows readers to catch their breath when Woolf rips our attention from actors to audience. But it is not an 'audience', which would imply 'the classical Latin *audientia* act of listening, attention',[8] or a group of passive spectators, but the much more chaotic, uncontrolled 'crowd'. No simple act of reception here. This is not the closed stage of naturalistic theatre but a more open stage, implying audience participation:[9] they are 'stamping their feet' while 'whistling'. Again the participle form renders the action ongoing. The narrator adds that whatever it is the crowd is gathered around sometimes bores them, at which point they are 'tossing' orange peel. To this anarchic action of actors and crowd Woolf adds another participant: a dog. The dual prepositional phrase 'which a dog would scramble for' modifies the action of tossing a piece of orange peel. Instead of going after the orange peel, the dog's modal 'would scramble' grammatically suggests repetition in the past.

Curiously, it is here that we have the one major variant in the sentence between the Harcourt and Hogarth Press versions. In the Hogarth edition, the audience is 'tossing a piece of orange peel on to the ice which a dog would scramble for'.[10] The grammatical and syntactic structure is still the same here, but the action is immensely less aggressive and judgemental; the Harcourt version suggests not bored but angry groundlings, who, theatrical records tell us, would show their displeasure by throwing cabbages and other garbage at the actors. The Harcourt variant also removes a reminder of the larger site of the action – the Frost Fair. Without this reminder, readers may not telescope out to the macrocosm, but remain focused on the microcosm. It is all too easy to read the sentence and forget that all we are witnessing is enacted on slippery ice. A few words alter reception at all levels: Orlando, the audience, and the readers.

All of this chaotic syntax is introductory and preparatory. It is visceral, visual, even tactile, olfactory and auditory. The actors and the first-level audience are completely unaware of Orlando, who, though accompanied by Sasha, is an audience of one, physically among the crowd but alone. Orlando hears something above the din, and we readers, if we are attentive, understand beyond sight, touch, smell and sound what Orlando experiences. Although the verbal forms suggest that the activity and noise continue, the word 'still' puts the brakes on the sentence, bringing us at last to the subject and predicate. The word actually does what it is; its form and content become one. With one word, the sentence switches abruptly from external, chaotic action to pure reception and response. Despite all the noise and bustle, the words uttered by the actors reach Orlando, but not in the cognitive sense: it is not the meaning of the words that infiltrates. Instead Orlando (and the reader) is seduced by sibilants in this, the only independent clause of the sentence: 'still the astonishing, sinuous melody of the words stirred Orlando like music'. It is not the meaning but the sound of the words that 'stirred' Orlando, as one grammarian put it, 'whatever that means'. The simile 'like music' modifies not 'Orlando' but the transitive verb 'stirred'. The semantics and syntax of the sentence leave both Orlando and the reader in the same state – with feeling more than meaning.

Slowing down our reading and focusing on exactly how this sentence works on us certainly creates what I referred to earlier as Ingarden's 'hiatus', not from 'vexation' but from 'vivid surprise'. To re-establish 'sentence flow' and to work toward cognition we must place the sentence in context. How does this sentence make us reappraise the sentences that precede it and anticipate those that follow? If we establish just how the sentence functions within this specific scene, we can then examine its function within the temporal and spatial framework of the novel. Here are the three preceding sentences:

> The main press of people, it appeared, stood opposite a booth or stage something like our Punch and Judy show upon which some kind of theatrical performance was going forward. A black man was waving his arms and vociferating. There was a woman in white laid upon a bed. (O 56)

In the first of these sentences readers not only hear, but are made complicit with the narrative voice; 'our' temporarily forces us to see the scene from the narrator's late-1920s perspective, rather than suspending our disbelief and letting us lose ourselves in the early seventeenth-century scene, and in Orlando's perspective. These sentences provide a correlative for rather than a description of the theatrical staging, as we are asked to envision first a Punch and Judy booth (or is it a stage?), and then the stage Orlando is viewing. In fact, what Orlando sees and what readers are asked to envision is nothing like a Punch and Judy show. There are live actors, not hand puppets or marionettes; the booths of Punch and Judy shows are quite small, while this stage is large enough to accommodate at least five or six actors; and Punch and Judy booths have no need for stairs. Readers must construct an image of this stage and performance, perhaps with the help of 1608 or 1683 woodcuts of the

Great Frost, perhaps from their own experience with pageant wagons or trestle stages in ubiquitous Renaissance Fairs.

The impressionistic stage is an apt setting for Orlando's impressionistic reception of what is being performed. Woolf's marvellous phantasmagoria, blending history, Jacobean and Restoration fanciful woodcut illustrations, and her own whim, form the Frost Fair setting. As Sasha and Orlando skate away from the Muscovite ship before encountering the theatrical spectacle, Orlando looks back, marvelling at 'the evening of astonishing beauty': 'Here was the fretted cross at Charing; there the dome of St. Paul's' (O 53). Woolf was certainly aware that in 1608, the year of James's Frost Fair, it would be another 100 years until St Paul's had a dome. Likewise, the multiple references to 'orange girls' hawking their wares to the crowd are, like the vision of the dome, appropriate to the eighteenth or nineteenth, but not the early seventeenth century. Oranges, especially in winter, were a luxury, selling for at least eight pence (8d) a piece. Samuel Pepys records that in 1668 they were still precious, though now indeed sold by 'orange women' at the theatres for 6d each, certainly still too dear for the groundlings.[11] For the price of an orange one of the spectators crowding around Woolf's icy stage could see eight productions at the Globe Theatre, obtain a place to sleep for a week, or purchase an excellent meal. The anachronisms, like the chaotic action and complex syntax, all help create the larger-than-life world of Orlando, contributing to what Sally Greene calls Woolf's 'renaissance imaginary'.[12]

Woolf's description of the Frost Fair theatrical production encapsulates the essence of the 'renaissance imaginary' she had outlined it in her 1925 essay 'Notes on an Elizabethan Play'. Even the worst of the Elizabethan plays, she argues, 'gives us the sense in our quiet armchairs of ostlers and orange-girls catching up the lines, flinging them back, hissing or stamping applause'. She contrasts this with the 'deliberate drama of the Victorian age [that] is evidently written in a study', where

> There is no stamping, no applause. It does not, as, with all its faults, the Elizabethan audience did, leaven the mass with fire. Rhetorical and bombastic, the lines are flung and hurried into existence and reach the same impromptu felicities, have the same lip-moulded profusion and unexpectedness, which speech sometimes achieves, but seldom in our day the deliberate, solitary pen. Indeed, half the work of the dramatists, one feels, was done in the Elizabethan age by the public. (E4 64)

Woolf seems to recognise here that the Victorian stage itself, with its proscenium arch, confines the chaos and forbids rather than invites participation. The architectonics of the proscenium arch renders the

Victorian audience passive. They cannot break the frame. Woolf is describing what Peter Brook would later call 'Deadly Theatre' – theatre that provides what is expected, that pacifies the audience, that is the theatrical equivalent of easy-listening music, that is driven by the economics of entertainment rather than an intention to make 'the stage a real place in our lives'.[13] When Woolf begins her sentence with 'Rough though the staging was', she anticipates Brook's 'Rough Theatre':

> Through the ages it has taken many forms, and there is only one factor that they all have in common – a roughness. Salt, sweat, noise, smell: the theatre that's not in a theatre, the theatre on carts, on wagons, on trestles, audiences standing, drinking, sitting round tables, audiences joining in, answering back.[14]

It is also helpful to contrast Woolf's imaginative reconstruction of the commoners as participatory audience in the seventeenth century with her view of the working-class audience witnessing a production of *Othello* in the early twentieth century:

> Seldom penetrated by love for mankind as I am, I sometimes feel sorry for the poor who dont read Shakespeare, & indeed have felt some generous democratic humbug at the Old Vic, when they played Othello & all the poor men & women & children had him then for themselves. Such splendour, & such poverty [. . .] Indeed, any interference with the normal proportions of things makes me uneasy. (*D2* 134)

There is a degree of self-deprecating posturing in this diary entry, and certainly Woolf's body of work demonstrates that her democratic and humanitarian concerns are more than 'humbug'. In fact, it was under the stage of the Old Vic that the young Virginia Stephen taught history and literature to working-class women.[15] It is clear, however, that Woolf misses the irony of her somewhat condescending comments about working-class access to Shakespeare's play. For her 'the normal proportion of things' is that cultured people read Shakespeare, whereas for Shakespeare himself and his early modern audience, the norm was that the plays were performed before an audience of all classes. Unlike Woolf, the privileged, aristocratic Orlando expresses no 'democratic humbug', but instead seems to see himself as the outsider. On that open-air stage, Shakespeare was for the masses, not for the insular reader.

As we return to the context of our sentence, to the groundling audience gathered around the makeshift stage, the narrator withholds information. Rather than informing readers that the play is *Othello*, the narrator shows us only what Orlando sees – a black man waving his arms, sounds (not words) coming out of his mouth, and a woman in white passively 'laid upon a bed'. Readers are left wondering just what it is that Orlando sees. Is there a black man on stage or a white actor in blackface, as he certainly would have been in Jacobean times? Orlando has accidentally come upon a performance that is just reaching its climax, and he has no clue about what is going on. Yet he seems to suspend disbelief almost immediately, and to him there is literally a black man on the stage. In two short sentences, Woolf lets us know where we are in the play – fifty lines into Act V, scene ii, just before Othello smothers Desdemona. Our sentence interrupts the action on stage, at first simply part of the meaningless noise and chaos, by causing readers to focus on the chaos of the entire theatrical event: staging, audience, hubbub, and physical action.

By the end of the sentence, the music of the words has stirred Orlando. Before meaning seeps in, Orlando focuses on the 'daring agility of tongue', reminding him of 'sailors singing in the beer gardens at Wapping' (O 57) – a seemingly inappropriate analogy. How are actors performing the climax of *Othello* anything like sailors singing in beer gardens, and in Wapping of all places? Subtly Woolf is telling us that Orlando, like Samuel Pepys after him, frequented waterfront dives such as 'The Pelican', known then as 'The Devil's Tavern' – now the more respectable 'The Prospect of Whitby'.[16] The words 'without meaning' that have already 'stirred Orlando like music' subsequently become 'as wine to him', that is, pleasantly intoxicating. In this 'stirred' and intoxicated state Orlando hears 'a single phrase' or unit of meaning (rather than merely units of sound) coming to him over the ice. Meaning, sound and action do not come together to form a reading or understanding of the scene from Shakespeare's play; instead, the words seem 'torn from the depths' of Orlando's own heart. Snippets of the play interact with Orlando's heightened emotions and confused senses, resulting in a state far more extreme than the usual theatrical suspension of disbelief: 'The frenzy of the Moor seemed to him his own frenzy, and when the Moor suffocated the woman in her bed it was Sasha he killed with his own hands' (O 57). Earlier we saw through Orlando's eyes a black man waving his hands over an unidentified white woman in a bed. When did Orlando become familiar with the details of the play? The frenzy? The Moor? This is another leap from chaos to order, from ignorance to knowledge. After all, the only fragmented unit of meaning shared with the reader, swooping over the ice and boring into Orlando's consciousness, is:

Methinks it should be now a huge eclipse
Of sun and moon, and that the affrighted globe
Should yawn – (O 57)[17]

The end of line 102, 'Should yawn at alteration', is lost on the wind, as the earth or all of nature (and the theatre that acts as a mirror to nature) gapes in fear and horror. Even if Orlando misses the self-referential, meta-theatrical reference to the globe/Globe, Woolf, the narrator and the reader do not.

A reference in Brenda Silver's *Virginia Woolf's Reading Notebooks* demonstrates that as early as 1909, Woolf was reading and taking notes on *Othello*. Silver records only the first sentence of the entry, 'this seems to me to be simpler than the other tragedies, because Othello & Desdemona stand out above all the rest, and draw all interest to them'.[18] In this early response to *Othello*, Woolf focuses on the 'love which turns to jealousy', and interestingly, her attention is almost entirely on the very scene that she will later have Orlando witness: 'The thing that [. . .] puzzles me is the slightness of proof in comparison with the gigantic effects which it produces'.[19] While Woolf, along with Desdemona, seems puzzled by Othello's tragic overreaction to circumstantial evidence and poisoned innuendo, her Orlando actually witnesses (or thinks he does) Sasha's almost bestial coupling with 'that hairy sea brute' who was 'like a dray horse' (O 52). Although Orlando has not yet observed the scene from *Othello* when he compares the sailor to a horse, the narrator renders readers complicit in recalling Iago who poisons Brabantio's mind with 'you'll have your daughter covered with a Barbary horse'.[20] The syntactic chaos of Woolf's sentence, the pandemonic scene it creates, and 'the frenzy of the Moor' lead Orlando back to his initial 'rage' and 'anguish', so much so that 'when the Moor suffocated the woman in her bed it was Sasha he killed with his own hands' (O 57). The groundling audience who presumably witnessed the entire play along with Woolf's imagined 'common reader' understand the dramatic irony of the moment and so sympathise with the innocent Desdemona, and may even be enraged by Othello's violence. Orlando, however, has moved far beyond mere suspension of disbelief to total, if momentary, identification. Whereas other audience members are empathising with Desdemona, the genteel, very white, somewhat effeminate Orlando becomes the raging beast – in his imagination. Here then is another gap, another hiatus, and so another leap in reception. With little warning, Orlando moves from passive to active, from androgynous wimp to masculine animal. Just as there is no order to the sentence or to the audience, there is no order or rationality to Orlando's thoughts or subsequent actions. Not only do his rage and identification with Othello precipitately thaw, but his depressive 'the life of man ends in the grave' gives way one sentence later to his manic, life-affirming 'Jour de ma vie!', signalling that the time to elope with Sasha had arrived (O 57). When she misses the rendezvous and boards the Muscovite ship (and presumably the Muscovite sailor), her actions confirm Orlando's dark, Othello-like perceptions.

Orlando's and Sasha's hot love-making on the cold ice during the 1608 Frost Fair represents a moment frozen in time, but their very heat presages the imminent thaw, after which time again inexorably moves forward. After the ice melts and 'the ship of the Muscovite Embassy was standing out to sea' (O 64), the first chapter abruptly ends. When Chapter II begins, Orlando finds himself exiled from court on a 'June morning – it was Saturday the 18th' (O 66), and falls into a six-day sleep-trance. When he awakes, specificity of time vanishes along with clarity of memory. Within a few pages, Orlando is reading Thomas Browne's *Religio Medici*, which was not published until 1642. Therefore, over thirty years have passed while Orlando remains virtually the same age he was eight pages earlier. Time has thawed, become fluid, though indeterminate (readers are given neither the title of the Browne book, nor the date). Virtually every comprehensive study of *Orlando* has dealt with the passage of time in the novel. Placing *Orlando* in the context of Woolf's other novels, Harvena Richter identified 'three modes of time': 'kinetic', which is 'time's movement, the emotional speed at which it passes';[21] 'time-dimensional', which is the 'ability to bring the past into the visible and tangible present';[22] and 'mnemonic', or the act of memory as a suggestion of the passage of time.[23] The mnemonic mode is seen in the act of 'dipping his pen in the ink' that brings Orlando back in time to remember 'the mocking face of the lost Princess' (O 79). The time-dimensional or 'contracted moment' comes at the end of the novel when twentieth-century Orlando sits in Queen Elizabeth's armchair: before her 'the gallery stretched far away to a point where the light almost failed. It was as a tunnel bored deep into the past' (O 319). Employing Richter's terminology, however, it is kinetic time that dominates in *Orlando*, and that we see in the Frost Fair episode and in our sentence.

The narrator of *Orlando* identifies her place in time with exactitude: 'the first of November, 1927' (O 78). This information is given in a twenty-line sentence, in which we learn that among the creations for which Nature is responsible is the 'unwieldy length of this sentence' (O 78). In the metatextual world of Orlando, time and sentences are closely related products of nature. The Great Frost freezes time and, in Richter's words, allows Woolf to prolong 'the moment of Orlando's passion for Sasha'.[24] This prolonged moment (extending over thirty pages of text) is paradoxically itself action-filled – kinetic. All sentences are representations of time, and our sentence is a microcosm of the frozen yet kinetic time in the Great Frost section of the novel. If we look at the sentence once more, we see that the postponement of syntactical closure suspends time. The third-person past indicative of the verb 'to be' places the staging at a moment in the simple past. But that moment is highly kinetic, even frantic; as we have seen, the present participles create action: 'running', 'stamping', 'tripping', 'whistling', 'tossing'. The temporal expressions 'sometimes' and 'would' suggest unpredictable yet repeated movement. So much action, so much Rough Theatre within a few lines of suspended syntax. Yet, all action ceases with the time-signifying adverb 'still'. As readers reach syntactical closure, as we finally reach the subject and predicate of the sentence, the focus turns to Orlando and one of his/her moments of epiphany. At the end of the sentence, the Rough Theatre of rushing actors, boisterous crowd and scrambling dog becomes for Orlando, now an audience of one, what Peter Brook calls 'Holy Theatre'. This 'Theatre of the Invisible – Made – Visible: the notion that the stage is a place where the invisible can appear has a deep hold on our thoughts', and this hold is like that of 'a magical thing called music'.[25] Here, finally, is what it means to be 'stirred' by Shakespeare's – and Woolf's – 'astonishing, sinuous melody of the words'.

Notes

1. Virginia Woolf, *Orlando: A Biography* [1928] (New York: Harvest/Harcourt Brace, 1956), pp. 56–7.
2. Prof. James Woolley, email message to author, 16 September 2015.
3. Roman Ingarden, *The Cognition of the Literary Work of Art*, trans. Ruth Ann Crowley and Kenneth R. Olson (Evanston: Northwestern University Press, 1973), p. 34.
4. Ibid. pp. 38–9.
5. Ibid. p. 41.
6. Roman Ingarden, *The Literary Work of Art: An Investigation on the Borderlines of Ontology, Logic, and Theory of Literature*, trans. George G. Grabowicz (Evanston: Northwestern University Press, 1973), p. 33.
7. Ibid. p. 107.
8. 'audience, n.', *OED Online*, available at <www.oed.com/view/Entry/13022> (accessed 3 April 2017).
9. Ingarden distinguishes between two forms of 'open stage': one 'formed and designed for an audience seen merely as an aggregate of "spectators"', while the other 'is intended for people who are no longer simply spectators but are, at least to a certain extent, participants in what occurs on stage'. Although for most of the audience the stage is 'open' in the former sense, for Orlando the stage is more like 'Old Greek tragedies, which formed a kind of mystery play in which the audience took part' (*Literary Work of Art*, p. 383).
10. Virginia Woolf, *Orlando: A Biography* (London: Hogarth Press, 1928), p. 54.
11. Samuel Pepys, *The Diary of Samuel Pepys*, vol. 2, ed. Ernest Rhys (London: J. M. Dent, 1908), p. 506.

12. Sally Greene, 'Entering Woolf's Renaissance Imaginary: A Second Look at the *Second Common Reader*', in Beth Rosenberg and Jeanne Dubino (eds), *Virginia Woolf and the Essay* (New York: St Martin's Press, 1997), p. 85. For an overview of research related to Woolf's view of Renaissance theatre, see Steven Putzel, *Virginia Woolf and the Theatre* (Madison, NJ: Fairleigh Dickinson University Press, 2012), p. 119.
13. Peter Brook, *The Empty Space* (New York: Simon & Schuster, 1996), p. 40.
14. Ibid. p. 65.
15. See Putzel, *Woolf and the Theatre*, p. 22.
16. One of the many taverns Pepys frequented was The Devil's Tavern. See Pepys, *Diary*, p. 574.
17. William Shakespeare, *Othello*, ed. M. R. Riddley (New York: Routledge, 1994), Act V, scene ii, pp. 100–2.
18. Brenda Silver, *Virginia Woolf's Reading Notebooks* (Princeton: Princeton University Press, 1983), p. 150.
19. Virginia Woolf, Holograph M22, The Berg Collection, New York Public Library.
20. Shakespeare, *Othello*, Act I, scene i, pp. 110–11.
21. Harvena Richter, *Virginia Woolf: The Inward Voyage* (Princeton: Princeton University Press, 1970), p. 150.
22. Ibid. p. 158.
23. Ibid. p. 163.
24. Ibid. p. 153.
25. Brook, *The Empty Space*, p. 42.

Chapter 12

In Amorous Dedication: The Phrase, the Figure and the *Lover's Discourse*
Amy Bromley

> But now and again a single phrase would come to him over the ice which was as if torn from the depths of his heart.[1]

In this sentence, Orlando experiences a physical, heart-wrenching identification with floating fragments of discourse. Like musical phrases, travelling through the air, 'over the ice', he feels the words as echoes of sounds which originate in his own being, and which are reflected back to him via the actor/character on stage. The words of the play are recognisable to him because the scenes of love and jealousy replicate a structure of feeling and of speaking – in phrases constructing a discourse, with its own grammar and vocabulary – in which Orlando (and *Orlando*) participates: they are fragments of a lover's discourse. Roland Barthes, in his creative-theoretical text *A Lover's Discourse: Fragments* (1977), demonstrates a theoretical 'Image-repertoire', or dictionary of terms for the figures by which lovers speak or think. The performative figures of this discourse are created through 'sentence-arias' in the lover's mind, and function like allegories or extended metaphors in that they come to stand for a concept such as 'waiting'.[2] Inspired by the sentence from *Orlando*, this chapter takes Barthes's *Lover's Discourse* as a reference point in order to show how *Orlando*'s lover's discourse works via the creation of figures, and how its figurative language creates the lover as subject. This is of particular interest in *Orlando*, since the text not only creates lovers within the narrative, but is itself also a fraught gift and love letter from Virginia Woolf to Vita Sackville-West. Its creation of the lover as subject is an inscription of Woolf as the lover of Sackville-West, and of Vita as Orlando. *Orlando* is a demonstration of a lover's discourse on multiple levels at once.

For Barthes, the lover's act of 'phrasing' repeatedly and almost nonsensically creates 'figures'. It creates 'figures' rather than 'concepts' because, as Barthes emphasises, they are embodied:

The figure is to be understood, not in its rhetorical sense, but rather in its gymnastic or choreographic acceptation; in short, in the Greek meaning: σχημα is not the 'schema', but, in a much livelier way, the body's gesture caught in action and not contemplated in repose: the body of athletes, orators, statues: what in the straining body can be immobilized.[3]

These figures of immobilised action build the grammar and vocabulary of an 'Image-repertoire' which is accessible to the lover, can be drawn on, is repeated and reinforced, and which links all lovers in a common language. This 'little language such as lovers use'[4] proceeds through fragmentary and repetitious echoing phrases. Although weighted with significance for the lover, this language does not fully signify in ordinary discourse: it is a kind of poetic language, yet it expresses itself through prose – the sentence rather than the poetic line is its unit of construction. Barthes writes: 'It is said that words alone have specific uses, not sentences; but underneath each figure lies a sentence, frequently an unknown (unconscious?) one, which has its use in the signifying economy of the amorous subject'.[5] These sentences are nevertheless incomplete, 'postulated' as 'a "syntactical aria", a "mode of construction".'[6] Of all its constitutive fragmentary sentences, the figure of 'waiting' is for Barthes illustrative of the lover's discourse itself:

> For instance, if the subject awaits the loved object at a rendezvous, a sentence-aria keeps running through his head: '*All the same, it's not fair . . .*'; '*he / she could have . . .*'; '*he/ she knows perfectly well . . .*': knows what? It doesn't matter, the figure 'Waiting' is already formed.[7]

Orlando is a text in which waiting for the beloved is a repeated scene: in addition to the memorable scene of waiting for Sasha, Orlando later spends time waiting for the Archduchess Harriett, and for Shelmerdine. In its fragmentary nature and its functioning through deferral, the lover's discourse builds the figure of 'waiting' into its mode of construction: 'Whence', Barthes writes, 'the emotion of every figure: even the mildest bears within it the terror of a *suspense*'.[8] Like the phrases which reach Orlando across the ice, and the play which he is witnessing, the lover's discourse performs through a set of (incomplete) posed images. Orlando first sees Sasha, also coming to him like the phrase across the ice, as 'a *figure*, which, whether boy's or woman's, for the loose tunic and trousers of the Russian fashion served to disguise the sex, filled him with the highest curiosity' (O 18; my emphasis). Thus the lover's drama of suspense is set into motion.

Orlando is consistently a lover (although not consistently the same lover of the same object: at times s/he is in love with Sasha, Shelmerdine, poetry, nature), and the discourse of love mutates with the protagonist and the centuries. The era of the text where Orlando is falling in and out of love with Sasha proceeds by a series of contortions and contradictions which dramatise the lover's discourse. Appearing where it does in the course of Orlando's love affair with Sasha – after he has seen her on the knees of a sailor, fainted with shock and anger, decided to believe her, spun her around on the ice, and so on – the sentence from which I started incorporates, and indeed approximates as fully as one sentence can, the contradictions of the lover's discourse that Barthes taxonomises. It begins with a contradiction – 'But'; situates a complex temporality with 'now and again'; and constructs semblance through simile, turning the whole sentence upon a figure: 'as if'. This sentence performs the condensed, yet aptly loaded, representation that happens in the lover's creation of mental and linguistic figures relating to the beloved and the love-plot. Furthermore, there is no punctuation in this sentence, leaving open multiple meanings: is it the 'single phrase' or 'the ice' which is 'as if torn from the depths of his heart'? Is it Orlando's heart or that of the actor/character on stage?

If we read it that the single phrase is as if torn from Orlando's heart, these phrases (from what figures recognisably as Shakespeare's *Othello*)[9] have a materiality, a shape and physicality: in the figurative language which Woolf uses, or which the biographer uses, omnisciently, they may be entities contained within Orlando's heart, or pieces of his heart itself. Whether this is Orlando's feeling or the biographer's construction of his feeling is a question that is inextricable from the functioning of the discourse itself: the figure upon which the sentence turns, 'as if torn from the depths of his heart', is a clichéd description of identification with the lover's discourse, and, through this cliché, is a phrase which itself performs that discourse. The lover's discourse of *Orlando* is a textual phenomenon and strategy which is always dualistically and simultaneously that of the biographer and of Orlando. It is also that of *Orlando*, of Woolf and her dedication of the book to her lover, Vita Sackville-West. In Woolf's mock-biography of Sackville-West, the two women are cited (or sited) in the position of biographer and of Orlando respectively; the composition and history of *Orlando* are thereby embedded within its textual discourse, and participate in constructing the lover's discourse.

The lover's discourse is only one type of language in the text, and does not work in isolation. In Mikhail Bakhtin's structural analysis of 'Discourse in the Novel' (1935), he contends that the comic-parodic mode is particularly demonstrative of the 'inherent stratification of literary language': that is, its hierarchical layering of many types or elements of discourse.[10] In *Orlando*, Woolf utilises the comic-parodic mode in her engagement with history and historiography, as well as with the signifying processes and discourses of gender, sexology, race, law, fiction, poetry and biography, to name a few. Such layering of discourses is in some ways unavoidable, as Bakhtin shows us, but in other ways, particularly through her use of the comic mode and 'staginess', which many critics have identified in this text,[11] it is deliberately deployed in the service of certain aesthetic and political ends: it enacts a subversion of the monological tyranny of categorisation in both arenas.

So why focus on the lover's discourse specifically? In addition to the motivating love plot within the text, I want to engage with Nigel Nicolson's often quoted description of *Orlando* as 'the longest and most charming love letter in literature', sent from Woolf to his mother, Vita Sackville-West.[12] For Bakhtin, the letter is a type of discourse which enters into the novel, and the textual history of *Orlando* as a kind of love letter cannot be separated from the discursive strategies by which Woolf sought to criticise and to 'revolutionise biography in a night' (along with historiography and the novel itself) (*L3* 429). Writing about the connections between *Orlando* and Woolf's 1907 mock-biographical sketch 'Friendships Gallery' – presented in purple ink and binding to its subject, Violet Dickinson – Karin E. Westman argues that critical focus on the dedications of these books is limiting: 'Both texts become *only* "love letters", to be read more for the affection conveyed than for the form and content of the narratives told'.[13] Westman's reading aims to re-focus on Woolf's experimentations with feminist biography and historiography, following a line of criticism which has, without question, been crucial in rescuing *Orlando* from its position as a mere 'writer's holiday' among Woolf's works (*D3* 177).[14] I argue, however, that such a criticism need not exclude the dedications. On the contrary, the affectionate intimacy of *Orlando* and 'Friendships Gallery' via their invocation of the love letter is inextricable from the multiple layers of discourse through which these texts and their feminist critique work.

A Lover's Discourse is also particularly appropriate for an analysis which begins from Woolf's investment in the sentence as a unit of meaning and expression. Barthes was generally interested in the sentence as the smallest possible iteration of discourse. In 'Introduction to the Structural Analysis of Narratives' (1966), he writes:

> From the point of view of linguistics, there is nothing to be found in discourse that is not to be found in the sentence. 'The sentence', writes Martinet, 'is the smallest segment that is perfectly and wholly representative of discourse'.[15]

Similarly, the grammatical construction of the lover's discourse proceeds through the single phrase, like those which Orlando hears (or intuits: they 'come to him') in our sentence. The 'single phrase would come to him' repeatedly; it is an action in past, present and future tenses ('now and again [...] would come [...] which was'). 'Now and again' encompasses the eternity of the arrival of this 'single phrase', like the eternity of Orlando him- and her-self as an historical figure. The phrase is duplicated and differentiated by the repetition of its 'coming' to him: it is many distinct phrases, but Woolf describes it as simultaneously a singular instance and multiple different ones which all follow the same pattern. The phrases are uniquely and collectively 'as if torn from the depths of his heart' (note that 'depths' is the only plural word in the sentence; the multiplicity of the phrases is constructed through the 'now and again' of 'a single phrase'). They are a projection outwards, and they 'come' to him as Sasha does not.

When it has become clear in the scene of waiting that Sasha is not coming, we are told that 'it was useless for the rational part of him to reason; she might be late; she might be prevented; she might have missed her way. The passionate and feeling heart of Orlando knew the truth' (*O* 34). Orlando's heart – from which in our sentence the intermittent 'single phrase' had metaphorically been torn – is a site of subjectivity (it 'knew'), of sensation ('feeling') and of physical space ('the depths of his heart'). It is a stage upon which scenes of emotion and selfhood are played. They are staged discursively, through an Image-repertoire shared with Shakespeare, and with an understanding beyond 'rational reason'.

This idea of staging is also played out in the form of Barthes's text, which is simultaneously a performative and structuralist engagement with the idea of a lover's discourse. He calls it 'a "*dramatic*" method which renounces examples and rests on the single action of a primary language (no metalanguage)':

> The description of the lover's discourse has been replaced by its simulation, and to that discourse has been restored its fundamental person, the I, in order to *stage* an utterance, not an analysis. What is proposed, then, is a *portrait* – but not a psychological portrait; instead, a structural one which offers the reader *a discursive site*: the site of someone speaking within himself, amorously, confronting the other (the loved object), who does not speak.[16]

If Orlando's heart itself is such a discursive site, there are also parallels here with Woolf's textual strategy and her dedication of the book to Sackville-West: the text is a 'portrait' of both Woolf herself and of Sackville-West ('who does not speak'); it is concerned with the staging of utterances; and it is the 'grand historical picture, the outlines of all [Woolf's] friends' such as she wanted to 'sketch' in her diary (*D3* 156–7). It is helpful to consider *Orlando* as a portrait in the Barthesian sense – as a 'discursive site' rather than a 'psychological portrait'.[17] This is in part because of Woolf's utilisation of the comic modes of caricature and parody, but also because of the dedication. The dedication – 'To V. Sackville West' – is a staged utterance which, in the signifying economy of the lover's discourse, is impossible and violent (insofar as the lover always already subjects the other, the beloved, to violence by making him or her the object of their affections). Barthes defines dedication as 'an episode of language which accompanies any amorous gift, whether real or projected; and, more generally, every gesture, whether actual or interior, by which the subject dedicates something to the loved being'.[18] The dedication itself is not a 'gift' – it 'accompanies' the gift, and signifies as a 'gesture'. The text, then, has a separate existence from the amorous dedication:

> Except for the case of the Hymn, which combines the dedication and the text itself, what follows the dedication (i.e., the work itself) has little relation to this dedication [. . .] it is interpretable; it has a meaning (meanings) greatly in excess of its address; though I write your name on my work, it is for 'them' that it has been written (the others, the readers). Hence it is by a fatality of writing itself that we cannot say of a text that it is 'amorous' but only, at best, that it has been created 'amorously'.[19]

In the case of *Orlando*, however, where Sackville-West is written into the gift of the text itself, we might claim that the dedication is part of the gift rather than separate from it, and that the text itself is therefore 'amorous': it performs the lover's discourse in the same way as Barthes's text does, but through different techniques and discursive practices, one of which is the portrait. Woolf was obviously aware of the amorous nature of her composition of this text, and her treatment and invocation of the language of love in *Orlando* can be both mocking and tender.

An ambivalence towards the discourse of love is evident in the repeated emphasis on the inadequacy of language and metaphors used in Orlando's attempts to capture his love: 'He called her a melon, a pineapple, an olive tree, an emerald, and fox in the snow all in the space of three seconds' (O 18). A few pages later, metaphor becomes simile:

> He would try to tell her – plunging and splashing among a thousand images which had gone as stale as the women who inspired them – what she was like. Snow, cream, marble, cherries, alabaster, golden wire? None of these. She was like a fox, or an olive tree; like the waves of the sea when you look upon them from a height; like an emerald; like the sun on a green hill which is yet clouded – like nothing he had seen or known in England. He wanted another landscape, and another tongue. English was too frank, too candid, too honeyed a speech for Sasha. (O 25)

While the biographer begins here with a sense of the ridiculous, he or she soon becomes caught up in Orlando's exoticising awe of Sasha. The series of images which describe and inscribe their love culminates in the recognisable scene – recognisable to all lovers because part of the Image-repertoire – of suspense as Orlando waits for Sasha to join him, to run away with him:

> All his senses were bent upon gazing along the cobbled pathway – gleaming in the light of the lantern – for Sasha's coming. Sometimes, in the darkness, he seemed to see her wrapped about with rain strokes. But the phantom vanished. Suddenly, with an awful and ominous voice, a voice full of horror and alarm which raised every hair of anguish in Orlando's soul, St Paul's struck the first stroke of midnight. Four times it struck remorselessly. With the superstition of a lover, Orlando had made out that it was on the sixth stroke that she would come. But the sixth stroke echoed away, and the seventh came and the eighth, and to his apprehensive mind they seemed notes first heralding and then proclaiming death and disaster. (O 34)

Woolf builds suspense in this passage, with the words 'anguish', 'awful and ominous', 'horror and alarm' deferring the moment when we realise that they are caused by St Paul's striking midnight, and moving to an increasingly definite sense of the performative: 'first heralding and then proclaiming'. This suspense, described and rooted in figurative terms (the repetition of 'seemed' emphasising semblance), conflates the ticking clock and the rain – the 'strokes' – in a metaphor which is both sexual and violent. The double sense of 'stroke', as the striking of the clock upon the hour and as a caress, is employed throughout this passage in 'the superstition of a lover' who intuits that 'it was on the sixth stroke that she would come'.[20] Orlando has also been 'struck in the face by a blow, soft, yet heavy, on the side of his cheek. So strung with expectation was he, that he started and put his hand to his sword' (O 34). It is the rain that strikes, but within the signifying economy of the lover, who is waiting in suspense, it becomes a repeated violence and slips via the figure of the 'strike/stroke' of the clock into a sexualised image. The 'soft, yet heavy [blow] on the side of the cheek' might be a kiss, and the moment when he 'put his hand to his sword' codes an earlier moment in the text, in the description of his first fascination with Sasha:

> his manhood woke; he grasped his sword in his hand; he charged a more daring foe than Pole or Moor; he dived in deep water; he saw the flower of danger growing in a crevice; he stretched his hand – in fact he was rattling off one of his most impassioned sonnets when the Princess addressed him: 'Would you have the goodness to pass the salt?' (O 20)

The constellation created here between the violence with which Orlando makes a 'foe' of the 'Moor' and his desire for the female body is overwritten with established literary codes of lovers' discourse – the 'impassioned sonnet' – which are then undercut with humour. This constellation is related to bodily recognition and identification with/in the lover's discourse, as expressed by the sentence describing Orlando's encounter with *Othello*. The dramatic situation played out on stage forms a figure from the Image-repertoire with which Orlando can identify – viscerally, 'as if [the phrases had been] torn from the depths of his heart'. We are not told which figures the phrases make – whether those of anxiety, madness, jealousy in Barthes's text – but they are figures that are created by, at the same time as they make possible, Orlando's identification with Othello: they are performed in interaction. As readers, we might in turn identify with Orlando's identification with the discourse of love. Barthes writes: 'A figure is established if at least someone can say: "That's so true! I recognize that scene of language".'[21] In this scene in *Orlando*, there is a convergence of the 'scene of language' and the scene in the play wherein Orlando recognises himself. The creation of the figure, however, is an expending of energy that leads the lover nowhere: much as Orlando furiously and passionately tries to describe Sasha, and repeatedly whirls her across the ice in the confined space of a river, the figures of the lover's discourse according to Barthes perform action and immobilisation at the same time. Emphasising the embodied nature of the figure, Barthes writes that the lover 'struggles in a kind of lunatic sport, he spends himself, like an athlete; he "phrases", like an orator; he is caught, stuffed into a role, like a statue. The figure is the lover at work'.[22]

The creation of the lover as a subject, a discursive site in interaction with another, is in some ways violent: the 'scene' in Barthes's schema is the lover's tiff, the argument – 'making a scene'. There is an inherent violence to scene-making in the lover's discourse. In the line which follows our sentence, 'the frenzy of the Moor seemed to him his own frenzy, and when the Moor suffocated the woman in her bed it was Sasha he killed with his own hands' (O 32). This identification calls out to be read against *Orlando*'s opening scene, in which he 'was in the act of slicing at the head of a Moor which swung from the rafters' (O 3).[23] It is a gesture, an action, and a scene in which we see Orlando 'in a kind of lunatic sport' – cutting a figure, so to speak, of the colonialist aristocrat/inheritor. There is also a gendered constellation here between the 'Moor' (both Othello and the head tied to the rafters), Orlando and Sasha which manifests a chain of displaced violence through the white male, the 'Moor' and the female body. Orlando literally comes to inhabit the figure of the female body, almost as though he becomes Sasha through the lover's identification; such an occurrence is prefigured in his love for her, with the doubling of certain textual markers in the biographer's narrative, such as the parenthetical references to the sexually disguising 'fashion of the time' in the initial description of both Orlando and Sasha. The lover's identification is both a mirroring projection, and an objectification and acquisition: 'Time went by, and Orlando, wrapped in his own dreams, thought only of the pleasures of life; of his jewel; of her rarity; of the means for making her irrevocably and indissolubly his own' (O 26). There is again a colonising violence here and, in the trajectory that Orlando's life follows, a complex relationship between the figure employed ('at work') in 'slicing at the head of a Moor' and in taking on a woman's body.[24]

There is an inability of language to capture such violent desires, but also a complicity in their manifestation: that is, there is violence in metaphor and figuration, in the 'remainder' which is left out of these 'single phrases'.[25] Woolf is alert to the shared laconic space of desire and violence, and it is presented in the metaphors she uses, for example in Orlando's projected longing for 'another tongue'. In this metaphor linking the body and language, Orlando's identification with phrases, or their spontaneous 'com[ing] to him', also looks forward to Bernard's collection and eventual denouncement of phrases in *The Waves*:

> My book, stuffed with phrases, has dropped to the floor [...] What is the phrase for the moon? And *the phrase for love*? By what name are we to call death? I do not know. *I need a little language such as lovers use*, words of one syllable such as children speak when they come into the room and find their mother sewing and pick up some scrap of bright wool, a feather, or a shred of chintz. I need a howl; a cry [...] I need no words. Nothing neat. Nothing that comes down with all its feet on the floor. None of those resonances and lovely echoes that break and chime from nerve to nerve in our breasts, making wild music, *false phrases*. I have done with phrases. (*TW* 227; my emphasis)

In attempting to metaphorise language itself, Bernard here both invokes and rejects the body as a site of sound and communication. At the same time as he ultimately displays scepticism towards phrases – rejecting in particular 'those resonances and lovely echoes that break and chime from nerve to nerve in our breasts', which resemble those felt by Orlando in our sentence – Bernard invokes the lover's discourse as a subversion of such 'false phrases', equating it with child-language, with the 'howl' and the 'cry'. The 'little language such as lovers use' is opposed to 'false phrases', but at the same time, there is a resonance between those 'lovely echoes' of 'wild music' and the phrases described in my chosen sentence. In *Orlando*, Woolf's parodic attempt to figure love in fragmented phrases or 'sentence-arias' highlights the impossibility of their full articulation. And yet, although figurative language will always be bound up with cliché and metaphor, to acknowledge this inadequacy in 'phrasing', rather than using apparently complete sentences, is a rhetorical strategy to represent or perform love as itself an approximation or an attempt. Love will always escape, be deferred or suspended in a figure: for example, in *Mrs Dalloway*, Richard is unable to tell Clarissa he loves her 'in so many words', and the flowers that he gives her are supposed to stand for the feeling that cannot be conveyed.[26]

By focusing on the figurative sentence wherein Orlando's heart becomes a discursive stage, I have suggested a reading of *Orlando* as an amorous portrait in a Barthesian sense, in which the dedication of the text as a metaphorical love letter emerges not merely as a gesture, but as part of the fabric of the text itself: it is figurative and performative at the same time. I want to end by posing the question of whether Woolf's performative dedication of *Orlando* to Sackville-West is a violent action – cutting a figure. There is an underlying violence to the imagistic performance of the amorous figure, and Woolf incorporates this violence into the very figures she uses – like the fox for which Orlando names Sasha: 'a creature soft as snow, but with teeth of steel' (O 20) – and in the phrases of our sentence, which are 'torn' from Orlando's heart.

Notes

1. Virginia Woolf, *Orlando: A Biography* [1928] (London: Vintage, 2000), p. 32.
2. Roland Barthes, *A Lover's Discourse: Fragments*, trans. Richard Howard (New York: Hill and Wang, 1978).
3. Ibid. p. 3.
4. Virginia Woolf, *The Waves* [1931] (London: Penguin, 1992), p. 227.
5. Barthes, *A Lover's Discourse*, pp. 5–6 (emphasis in original).
6. Ibid.
7. Ibid. (emphasis in original).
8. Ibid. p. 6 (emphasis in original).
9. See Steven Putzel's essay in this volume, pp. 000–000.
10. Mikhail Bakhtin, 'Discourse in the Novel', in M. Bakhtin, *The Dialogic Imagination: Four Essays*, trans. Caryl Emerson and Michael Holquist (Austin: University of Texas Press, 1981), p. 301.
11. See Celia R. Caputi Daileader, 'Othello's Sister: Racial Hermaphroditism and Appropriation in Virginia Woolf's *Orlando*', *Studies in the Novel*, 45.1 (Spring 2013), p. 63.
12. Nigel Nicolson, *Portrait of a Marriage* (New York: Athenaeum, 1973), p. 202. Nicolson's comments are somewhat of a back-handed compliment in light of Woolf's own feelings about the word 'charming'. In her essays, including 'Professions for Women' (1941; *E6* 479–84) and 'George Eliot'

(1925; *E4* 170–80), she considers charm to be an infantilising and submissive quality projected onto female writers by their male peers.
13. Karin E. Westman, 'The First *Orlando*: The Laugh of the Comic Spirit in Virginia Woolf's "Friendships Gallery"', *Twentieth Century Literature*, 47.1 (Spring 2001), p. 43. See also Julia Briggs, *Reading Virginia Woolf* (Edinburgh: Edinburgh University Press, 2006), pp. 25–41, in which Briggs discusses Woolf's impulse to disguise her personal intimacy with Dickinson in 'Friendships Gallery' via a 'mock-heroic' mode that is characteristic of Woolf's ambivalence towards biographical projects more generally (p. 30).
14. See also Judy Little, 'The Politics of Holiday: Woolf's Later Novels', in J. Little, *Comedy and the Woman Writer: Woolf, Spark and Feminism* (Lincoln: University of Nebraska Press, 1983), pp. 66–88, and Angeliki Spiropoulou, *Virginia Woolf, Modernity and History: Constellations with Walter Benjamin* (London: Palgrave, 2010).
15. Roland Barthes, *Image-Music-Text*, trans. Stephen Heath (London: Fontana Press, 1977), p. 82.
16. Barthes, *A Lover's Discourse*, p. 3 (my emphasis).
17. Westman claims that Woolf's mock-biographer's technique shifts the emphasis from 'intellectual development to a broader psychological portrait of his subject, one that could capture the "flight of her mind"' ('The First *Orlando*', pp. 58–9). This reading elides Woolf's manipulation of discourse and ironic distance from the figure of the biographer.
18. Barthes, *A Lover's Discourse*, p. 75.
19. Ibid. p. 78
20. See also in this volume, Jane Goldman's reading of arrival and orgasm via the sentence 'The Queen had come' (pp. 15–31).
21. Barthes, *A Lover's Discourse*, p. 4.
22. Ibid. pp. 3–4.
23. Although she does not deal specifically with the violence of love and discourse, Daileader has begun such a reading in her essay cited above.
24. Daileader notes that *Othello*, as 'Shakespeare's tragedy of interracial love and murder [,] seems to be everywhere and nowhere in the novel', and points out that Orlando's name and Othello's are close: a 'seven letter name beginning and ending in the round vowel. If this resemblance is accidental, Woolf's shorthand for the novel in her letters "O–o" hints further at an unconscious association' ('Othello's Sister', p. 57). She suggests that in the failure of Orlando's plan to elope with Sasha (after seeing the performance of *Othello*), Woolf writes an 'anti-*Othello*. It is almost as if Woolf sat down to write the story of an Othello whose Desdemona betrays him *before* their marriage, and then eludes (ingeniously and to feminine applause) his jealous rage' (p. 57).
25. See Jean-Jacques Lecercle, *The Violence of Language* (London: Routledge, 1990).
26. *Mrs Dalloway* [1925] (London: Penguin, 2000), p. 129.

Chapter 13

A Spirit in Flux: Aestheticism, Evolution and Religion
Todd Avery

Orlando, it seemed, had a faith of her own.[1]

At a pivotal moment in Paul Roche's novel *Vessel of Dishonor* (1962), Father Martin Haversham, a scrupulous young Catholic priest, tries to 'blank religion out of his mind'.[2] Lying in bed one night in London during the Second World War, fatigued by pastoral ministry, he reaches over and haphazardly grabs the volume atop a stack of books. Woolf's *Mrs Dalloway* teaches him a life-altering lesson in spiritual economics:

> There were other realities besides the religious, and the human spirit must try to grasp them. Life was the context of religion and not the other way round. Life was the only stuff of which religion could be made; there was no such thing as religion without life.[3]

Thereafter, for Haversham, to live religiously means discovering a new vocation that involves immersion, and the celebration of spiritual fecundity, in the very physicality of life.

The melodramatic romance of a man torn between spirit and flesh, Roche's semi-autobiographical novel represents a powerful testament to the keenness of Woolf's own spiritual insight. Father Martin's formal religious training pressures him to locate spiritual truth *hors de combat*, among 'the PRIESTS', who, notwithstanding their sometimes admirable benevolence, prefer 'higher things'. Woolf helps him discover truth within the vicissitudes of everyday life. *Mrs Dalloway*, with what Father Martin sees as its sanctification of the ordinary, inspires him to redefine his understanding of life and religion and of their interdependence. By the end of the novel, Martin has left the priesthood, and feels that 'he was at last fulfilling his humanity, his natural destiny. He was alive – as he had never been in religion'.[4] Moreover, 'reaching down into the springs of his creaturehood', Martin begins to feel 'something human and divine [...] within him'.[5] In good part, Martin's path to an immanently and exclusively human spirituality follows through Woolf's serendipitous intercession. As a contributor to the 'spiritual' movement in early twentieth-century British literature, Woolf, Pericles Lewis writes, felt compelled 'to consider the spiritual possibilities of life outside a church or synagogue, even as the broader culture remained largely – and traditionally – religious, particularly in the English-speaking world'.[6] For Woolf, the sacred and spiritual remained very much alive, despite her dubiousness towards organised religion. Lewis explains: 'Woolf protests her incomprehension of religion, but [. . .] she seeks new forms of the sacred that will accommodate the pluralism of modern life'.[7] A sense of the sacred, the mystical, and the numinous permeates Woolf's fiction.

The playfully genre- and gender-bending *Orlando* traces a spiritual quest of sorts, while commenting on spirituality, and religiosity, as a psychological and historically conditioned expression of a fundamental creative impulse. The novel is chock-full of the appurtenances of Christianity. There are chapels; church bells and clocks; a monk; a prayer book once owned by Mary Queen of Scots; and, in a moment that recalls Lily Briscoe's imagining of the mind as 'a high cathedral-like place', there is a 'cathedral tower which was [Orlando's] mind' (*O* 208).[8] Orlando possesses 'a very complicated spiritual state' (*O* 208), which apparently shapes itself into 'a faith of her own' (*O* 128). What is the specific content of this faith? What role does it play in *Orlando*'s pursuit of that most elusive fact and concept, 'life'? The obvious answer to the question, 'What does Orlando believe in?' is, in a word, Literature: 'The poet's', Orlando thinks, 'is the highest office of all' (*O* 128). Is there, however, a spiritual foundation to that aesthetic conviction?

As in so many of Woolf's fictional works, the spirituality of *Orlando* emerges from a deep wonder before the mystery, strangeness and absurdity of life. In her fiction, Woolf continually renews her 'spiritualist' credentials by 'look[ing] deep into the darkness where things shape themselves' (*O* 239) – that is, into the depths of the mind – and finding there an obscurity rich with possibility and deserving of celebration, even a kind of worship. In the mind's depths, Woolf discovers religion as a 'reflection' of an 'intellect' which is 'divine and all worshipful' (*O* 156). Woolfian worship is not conventional. Just as Orlando has 'no traffic with the usual God' (*O* 158), so too Woolf has no truck with traditional religious institutions or rituals. Religiosity, for Woolf, resembles her Bloomsbury friend Lytton Strachey's definition of religion as an acute feeling of the true worth of things of great value.[9] It is also conditioned by a particular 'attitude towards oneself and the ultimate', as John Maynard Keynes defined the religious mentality.[10] Woolfian worship is a type of reverence, a venerative disposition towards the world and towards the mind's engagement with it.

Woolf uses the words 'reverence' and 'reverent' in *Orlando* nine times, mostly to describe her hero/heroine's worshipful attitude towards literary and artistic creation. It is significant that Woolf introduced the term 'spiritual' as a defining characteristic of modernist writing at the very time when she was beginning to forge the aesthetic methods that would soon issue in the series of novels, from *Jacob's Room* to *The Waves*, that express reverence towards existential facts larger than the individual self – life's fleeting impermanence and the radical interconnection of human minds. The spiritual inspiration that *Mrs Dalloway* offers Roche's protagonist emerges from Woolf's seismographic sensitivity to spiritual aspects of everyday life. *Orlando* develops a stranger spirituality, one precariously grounded in Herakleitean flux, and embracing core elements of aestheticism and of the evolutionary theory that inspired it.

Aestheticism

As Perry Meisel long ago demonstrated, Woolf's 'spiritual' challenge to Edwardian fictional 'materialism' was inspired by Walter Pater's 'Conclusion' to *The Renaissance* (1873).[11] In Woolf's hands, art for art's sake becomes the springboard into a new spirituality. This aspect of her argument is clearest in her reflections, in 'Modern Fiction' (1925), on the 'spiritual' Joyce, who, 'to reveal the flickerings of that innermost flame which flashes its messages through the brain', invents new methods 'to support the imagination of a reader when called upon to imagine what he can neither touch nor see' (*E4* 161). To define spiritual modernism, Woolf invokes the spectre of an invisible and untouchable world, slipping into a register that verges on the religious: does not the imagining of, and faith in, a truth unavailable to the senses reside in the heart of religious experience?

Near the end of 'Modern Fiction', Woolf admires recent Russian writers in whom 'we seem to discern the features of a saint' (*E4* 163). She defends the special qualities of the English novel, but regrets its spiritual insufficiency beside the Russian: 'It is the saint in them which confounds us with a feeling of our own irreligious triviality, and turns so many of our famous novels to tinsel and trickery' (ibid.). Woolf spent little time fretting about her irreligiosity; for her the most important thing that can be neither touched nor seen resides in 'the dark places of psychology' (*E4* 162). It is there that the spiritual disposition of the modern novelist will find the proper material for a new, and exclusively human, reverence. One sentence in particular in the 'Mr Joyce is spiritual' passage from 'Modern Fiction' opens a door onto an unexpected landscape of interpretive possibility: 'Let us not take it for granted that life exists more fully in what is commonly thought big than in what is commonly thought small' (*E4* 161). The ordinary and the everyday, and the most intimate and private psychological experiences, represent not only valid occasions for aesthetic representation, but also as interesting opportunities for spiritual reflection, as do grand events in the world outside our minds, let alone any supernatural world. Woolf's adjuration recalls the first and third Beatitudes;[12] the Coleridgean conviction that the best prayers show love for 'all things great and small';[13] and Cecil Frances Alexander's well-known 1848 Anglican hymn 'All Things Bright and Beautiful', with its celebration of 'all creatures great and small'.[14] Woolf showed with particular intensity during the years surrounding *Orlando* that there is more material for spiritual insight and reverence in the elusive, everyday workings of the small individual mind – thinking, speculating, loving, trying to connect with the minds of others, shattering into madness, imagining, creating art – than in large religious institutions with their big dogmatic certainties and metaphysical complacencies. As Michael Lackey writes, in the face of institutional inertia as well as the general untenableness of faith in a supreme being, Woolf thought 'atheism necessary for the development of healthy human relationships' because it 'eliminate[s] [. . .] the dehumanizing and oppressive patterns of thinking built into the epistemological act of believing in God'.[15] For Woolf, the spirit lives in no church: the mind supplants the church and becomes a cathedral of its own, and it is in the workings of the individual mind and its engagements with the world outside it that, as the proper object for reverence, the spirit resides.

The Woolfian spirit, however, is housed in a Woolfian mind; however cathedral-like it may be, this is a mind in elemental motion. This modern mind is forever elusive, fleeting and evanescent. Orlando's religion itself, her very faith, also eludes precise definition. *Orlando*'s biographer-narrator tells us that 'Orlando, it seemed, had a faith of her own' (*O* 128). But where does the emphasis fall in this seemingly casual observation? It is not at all clear that Orlando actually possesses a faith of her own, however conventional or unconventional. Orlando does not unequivocally *have* a faith of her own; she only *seems* to have one. Moreover, what is the attitude of the narrator towards this putative possession of an idiosyncratic faith? That little qualification, 'it seemed', inhabits a sentence of indeterminate tone: is the narrator surprised? Supercilious? Admiring? Is she throwing us a knowing wink? Is the narrator teasing us, leading us on a wild goose chase by hinting at a religiosity that may or may not be there? This indeterminacy embodies the tenuousness of biographical understanding as much as Orlando's physical transformation from one sex into another embodies the impermanence of biological identity. This narrative attitude owes much to aestheticism, but also expands beyond it and draws on conceptual resources made available by modern science.

Evolution

What happens to spirituality, never mind any kind of formal religiosity, when the individual mind, spirit, or self – when any seemingly stable aspect of identity, and when identity as such, like genetic sex – loses coherence and fixity, grows disconnected and even incoherent? What is there for the spiritual modern to revere if the dark places of psychology harbour the profoundest confusion of identity, a radical unmooring of self, like the abdication of Orlando's 'Captain self' (O 227)? What to revere if it is true of every moment, as aestheticist ontology and epistemology insist, that 'it is an open question in what sense Orlando can be said to have existed at the present moment' (O 225)? Orlando's is a modern mind, a mind in flux contained by a body in flux, in a world of continuous change where, as Pater writes, 'to regard all things and principles of things as inconstant modes or fashions has more and more become the tendency of modern thought'.[16] By explicitly locating modernist spirituality in relation to Paterian aestheticism, Woolf implicitly stages it as a response to the most powerful stimulant to Pater's own thinking on art and identity. Her argument derives directly from Pater but indirectly from Charles Darwin, whose theory demands a thorough rethinking of human nature, and attendant of the intellectual legitimacy of religion. At the philosophical core of Darwin's theory is the introduction of time into essence, change into biological being. In demonstrating the changeability of species, he puts physical life, as Pater puts it, into 'perpetual motion'.[17]

The spirit of *Orlando* is the spirit of evolution. It is the story of a life that spans an unusual length and that, far from being fixed in even its reproductive organs, undergoes mutation at the most basic biological level in an instant of special change which, precisely because it is a change from one definite biological thing into another, mocks (performs and undercuts) the idea of special creation. It is a story about inheritance, both biological and economic; about descent and modification; about mutability. It is also the story of an identity in flux, a self in motion both in the external, physical world and 'in the cathedral tower which was her mind' (O 122). The instability of Orlando's physical self finds a psychological analogue in the internal incoherence of her mind, which is 'a phantasmagoria [...] and meeting-place of dissemblables' (O 130).

For *Orlando*'s biographer-narrator, institutionalised religion often serves as a compensation for moments of 'disillusionment'; in such moments, 'women turn nuns and men priests' (O 149). This voice also, however, figures disillusionment and the obscure, kaleidoscopic, unstable mind itself as the source of a richer spiritual inspiration. Religion, for Orlando, reflects the obscurest, most primitive depths of the mind, of the darkness where things shape themselves. It is simultaneously a physical and a spiritual phenomenon. In the 'intimate, imaginative sphere', Lewis writes, Woolf discovers 'a remnant of religious life and locus of mystical experience'.[18] Neither the seeming of Orlando's identity nor the dubious existential status of his/her faith undermines religion, or spirituality, as such. For Woolf also embraces a radical, and specifically Darwinian, understanding of the spiritually creative powers of the mind. The intellect, for Orlando, however unstable, is 'all worshipful' – and it is the *fons et origo* of religion. Its worshipfulness consists in its creative power. In this, there is a strong echo of Darwin's ideologically disruptive notion that the human mind, a highly 'elevated' product of 'long-continued' physiological and cultural development, creates God, and not the other way around.[19] Until, and even to a certain extent after, the entrance of her future husband, Marmaduke Bonthrop Shelmerdine, Orlando's 'faith of her own' consists in a reverence towards literature and the activity of literary creation. It is no accident that Orlando's writing career begins and ends with mythical subjects, nor that his or her *chef d'oeuvre* branches like the Darwinian tree of life. Located against a background of long-continued biological and cultural development, and despite the tenuousness of all physical, mental and conventional religious certainties, Orlando's aestheticist spirituality constitutes a relatively still point in his, then her, turning world.

Theological modernism

Is Orlando's aestheticist and evolutionary spirituality also a still point in *Orlando*'s turning world? How far might Orlando's worship of literature indicate the workings of a spiritual sensibility in the telling of his or her life? Like *Orlando* as a whole, the passage in which Woolf raises the possibility of Orlando's having 'a faith of her own' contains not a little humour. When Orlando takes contemplative refuge in the chapel of her home after returning to England in the eighteenth century, she opens a family prayer book which 'had been held by Mary Queen of Scots on the scaffold' (O 127). This volume inspires 'pious thoughts' in Orlando; it also contains 'a crumb of pastry' between the pages – an intrusion of the everyday into the precincts of the holy, now augmented by Orlando's own contribution of 'a flake of tobacco' from the cheroot that she calmly smokes (ibid.). In addition to this blending of the sacred and the profane, the venerative and the vulgar, the reverence of Orlando's contemplation is undercut by the narrator in a comical reduction of spiritual matters to mundane questions of grammar, and the apparent elevation of the latter to spiritual significance. Orlando characterises the multiple 's'es in her poem 'The Oak Tree' as 'sinful reptiles', and she identifies the even more heinous present participle as 'the Devil himself' (O 128). Here as throughout *Orlando*, with its rapid shifts in tone, Woolf blends the satirical with the earnest: the spiritual atmosphere of the text is composed of tonalities as subtly compounded as those that constitute Orlando's own 'spiritual state'. Ultimately, the passage that describes Orlando's faith represents if not an earnest then at least a serious acknowledgement of the 'high office' of the craft of writing – 'office' vibrating, of course, with vocational significance.

The spiritual, non-doctrinal idea of development and change that Woolf embraces, even while gently mocking the seriousness with which Orlando takes the craft of writing as a marker of her spiritual depth, is not necessarily irreligious in a theological context. 'Religion' is hardly a signifier with a fixed meaning. Does Woolf, despite her hostility to organised religion, articulate a spiritual vision that accords with contemporaneous theological efforts to synthesise metaphysical belief and scientific understanding – efforts that invited the most extreme derision of patriarchal ecclesiastical Authority? In her attack on her Edwardian 'materialist' forebears, Woolf repeats the criticisms levelled at Victorian utilitarianism by so many aesthetes and decadents, many of whom turned to religion as a source of more enduring and humanising spiritual values. Does Woolf, in *Orlando*, work towards a synthesis of rationality and imagination that embodies a spirituality grounded in the flux of 'sacred communion'?[20] How does Woolfian spirituality, as articulated through the Darwin-inflected, Pater-inspired impressionism of the genre-bending *Orlando*, converse with the major doctrinal movement of the Christian early twentieth century? How does Woolf talk with the original Modernists?

Woolf had no particular interest in Roman Catholicism, and it would be absurd to claim that she was in any way influenced by, or even that she cared in the slightest about nuances of doctrinal developments in the Catholic Church. However, just as the British aesthetes and decadents of the late nineteenth century found more sustenance in what they saw as the aesthetically rich Christianity of Catholicism than in their Protestant heritage, so too does Woolf's own aestheticism harmonise with certain major trends in late nineteenth- and early twentieth-century Catholic thinking. Specifically, the evolutionary spirituality of Catholic Modernism embraces the theologically radical notion that, as Orlando thinks, 'thoughts are divine' (O 128). As Pope Pius X put it early in the century in a feverish denunciation of the idea, for the Modernists, Biblical exegesis required no faith in 'the supernatural origin of Sacred Scripture'; they interpreted scripture 'the same as any other merely human document'.[21] Relatedly, Pius condemned the Modernist presumption of immanent and evolving truth: the assumption that 'Truth is no more immutable than man himself, since it evolved in him, with him, and through him'.[22] These statements are taken from the syllabus *Lamentabili Sane Exitu* ('With Truly Lamentable Results'), the first of two documents issued with the Papal imprimatur in 1907 condemning the increasingly popular doctrines of Modernism. The *Lamentabili* condemns sixty-five Modernist propositions, all of which assume doctrinal development and change. This theme courses throughout the propositions; its connections to broader currents in modern thought are especially clear in some of the later propositions:

> 53. The organic constitution of the Church is not immutable. Like human society, Christian society is subject to a perpetual evolution.
> 64. Scientific progress demands that concepts of Christian doctrine concerning God, creation, revelation, the Person of the Incarnate Word, and Redemption be re-adjusted.
> 65. Modern Catholicism can be reconciled with true science only if it is transformed into a non-dogmatic Christianity; that is to say, into a broad and liberal Protestantism.

For Pius, the idea of doctrinal change threatened the fabric of Catholic belief in the same way that evolutionary theory in biology had challenged the metaphysical theory of special creation. Both evolution and theological Modernism introduce time into essence, change into dogma, with far-reaching ideological consequences.

Pius was constitutionally and dogmatically opposed to doctrinal evolution, transformation or readjustment. The *Lamentabili* lists some instances of Modernist 'error', but his second encyclical of 1907 challenges them in a sustained argument. *Pascendi Dominici Gregis* ('Feeding the Lord's Flock') condemns the 'evolutionary' tendencies in Modernism; it systematically attacks Modernism in philosophy, theology, history, criticism and apologetics; it criticises the core Modernist assumption of the 'unstable' character of 'dogmatic formulas'; and it denounces as heretical the idea of 'theological immanence' – the conclusion that follows from this line of reasoning: 'The [Modernist] philosopher has declared: The principle of faith is immanent; the believer has added: This principle is God; and the theologian draws the conclusion: God is immanent in man'.[23] In such core Modernist convictions, Pius sees a grave threat to truth, orthodoxy and hierarchical authority. At root, his diatribe in all its multifaceted complexity resolves into a condemnation of 'the general principle that in a living religion' – as in a living individual or species – 'everything is subject to change, and must in fact be changed. In this way [Modernists] pass to what is practically their principal doctrine, namely, evolution. To the laws of evolution everything is subject – dogma, Church, worship, the Books we revere as sacred, even faith itself'.[24]

The forms that Modernism takes include 'arts entirely new'[25] and an unquenchable 'passion for novelty' that finds voice 'in every page';[26] a 'doctrine of experience [as source of truth] united with that of symbolism';[27] artistic and intellectual expressions 'applied with destructive effect to tradition';[28] a fetishisation of 'internal impulses or necessities';[29] and the axiomatic conviction that 'there is [. . .] nothing stable, nothing immutable'.[30] In summing up, the *Pascendi* calls Modernism 'the synthesis of all heresies':[31] 'with feverish activity', it claims, the Modernists 'leave nothing untried in act, speech, and writing'.[32] In its febrile pursuit of novelty in a world in flux, Modernism threatens the historically recent notion of Papal infallibility as thoroughly as Luther's theses had challenged Papal authority 400 years before; it challenges the 'check [on] unbridled spirits' imposed by the sixteenth-century Council of Trent, the doctrinal epicentre of the Counter-Reformation.[33] It would be difficult to devise a more textbook definition of cultural modernism than the definition of theological Modernism contained in the Pionine *Pascendi*.

Such a complex, multiform movement as modernism in either theology or the arts cannot be reduced to a single controlling idea. In the theological arena, though, Pope Pius X makes a strong case that evolution is just such a thing. Evolutionary ideas continued to percolate through the modernist era, and the *Pascendi* is a sign of the times that also produced *Orlando*. *Orlando* borrows from aestheticist principles and from a Darwinian mentality, telling the life of an artist-in-progress, a long story of gradual change including a sudden moment of physical transformation in which Orlando's change of sex suggests the mutability of species. 'Yet still', Orlando thinks after returning to England in the eighteenth century, 'for all her travels and adventures and profound thinkings and turnings this way and that, she was only in process of fabrication. What the future might bring, Heaven only knew. Change was incessant, and change perhaps would never cease' (O 130). Orlando's life represents an ever-evolving work-in-progress over a span whose protracted length, ironically mimicking the long lives of the first men and women of Genesis, speaks to the modern geological and biological recognition of life's long and slow development.

A goose and a dove

Orlando's life is also a spiritual life. Orlando is a writer with a mind like a cathedral tower who, despite a creative mediocrity, perseveres in his or her dedication to the craft of the poet. This is 'the highest office of all', which, true to the ecclesiastical connotation of that resonant word, Orlando approaches 'with all the religious ardour in the world', erasing the line between art, ethics and religion (O 128). Orlando's devotion to writing is a spiritual devotion: in addition to being a writer, Orlando also has a great capacity for spiritual self-analysis and, in 'reflect[ing] on her sins and the imperfections that had crept into her spiritual state', she goes so far as to develop 'the intolerance of belief' (ibid.). Despite such sporadic intolerance in the protagonist, *Orlando* ultimately celebrates creative inspiration as akin to spiritual insight.

Orlando's biography accelerates towards an epiphany that locates aesthetic delight within a spiritual framework and as a type of sacred experience. The chiming of a church clock in the novel's final pages leads Orlando 'to look deep into the darkness where things shape themselves' (O 239). There, Orlando's mind moves from matter to spirit, from memory of real things (of seeing Shakespeare, of Sasha, of a boat on the Serpentine) to faith in things unseen (her husband's 'brig was through the arch and out on the other side; it was safe at last!' (O 240)). These unseen things inspire a redemptive 'Ecstasy!' in a simultaneously deeply embodied and ecstatically disembodied moment of vision (O 240). Orlando's ecstatic fantasy, before the stroke of midnight recalls her to the dark and windy present, reveals to her under a rising moon 'the great house with all its windows robed in silver. Of wall or substance there was none. All was phantom' (ibid.). This fantasy abruptly ends with a royal hallucination in which Orlando welcomes to her home Elizabeth I, 'a Queen once more stepp[ing] from her chariot'. This is a posthumous and other-worldly event, taking place in a mystical afterlife, for it is not a living host but 'the dead Lord, my father, [who] shall lead you in' (O 240).

Here religiosity finds a phantasmagoric paradoxicality. In this mystical moment of imagination, prompted by the chiming of a church clock, a dead queen is welcomed into the house of Orlando's fathers by a suggestive apposition: 'The dead Lord, my father'. This is not to say that Orlando – or Woolf – actually thinks of the father as a divinity. But the phrasing, in the context of successive apparitions, points to Woolf's intention to set religious discourse productively at play with that of artistic vision. *Orlando*'s opening paragraph assumes the certainty of Orlando's Christianity, when this child of a father who once killed a 'vast Pagan' himself slashes with his blade at the head of a Moor in his attic (O 11). As Lackey explains, Woolf implies Orlando's Christian identity, by deflecting attention from it, in contrast to the way she vertiginously expresses dubiousness about Orlando's sex when stating that it cannot be doubted.[34] This first paragraph ends with a casual assumption of the death of God – Orlando's house is the 'house of the Lord', but this is a dead Lord. Regardless of the religious ambiguity, *Orlando* concludes with a joyous epiphany. In the novel's exuberant penultimate paragraph, the spiritual ecstasy of intimate personal relations replaces divinely mandated aristocratic duty in Orlando's mind. Orlando achieves her keenest spiritual insight here, when she sees the wild goose of inspiration taking flight over the head of her husband who descends, apparitionally, from his aeroplane which 'hovered above her' (O 240). This is a moment rich with spirituality, as the hovering of the aeroplane and the appearance of the goose both echo John the Baptist's vision of the descent of the Holy Spirit from heaven in the shape of a dove onto the head of Jesus.[35]

Woolf's great protagonists from the mid to late 1920s achieve a sort of secular saintliness by pursuing a purity of purpose that grants them eternal moments of vision or being, epiphanies. Clarissa Dalloway has her party; Lily Briscoe her vision; Orlando sees her goose. In all of these cases, Woolf's heroines commit themselves to the messy spirituality of art and human relationships in the world, while rejecting the comparative and, for Woolf, the untenable simplicity of religious orthodoxy and metaphysical certainty. Ultimately, it is in the everyday and ordinary experience of her marriage, just as in the hostess's quotidian experience of throwing a party or the painter's habitual effort to see, that Orlando achieves a mystical insight. For her, as Roche noticed of Orlando's creator, 'the very stuff of life', however ordinary, is 'the only stuff of which religion could be made'.[36] This is a conviction that drives Woolf's fiction, and which the religiously attuned Roche saw so clearly in his story of a priest torn between higher and lower vocations, who discovers an alternative and life-saving spirituality in Woolf's fiction. It seems fitting that *Orlando* was published the same week that an obscure Spanish priest named Josemaría Escrivá, the controversial founder of Opus Dei, had his own vision of the sanctification of the ordinary, of the idea that holiness, the work of God, lay within the practice of daily life.

Notes

1. Virginia Woolf, *Orlando: A Biography* [1928] (New York: Harcourt, 2006), p. 128.
2. Paul Roche, *Vessel of Dishonor* (New York: Signet, 1963), p. 143.
3. Ibid. p. 143.
4. Ibid. p. 218.
5. Ibid. p. 221.
6. Pericles Lewis, *Religious Experience and the Modernist Novel* (Cambridge: Cambridge University Press, 2010), p. 3.
7. Ibid. p. 143.
8. Virginia Woolf, *To the Lighthouse* [1927] (New York: Harcourt, 1955), p. 194.
9. Lytton Strachey, 'Should We Have Elected Conybeare?' in Todd Avery (ed.), *Unpublished Works of Lytton Strachey: Early Papers* (London: Pickering & Chatto, 2011), p. 72.
10. John Maynard Keynes, 'My Early Beliefs', in S. P. Rosenbaum (ed.), *The Bloomsbury Group: A Collection of Memoirs and Commentary* (Toronto: University of Toronto Press, 1995), p. 86. The Bloomsbury Group's attitudes towards and engagements with religion represent, with few exceptions, a critical *terra incognita*.
11. Perry Meisel, *The Absent Father: Virginia Woolf and Walter Pater* (New Haven: Yale University Press, 1980).
12. *Matthew* 5:3, 5.
13. Samuel Taylor Coleridge, 'The Rime of the Ancyent Marinere', in William Wordsworth and Samuel Taylor Coleridge, *Lyrical Ballads and Related Writings*, ed. William Rickey and Daniel Robinson (Boston. MA: Houghton Mifflin, 2002), p. 42.
14. Cecil Frances Alexander, *Hymns for Little Children* (London: J. Masters, 1871), p. 27.
15. Michael Lackey, 'The Gender of Atheism in Virginia Woolf's "A Simple Story"', *Studies in Short Fiction*, 35 (1998), pp. 50, 59.
16. Walter Pater, *Studies in the History of the Renaissance* (Oxford: Oxford University Press, 2010), p. 48.
17. Ibid. p. 118.
18. Lewis, *Religious Experience*, p. 146.
19. Charles Darwin, 'The Descent of Man', in *Darwin*, ed. Philip Appleman (New York: Norton, 2001), p. 249.
20. Lewis, *Religious Experience*, p. 153.
21. Pope Pius X, Lamentabili Sane Exitu: *Syllabus Condemning the Errors of the Modernists* (3 July 1907): §12, available at <www.papalencyclicals.net/Pius10/p10lamen.htm> (accessed 18 September 2015).

22. Ibid. §58.
23. Pope Pius X, *Pascendi Dominici Gregis: On the Doctrine of the Modernists* (8 September 1907), available at <www.papalencyclicals.net/Pius10/p10pasce.htm> (accessed 18 September 2015).
24. Ibid. §26.
25. Ibid. §1.
26. Ibid. §42.
27. Ibid. §15.
28. Ibid.
29. Ibid. §21.
30. Ibid. §28.
31. Ibid. §39.
32. Ibid. §43.
33. Council of Trent, 'Decree Concerning the Edition and Use of the Sacred Books' (18 April 1546), §2, available at <www.ewtn.com/library/COUNCILS/TRENT4.htm#1> (accessed 18 September 2015).
34. Michael Lackey, 'Woolf and the Necessity of Atheism', *Virginia Woolf Miscellany*, 53 (Spring 1999), p. 3.
35. *John* 1:32. This echo is probably mere coincidence; Woolf's wide reading did not include the Bible until the mid-1930s. See Diane F. Gillespie, '"Woolfs" in Sheep's Clothing: The Hogarth Press and "Religion"', in Helen Southworth (ed.), *Leonard and Virginia Woolf, the Hogarth Press, and the Networks of Modernism* (Edinburgh: Edinburgh University Press, 2010), p. 77.
36. Roche, *Vessel*, p. 143.

Chapter 14

Sir Thomas Browne and the Reading of Remains in *Orlando*

Benjamin D. Hagen

For though these are not matters on which a biographer can profitably enlarge it is plain enough to those who have done a reader's part in making up from bare hints dropped here and there the whole boundary and circumference of a living person; can hear in what we only whisper a living voice; can see, often when we say nothing about it, exactly what he looked like, and know without a word to guide them precisely what he thought and felt and it is for readers such as these alone that we write – it is plain then to such a reader that Orlando was strangely compounded of many humours – of melancholy, of indolence, of passion, of love of solitude, to say nothing of all those contortions and subtleties of temper which were indicated on the first page, when he slashed at a dead nigger's head; cut it down; hung it chivalrously out of his reach again and then betook himself to the window-seat with a book.[1]

Virginia Woolf's sentences prompt us – indeed, they train us with continued engagement – to become more agile, creative and discerning readers. Many of *Orlando*'s sentences press this training even further, enjoining us to problematise reading itself as a notion or concept and to reflect on our own reading habits and practices. In this chapter, I examine one of these sentences and explore how its encouragement and theorisation of a reflexive, curious and ethical mode of reading opens us to a host of disturbing and disturbingly related contexts: namely, the mostly unexamined influence of Sir Thomas Browne on Woolf's thought,[2] the philosophical implications of her fascination with ruins and remains, as well as the legacy and contemporaneity of colonialist and imperialist violence. Problems of reading – what it is or might be, how one might go about it, what sort of obstacles might interrupt it – link together these and other contexts in *Orlando*, which suggests that some acts of reading (perhaps our own, perhaps even Woolf's) are complicit with human cruelty, violence and indifference. But since one might play 'a reader's part' (*O* 73) in any number of ways, Woolf's ideal mode of reading – an autocritical and reparative work of engaging with the living and the dead – strives to interrogate one's own potential complicities, to undo the violent translation or figuration of humans (into savages, for instance), and to learn to encounter and to be encountered by others.

In the novel's second chapter, we learn that Orlando is 'afflicted with a love of literature', 'infected', that is, 'by a germ [...] which was of so deadly a nature that it would shake the hand as it was raised to strike, cloud the eye as it sought its prey, and make the tongue stammer as it declared its love' (O 73–4). Woolf's ironic description of this fatal reading disease follows one of her most interesting and disquieting sentences, cited in epigraph to this chapter. Several problems take shape in this sentence: (1) the syntactic and thematic dissonance between plainness and contortedness, clarity and obscurity; (2) the collaborative and competitive roles of biographer and reader; (3) the impossible translation of partialities into wholeness; (4) the sketch of Orlando as an inharmonious admixture of affects, attitudes and energies; and (5) the juxtaposition of Orlando's solitary communion with a book beside 'the head of a Moor', hung from the rafters of his family's great house: a toy in the solitary games of a young man and a trophy of imperial conquest (O 13). But it is reading which connects and situates these problems with each other. The biographer's later diagnosis of Orlando's love of literature (which manifests as a debilitative, compulsive, anti-social mode of reading) reacts against the young man's decision to seclude himself with the writings of Sir Thomas Browne. This seclusion also inspires the biographer's statement about the readers for whom she writes, readers who are not boringly passive but actively, almost suprasensibly constructive. While the biographer seemingly cannot 'profit' from enlarging this scene of reading into a scene of living, she acknowledges that she still needs readers of another sort to fill in the gaps she leaves throughout her work, transmuting 'bare hints' into a 'living person', whispers into a 'living voice', 'nothing' into a faithful vision, and silence into precise intuitions of private thoughts and feelings (O 73). Such work is neither metonymic (treating parts as if they stood in for wholes) nor metaphoric (translating parts into other objects, codes or paradigms). Rather, the work is paradoxically speculative and materialist, conjuring an imagined sense of wholeness from remains it neither displaces nor substitutes. They must *remain* remains.

The fundamental irony of this opposition between 'readers such as these' and lovers of literature is that the biographer expresses this opposition in a twisted syntax and deliberately clumsy prose, which might cause many readers to pass over this sentence several times in order to straighten out its parallelism, to make sense of its punctuation, and to bypass its clumsiest bit ('and it is for readers such as these alone that we write') in order to link up its opening statement – 'it is plain enough to those who have done a reader's part' – with her main point – 'it is plain [...] that Orlando was strangely compounded of many humours' (*O* 73). Woolf's sentence, then, is a reading challenge in form and content, which ironically withdraws from, even as it directly concerns, a young man who is reading in the dark, and which thus refuses to enlarge on a scene of reading even as it proceeds to muse on reading.

If reading is a common component of the problems outlined above, so is the fact that Orlando is reading 'one of the [...] longest and most marvellously contorted cogitations' of Sir Thomas Browne, learned doctor and Renaissance prose stylist (*O* 73). Though the 'for' which opens the sentence signals a withdrawal from the 'matters' at hand – namely, the activity of Orlando at his reading table – the good doctor nevertheless seems to haunt its contorted style. As if infected by the germ of Orlando's illness (the 'love of literature'), as if Browne's sentences themselves were contagious, the warped syntax imitates the daunting pages of *Religio Medici* (1643) as well as those of *Urn Burial* (1658). 'Accustomed as we are', Woolf writes in her 1919 essay 'Reading',

> to strip a whole page of its sentences and crush their meaning out in one grasp, the obstinate resistance which a page of *Urn Burial* offers at first trips us and blinds us [...] We must stop, go back, try out this way and that, and proceed at a foot's pace. (*E3* 158).[3]

Indeed, Woolf regularly associates Browne with the challenges and pleasures of reading. He is, after all, the second 'illustrious' and inspirational friend listed in *Orlando*'s Preface, and in her essay 'Hours in a Library' (1916), Browne's name appears beside those of Milton and Shakespeare, a trio that still 'gives [one] [an] absolute certainty of delight' (*E2* 60). '*Urn Burial*', she writes in 'Sir Thomas Browne' (1923),

> is a temple which we can only enter by leaving our muddy boots on the threshold [...] It is a difficult book to read, it is a book not always to be read with pleasure, and those who get most from it are the well-born souls. (*E3* 369–70)

'To read Sir Thomas Browne', she concludes, 'is always to be filled with astonishment' (*E3* 371). Elsewhere she champions his 'sublime genius',[4] his 'splendour',[5] and the occasionally poetical achievement of his prose. 'Poetical' here does not necessarily imply lyricism or figuration but, rather, a mode of marshalling and delivering facts in such a way that 'shift[s] the value of familiar things' without sacrificing a passion for the knowledge of the very materiality of these things.[6] Browne's prose thus explores echoes and fragments as they are – as pieces of lost wholes – and works on the imagination of his reader without translating or figuring these pieces as something other than they are. It is yet another irony of this sentence, then, that the fictional biographer who turns away from a fictional reader of Browne nevertheless exhibits the capabilities and sensitivities of the actual novelist who has read and studied Browne's 'crabbed sentences' with pleasure (E3 158).

Woolf's Brownian sentence encourages, at the level of style and syntax, the very mode of reading which Orlando himself exhibits – a reading which slows action, introduces doubt into forward progress, halts or opposes violence, learns to love and inhabit 'the region of beauty' (E3 159) with pleasure and delight – that is, the very sort of reading against which the biographer opposes her active, collaborative and ideal reader: the one who plays her part well, and who learns to explore remains which refuse to revive (O 65). In other words, this sentence seems to call simultaneously for two very different readers: a reader who tarries with idiosyncratic difficulty (and does so with pleasure and love) and a reader who learns to honour absent wholes through imaginative speculation.

In the context of Woolf's contemporaneous essay 'The New Biography' (1927), this opposition of reading modes in *Orlando* resonates with the primary but impossible aim of life-writing: namely, the task of 'weld[ing]' truth and personality, 'granite-like solidity' (the material remains of a life) and 'rainbow-like intangibility' (the elusive *thisness* of the biographical subject) 'into one seamless whole' (E4 473). While Woolf casts the biographer's desire for readerly aid in an ironic tone that teases naïveté and ineptitude, the desire still seems sincere and makes good sense, since even twentieth-century biographers fail to achieve 'that perpetual marriage of granite and rainbow' which one might simply call *life* (E4 478). While, in Woolf's view, Harold Nicolson may achieve the revelation of a 'figure' approaching 'a real human being' through a 'mixture of biography and autobiography, of fact and fiction', that which biography in general requires and Orlando's biographer in particular desires – that is, life-size wholeness – is still missing (E4 477). For Woolf, then, how to write life remains an open problem, not because of language's limited capacity to express its complexity or the depths of personality but because of the challenges of scale, selection, suggestion and sensibility involved with the task, problems haunted immanently by the seemingly irresolvable truths of fact *and* fiction.

Yet in the context of Woolf's writings on Browne, the opposition between reading modes in *Orlando* and the amalgamations of truth and personality in 'The New Biography' seem to resolve and form a *composition* of reflexive concerns and orientations toward others, the world, and oneself. Indeed, Woolf's interest in Browne seems anchored in the split focus of his writing. Though he does not write what we might categorise as biography, his essays and books seem to express the truth that biographies (at least for Woolf) so rarely succeed in capturing: namely, the 'lonely life within' (*E4* 58). He is, Woolf claims, 'the first of autobiographers' (*E4* 59). Though he compiles 'notes on elephants or bubbles or Icelandic flora and fauna', he also attends to matters of the body and provides a composite portrait of his own soul.[7] 'Strange beyond belief', Woolf writes in 'Reading', 'are the capacities that he detects in himself, profound the meditation into which the commonest sight will plunge him, while the rest of the world passes by and sees nothing to wonder at' (*E3* 156). Admiring that 'the door of his mind' seems to split and open 'more and more widely' 'for any curious thing that chooses to enter in' (*E3* 154), Woolf sees in Browne the same composition of self-reflexive curiosity and creativity which the Brownian sentence in *Orlando* enjoins from its readers: a simultaneous orientation toward the self (what sort of reader am I? what sort of reader have I been?) and toward the adjacent pieces and fragments of other worlds, lives, objects and selves that the reader might encounter in any given text (no matter how distanced, obscured or fantastical). In short, Woolf sees Browne as a composite model of the lover and the truth seeker. This double ethos of reading develops Woolf's earlier sense, in 'Hours in a Library', of 'true' reading as a matter of 'intense curiosity' (*E2* 55) and her later theory – in 'How Should One Read a Book?' (1932) – that the reader must learn to 'open his mind as widely as possible' in order to become the 'fellow-worker and accomplice' of the authors whom he reads (*E5* 573–4).

But there are darker aspects to this complex orientation. Though Browne might pause to fancy 'a flower on a walk, or a chip of pottery', the good doctor also finds himself interested and invested in 'the thousand doors that lead to death' (*E3* 154–5). Browne's 'study', as he puts it, 'is life and death', and he 'daily behold[s] examples of mortality, and of all men least' does he 'need artificial *memento*'s, or coffins by [his] bed side, to minde' him of his eventual destination.[8] This dark side of Browne, I contend, also haunts *Orlando* and this sentence. Indeed, Orlando sits to read Browne after a tour of his family's 'ghastly sepulchre', and though his depressed intuition that 'life was not worth living any more' may ultimately be motivated by his forlorn 'desire [for] a woman in Russian trousers', there is an unmistakable parallelism between the reading task set by the difficult Brownian sentence above and Orlando's descent among the hints and whispers of the departed: among ten generations' worth of piled coffins, a random thigh bone and skull and the 'skeleton hand' which prompts him to begin a speculative query (*O* 70–2). He wonders, 'whose hand was it? [. . .] The right or left? The hand of man or woman, of age or youth? Had it urged the war-horse, or plied the needle? Had it plucked the rose or grasped the steel?' (O 71).

Orlando tarries with bones, and in the Brownian sentence above the reader must tarry with a stuttering syntax, a jumbled subject, and that dangling head (to which I will turn shortly). Quite suddenly, the work of the biographer's ideal, curious reader begins to resemble a dalliance among bodily remains, an interrogation of bones which will not sing, an art of lingering with fragments and imagining the absent wholes they evince. Orlando mutters: '"Nothing remains of all these Princes [. . .] except one digit"', and in doing so he speculates and invents, 'indulging in some pardonable exaggeration of their rank' (O 71). In Woolf's Brownian sentence, one learns that the biographer's ideal reader must likewise become a speculative conjuror and composer, 'making up [. . .] the whole boundary and circumference of a living person' from nothing but 'bare hints' and whispers (O 73). Among the remains of his relatives, Orlando encounters and quickly abandons an identical challenge before retreating to read *Urn Burial*, reading remainders – literally, human remains – as signs of what once was, what is not, what cannot now be known, and what lies beneath what is: 'all pomp is built upon corruption [. . .] the skeleton lies beneath the flesh [. . .] we that dance and sing above must lie below' (O 71). Poems, novels and memoirs are, after all, well-wrought urns, and the challenge of such 'ashes' and 'reliques' and 'vessels', in Browne's words, is that they too may 'silently [express] old mortality, the ruines of forgotten times, and can only speak with life, how long in this corruptible frame, some parts may be uncorrupted; yet able to out-last bones long unborn, and noblest pyle among us'.[9] Whether reading thigh bones or Thomas Browne, then, Orlando's activities in his family crypt and at his bedroom desk associate reading with a tour of ruins and remains.

In *Urn Burial* especially, Browne anticipates this association. This strange work was inspired by the 1655 discovery in Norfolk of several dozen ancient urns filled with ashes, bones and a variety of objects. Far from tracing the origins of these urns, Browne, who resided near the site of discovery, withdraws from them, like Orlando from his family crypt, to survey instead a history of cultural methods of interment as well as the various logics and anxieties associated with these methods. Some cultures, for instance, have burned the bodies of the dead, while others abhor fire and prefer 'precious Embalments, depositure in dry earths, or handsome inclosure in glasses' to conserve and preserve corpses.[10] Browne thus makes up from the bare hints of the ancient urns a brief history of human interment, which seems to inspire and attract

Orlando's pessimism as he tours his family crypt. This history climaxes in the sobering prose of *Urn Burial*'s final section:

> Oblivion is not to be hired. The greater part must be content to be as though they had not been [. . .] Since our longest Sunne sets right descensions, and makes but winter arches, and therefore it cannot be long before we lie down in darknesse, and have our light in ashes. Since the brother of death daily haunts us with dying *memento's*, and time that grows old it self, bids us hope no long duration: Diuturnity is a dream and folly of expectation.[11]

Browne does not reach this conclusion by writing and thinking in isolation, but, as his footnotes demonstrate, through the study of ancient texts, which is to say, through learning to read – as Orlando quite literally reads – *in the dark*.[12] There is a good deal of obscurity in the reading and writing task Browne assigns himself. There can be 'no authentic account' of this method; 'no authentic decision' about that one;[13] 'no assured period' in which to locate this or that practice or relic; 'no good account of covering' this or that body;[14] for 'the certainty of death is attended with uncertainties, in time, manner, [and] places' and with a good many obscurities that pose impossible problems 'not to be resolved by man, nor easily perhaps by spirits'.[15] But why dally with death and decay or apprentice oneself to the imminent void? Why become a curious reader of such remains when fostered ignorance of one's inevitable end keeps corrosive and depressive sorrows at bay? Perhaps because reading – for both Browne and Woolf – is a learned effort to negotiate and navigate the dark, an activity which accepts with austerity and courage one's mortal predicament, which affirms the pleasures of discovery (of urns, of books, of lovers), and which relishes the thought-adventures which await one among 'the treasures of oblivion', those 'heapes of things in a state next to nothing almost numberlesse'.[16]

This speculative link between reading, ruins and remains not only haunts but, moreover, motivates and orients Woolf's own engagement with literary and nonliterary texts. 'The Pastons and Chaucer', the first essay of *The Common Reader: First Series* (1925), for instance, begins with a sketch of ruined walls and a tale – pieced together from extant family letters – of John Paston's bare, unadorned grave. Though Woolf makes much of his son John's fascination with Chaucer, there is still the sheer material bulk of the four-volume collection of family letters she reviews, in which Sir John the younger is 'swallow[ed] up [. . .] as the sea absorbs a raindrop' (*E4* 34). In the immensity of this multi-generational archive, only two major things seem to remain of this single life lived in these now ruined walls: the fact that he never erected his father's gravestone and that he (like Woolf) adored Chaucer. The themes of death, ruin and loss continue through the volume. 'On Not Knowing Greek' concludes with the vision of a shadow, 'a sadness at the back of life', in which all humans live; this shadow and the depths of passing time have also swallowed up and obscured the ancients, even if schoolboys and scholars fantasise their close familiarity (*E4* 50). Elsewhere Woolf is drawn to 'The Lives of the Obscure' fading in some 'out-of-date, obsolete library', 'nameless tombstones' passing themselves off as books (*E4* 118); to figures like Margaret Cavendish, Duchess of Newcastle, alive 'only in a few splendid phrases that Lamb scattered upon her tomb' and whose 'real life [. . .] moulder[s] in the gloom of public libraries' (*E4* 81); and even to the recently deceased Joseph Conrad (*E4* 227-33). Whether canonical or obscure, most of the essays linger in some way with the shadows and at the ruinous boundary between what is irretrievably lost and what somehow remains, composing sketches, proffering arguments about quality and value and taste, and even speculating – as in the case of Jane Austen – about what would have happened had the author 'lived a few more years only' (*E4* 154). Woolf's engagements with these matters in *The Common Reader* anticipates the call of Orlando's biographer in the sentence above: she tarries among obscurities, feels her way among shadowed library shelves, pieces together a scene or sketch when she can, and always asks after what or whom remains, and what sort of effect the various traces of the dead might make on the present and on oneself. Thus, as with Browne, the curious view outward toward what one reads doubles as an examination of the self, of the present (as in the essays 'Modern Fiction' and 'How It Strikes a Contemporary'), and also of the fleetingness which the self shares with those whom one reads.

But what is one to do with the Brownian sentence's final reading challenge, that unsettling ruin and remainder swinging from the rafters on the novel's first page, that 'dead nigger's head' (*O* 73), the haunting 'head of a Moor' (*O* 13) that resurfaces in the second chapter? How does one square the recollection of Orlando's desire for literary companionship and his melancholic 'love of solitude' with his continuing indifference toward the decapitation and ornamentalisation of a human being? Or the deaths of those whose 'many heads' 'of many colours' his many 'fathers [. . .] had struck [. . .] off many shoulders' (*O* 13)? Though the novel does not appear to make much of this head, it is nevertheless the first sign of death in *Orlando* as well as a disconcerting response to Browne's rhetorical opening in *Urn Burial*: 'But who knows the fate of his bones, or how often he is to be buried?'[17] Sometimes one is *not* buried; sometimes one remains, though not in the ways Woolf studies in *The Common Reader*, and not in the ways the culprits of this decapitation remain in the family crypt below (seemingly free from mistreatment or misappropriation or theft or figuration). As the rather strange history of Browne's own skull attests, however,[18] the sadness at the back of life no doubt affects both conquered and conqueror – coloniser and colonised – and it does so variably and indifferently. Yet the head of the human being killed by Orlando's father(s) is itself indifferently figured as the trophy of successful conquest, and despite his love of death, Orlando fails to recognise ruin in a face which has been transfigured and de-faced.

And yet one who does a reader's part in attending to pieces, ruins, remainders, whispers, obscurities and silences might see a different work *at work* on the first page of the novel and in the later sentence I have been examining. We might see the reproduction, after all, of racial and cultural inequalities in the play of the young man. Indeed, the violence of imperialism, war and religion begins – as *Orlando* itself begins – in secluded child's play, the violence of which the surrounding culture mutes, adores and passes off as necessary for growth, camaraderie and manliness. 'Whatever innate impulse toward rambunctiousness Orlando may possess', Kathy J. Phillips writes, 'it takes long practice sessions in the attic to magnify his aggression into the capacity for murder [. . .] and to hide the details of violence in a romantic fantasy'.[19] This play, as the biographer tells us, substitutes and stands in for what Orlando cannot do *now* – at sixteen he is 'too young to ride' and must be content to 'lunge and plunge and slice at the air with his blade' (O 13). When we do a reader's part and *de*figure this trophy back into a human head and recognise in its face something other than a 'grinn[ing]' 'enemy' (O 14), we might learn that this play simulates the repetition of this nameless, irretrievable person's slaying and participates in the ongoing atrocities of colonial and imperial violence which Woolf associates – and which Eric Cheyfitz so damningly identifies – with the European Renaissance (the era in which *Orlando* opens). That Orlando loves literature, solitude and death, that he embodies pieces of the novel's notion of an ideal reader, does not mean that he is free from complicity in this history of conquest, cruelty and indifference. Indeed, as Cheyfitz teaches us, the history of eloquence – of metaphor and translation – is itself complicit in the originary, compulsive and violent distinction between 'savage humanity' and 'civilization'.[20] Indeed, to interrogate the role of this dangling human remainder leaves one with many problems: can reading become more than an occasion to hide from one's complicities? Does withdrawing to a 'window-seat with a book' amount to a wilful evasion of that part of oneself which refuses to engage the misery of this hanging human head (O 73)? Can one learn *to face* and to be encountered by the violence in which one has participated? Can reading become an ethical mode of staying the hand as it is raised to strike? Of seeing what one has not yet seen?

Woolf herself is not free from complicity in this legacy of ruin, death and loss. Her essay 'The Elizabethan Lumber Room' (1925), which ends with several paragraphs dedicated to Browne, begins with reflections on 'the fruit of innumerable voyages, traffics, and discoveries to unknown lands in the reign of Queen Elizabeth' (*E4* 53). The purpose and tone of these pages – rendered in free indirect style – is unclear. Though Woolf alludes to signs of imperial violence, the swiftness of these allusions recalls Orlando's indifference and the 'many humours' of which he is 'strangely compounded' (*O* 73). Indeed, one might encounter whispers of critique here, bare hints of Woolf's widely recognised anti-imperialism, but her repeated use of the term 'savage' (*E4* 54–6) – which recalls the biographer's reference to 'barbarian fields' and the 'vast Pagan' whose head is translated into imperial ornamentation – signals her entanglement in the translation and figuration of other peoples as uncivilised barbarians (*O* 13). But Woolf's complicity need not entangle us in a project of critical defensiveness, for as we learn from Browne and from Woolf, curious readers can defy the violence of figuration and accomplish a great deal with mere whispers and hints through a sort of reverse translation.[21] *Orlando* repeats the vision of the hanging head, after all, and it returns its gaze to us, affording us an opportunity to interrogate not only the history of violence to which it testifies, but also whether or not we failed to read its gaze as a human gaze the first time around.

Notes

1. Virginia Woolf, *Orlando: A Biography* [1928] (New York: Harcourt, 1956), p. 73.
2. Despite wide critical familiarity with Woolf's interest in Renaissance literature, I have found only three short essays which attend to the Woolf/Browne connection. See Pamela Caughie, 'Sir Thomas Browne and *Orlando*', *Virginia Woolf Miscellany*, 25 (1985), p. 4; David Galef, 'Mrs Woolf and Mr Browne', *Notes and Queries*, 36 (1989), pp. 202–3; and Sally Green, 'Brownean Motion in "Solid Objects"', *Virginia Woolf Miscellany*, 50 (1997), pp. 2–3.
3. 1919 seems to have been a significant year for Woolf's interest in Browne. 'I have read him fairly often', she writes in her diary after rediscovering his work (*D1* 297). And in *Night and Day* [1919] (New York: Harcourt, 1948), Ralph Denham studies 'a small and lovely edition of Sir Thomas Browne' (p. 75).
4. 'The Elizabethan Lumber Room' (1925), *E4*, p. 58.

5. 'The Modern Essay' (1925), *E4*, p. 218.
6. 'Impassioned Prose' (1926), *E4*, pp. 367, 363.
7. Stephen Greenblatt and Ramie Targoff, 'Introduction', in Sir Thomas Browne, *Religio Medici and Urne-Buriall*, ed. S. Greenblatt and R. Targoff (New York: New York Review Books, 2012), p. ix.
8. Browne, *Religio Medici and Urne-Buriall*, p. 94.
9. Ibid. pp. 93–4.
10. Ibid. p. 99.
11. Ibid. pp. 135–6.
12. Cf. *O* 76: 'For when he had read for an hour or so in Sir Thomas Browne . . . the bark of the stag and the call of the night watchman showed that it was the dead of night and all safe asleep'.
13. Browne, *Religio-Medici and Urne Buriall*, pp. 107–8.
14. Ibid. pp. 110, 113.
15. Ibid. pp. 117, 133.
16. Ibid. p. 141.
17. Ibid. p. 93.
18. Given the posthumous afterlife of Browne's skull – stolen from his grave in 1840 – it is tempting to interpret Orlando's choice of reading material as an ironic frame through which Woolf invites us to read the dead black man's head. Browne and the black man are vulnerable to a similar fate, though their figuration is quite different and unequal. Browne's skull becomes a sign of value/profit as well as enduring genius; the black man's skull constitutes a sign of his savageness and the British strength and progress that overcame it. Whether or not Woolf knew this history, she was well aware of a 'great renewal of interest' in Browne (*E3* 368), evinced by the 1923 Golden Cockerel Press's editions of his work. These editions themselves may have been inspired by the eventual re-interment of Browne's skull in 1922. See Colin Dickey, *Cranioklepty: Grave Robbing and the Search for Genius* (Lakewood, CO: Unbridled Books, 2009).
19. Kathy J. Phillips, *Virginia Woolf Against Empire* (Knoxville, TN: University of Tennessee Press, 1994), p. 186.
20. Eric Cheyfitz, *The Poetics of Imperialism: Translation and Colonialization from* The Tempest *to Tarzan*, expanded edn (Philadelphia: University of Pennsylvania Press, 1997), p. 113.
21. I want to thank Elsa Högberg for suggesting the phrase 'reverse translation' for this ethical and defigurative mode of reading.

Chapter 15

The Negress and the Bishop: On Marriage, Colonialism and the Problem of Knowledge

Randi Koppen

And so they would go on talking or rather, understanding, which has become the main art of speech in an age when words are growing daily so scanty in comparison with ideas that 'the biscuits ran out' has to stand for kissing a negress in the dark when one has just read Bishop Berkeley's philosophy for the tenth time.[1]

What I have just cited is hardly the most memorable or resonant of *Orlando*'s sentences. It does not draw attention to itself through thickness of style – the joys of ventriloquism, parody and pastiche that energise this writer's holiday. If Woolf is citing anyone in this sentence it is herself: the lightness of touch that defines her essays. And yet, like every phrase of *Orlando*, it has its work cut out, not so much in moving the narrative forward as in carrying and indexing, freighting, nudging and winking, a signifying practice that by necessity breaks the limits of the sentence and sets it in connection with a wide field of signification. As such the sentence exemplifies the fundamentally allusive nature of Woolf's writing, where even the most fleeting reference has complex resonances, inviting a work of reading that never finishes.

The question that will occupy me in this chapter is where we are invited to look, and what the allusion nudges us to see, a question complicated by another typical feature of Woolf's textual practice: the unequal juxtaposition. I'm thinking of the Woolfian constellation that transposes and reframes by establishing links between the radically disparate, like those fortuitous 'swift marriages' Woolf speaks of in 'Craftsmanship' (1937; E6 91–102) – the promiscuous mating of words brought about by their free-floating traffic along lines of contiguity and association. *Orlando*'s marriage of Bishop and negress is one such constellation of the 'freakish and unequal',[2] an oxymoronic mating of chains of signification which, I want to suggest, nudges us in the direction of Woolf's first novel, *The Voyage Out* (1915), and its story of the formation of the woman artist in its initial, painstakingly serious form.

Like Orlando's adventures in foreign parts, Woolf's first voyage out has its own 'bishop and negress' whose presence behind *Orlando*'s allusive register opens up a reading of the later novel as a playful return to the first, a second take on the concerns that my sentence frames: questions of marriage, of language and what we have in common, but also of the colonial origins of modernist aesthetics and lifestyles. The proposed constellation of *Orlando* and *The Voyage Out* gives us two stories of formation that present heterosexual marriage as the decisive step in a process of maturity, while introducing a 'native' other – a 'negress' – as the third, mediating term in the question of union. It also gives us two takes on the *Künstlerroman*; one comic, one tragic; one set in a carnivalesque Orient partly mediated through parodic versions of colonial genres, letters and diaries; the other placed in a pseudo-Amazonian landscape arising out of a colonial imaginary. In what follows, the reading practice I propose as a means to trace the movement of this return will be guided by the textual practice which Woolf's exemplary sentence thematises and performs: a modernist hermeneutics that keeps an eye out for nudges and winks, substitutions and metonymic displacements, welcoming links between the disparate, and appreciating the value of the malapropos.

Jokes and their relation to the unconscious

The rules of syntax tell us that the first unit in our example – 'And'– is a sentence connector, a coordinating conjunction that works with 'so' as a linking adverb to indicate sequential order, a result or conclusion to what has gone before. What it sets out to articulate is the mode of discourse that proceeds from romantic union, as in Orlando and Shelmerdine's meeting of perfectly sympathetic minds: the understanding (rather than talking) that is called for when the available linguistic resources fall short of the experience of being modern. As so often though, the Woolfian sentence takes liberties, proceeding to speak of the wrong thing, the freakish and outlandish, carrying lovers' talk to sexual transgression. And so, as we shall see, the semantic field widens, proceeding by knowing winks to Vita and Harold Nicolson's unconventional marriage along with nods to Bloomsbury's philosophical debates, polymorphous sexual identities and a history of imperial conquest.

At the most immediate level what is uttered here is a joke, a joke whose humour arises from the 'swift marriage' at the end of the flight of fancy – the 'freakish and unequal' juxtapositions of biscuits and philosophy, Bishop and negress, and the juxtaposition of comic emergencies:

the depletion of biscuits and the depletion of words; the marine explorer down to his last provisions and the sexually frustrated imperialist on a diet of dry philosophy. The point of the joke, or one of them, is the novel's figuration of modern marriage as a state of androgynous union. It describes the sympathy that defines the relationship of the modern couple imbued with the modern spirit, a perfect understanding of a very different calibre than that of their Victorian forebears. Orlando at least understands that language in the modern age has to work by metaphor and metonymy, and that some experiences have to pass as others in order to get past the censor. As 'tolerant and free-spoken as a man', s/he understands and dares to say that 'negresses are seductive'; 'as strange and subtle as a woman', Shelmerdine exhibits the depth of one who speaks in riddles – in the substitutions and displacements of a Freudian dream language (O 179). Considered in this light, the joke appears to nudge us towards an ideal of modernist language, combining simplicity with depth, clarity with image, and anticipating the androgynous writing elaborated in *A Room of One's Own*. As we shall see, however, the allusive net cast by this sentence reaches much further, casting into doubt who or what is the butt of the joke.

For Freud, as Jaime Hovey reminds us in her reading of *Orlando*, the joke is a 'double-dealing rascal' whose meaning often turns on substitution, displacement, dissimilarity and the 'bringing forward of what is hidden'.[3] What Hovey finds hidden in Woolf's sentence, what the joke brings to light, is a cultural displacement of one taboo onto another. As Hovey observes, in the lovers' intimate code the figure of the 'negress' is appropriated, on the one hand, to triangulate the modern couple's 'polymorphous sexuality and fluid gender identification' and, on the other, to 'mark the closeting of [Orlando and Shelmerdine's] queerness'. 'Assenting to the cultural values that exoticize their homosexual, interracial, and cross-class sexual tastes,' Hovey writes, 'Orlando and Shelmerdine agree to closet their sexuality, to kiss their unacceptable sexual objects – their "negresses" – in the dark'.[4] In Hovey's reading, what the joke turns on and allows to surface is a form of cultural masquerade and the appropriations, projections and displacements on which it depends. The displacement that is brought to light is the appropriation of the 'negress' in a racialised erotic language that enables a coded and playful articulation of modern subjectivities, an articulation, moreover, that simultaneously reconfigures and domesticates imperialist dynamics in the political evasions of modern orientalism, primitivism and exoticism.

Rather than define a modern ideal, then, the 'understanding' our sentence describes is a crossing-over to the place of the other that depends on the appropriation of a third term – the racial other whose difference is subsumed in a signifying practice that can be little more than a fashionable form of euphemism. If this is what the 'double-dealing rascal' brings to light, the question is whether this is a revelation our sentence makes in spite of itself: whether the joke connects with a larger anti-imperialist project articulated by the novel as a whole, or is best understood as emanating from a textual unconscious. Or, differently formulated: whether the butt of Woolf's joke is a liberal metropolitan elite, exemplified by the Nicolsons but including herself, who are immersed in modern forms of orientalism yet imagine themselves to occupy a position outside a racist and colonialist Establishment, naïvely thinking of individual liberalism and polymorphous desire as effective antidotes to the oppression of colonial structures.

Woolf's Bishop

Leaving aside these unresolved questions for the moment, let us return to our sentence and pose another, taking into consideration the part of the joke Hovey leaves out: where does Woolf's Bishop nudge us to look, and what, if anything, is framed in the 'freakish and unequal' constellation of Bishop and negress? Most immediately, what George 'Bishop' Berkeley metonymises in the sentence is an early twentieth-century philosophical debate between young and old, realism and idealism, in which Berkeley represents the old, and male Bloomsbury represents the young. More generally, we may say that the bishop flags the problem of knowledge as it figures in Woolf's writing: questions of the truth status of our sense perceptions, how we see and think we might come to know common objects, and of what we have in common – the commensurability of subjective worlds and perspectives. These are questions that fuel Woolf's modernist aesthetic as much as her thematic.

As is well known, G. E. Moore constructed the argument of his 'Refutation of Idealism' (1903) against Berkeley's idealist proposition that reality is mental, that a thing must be perceived in order to exist, and Moore had a liberating influence on Cambridge philosophy and the male members of Bloomsbury who had been 'Apostles'. Woolf herself was familiar with Berkeley's philosophy through her father's *History of English Thought in the Eighteenth Century* (1876) as well as her own reading of Berkeley and Moore. Of Woolf's novels, as Gillian Beer was the first to show, *To the Lighthouse* focuses the Berkeleyan preoccupation with questions of perception, perspective and knowledge most clearly, creating an elegiac form that carries out that hypothetical extension of the subject's powers of observation, which Leslie Stephen had evoked as a means to imagine the object without a subject.[5] Philosophical speculation translates into formal experiment with the unoccupied perspectives of 'Time Passes', a writing that deliberately obliterates any suggestion of a single perceiver. The notion of an 'eyeless' vision, a 'world seen without a self' (*D3* 203; *W* 221),[6] also motivates Woolf's narration in the interludes of *The Waves*, indicating the extent to which philosophical speculation – the Bishop's questions of perception and knowledge – served to invigorate aesthetic enquiry along with a sense of narrative experiment as an instrument for obtaining knowledge. Her fiction interrogates the related problems of knowledge and language both in everyday communication and in fictional language as it transcends perceptual and imaginative limits through synoptic pictures which do not assert a common sense perspective on reality, but seek to establish what we have in common even while imagining otherness and difference – what is there when *I* am not.[7]

As cultural practice and a body of texts, philosophy is ambivalently coded throughout Woolf's writing, one moment associated with modern rationality and liberating thought-experiments, the next representing a paternally sanctioned civilising project caught up in material conditions and relations of power. Three of her novels consider philosophy in the context of women's education, specifically the available forms of *Bildung* for young middle-class women bound up with cultural expectations of courtship and marriage. In *The Voyage Out*, Moore's philosophy is proffered as a point of orientation in Rachel's process of formation, while in *Jacob's Room*, Berkeley's philosophy figures in connection with the education of women, women's ignorance and boredom.[8] The 1907 section of *The Years*, set at roughly the same time as *The Voyage Out*, depicts Sally reading Berkeley's 'faded brown book' as she waits for her parents and Maggie to return from a dance.[9] Attempting one of the Bishop's mental exercises, which involves lying completely still to 'let herself be thought', Sally finds 'idealism' comically disturbed by the reality of her body, her own girlish fantasy of romantic union and 'what people say to each other at parties' (*Y* 119). Next, the backdrop of middle-class courtship and marriage leads to another mental exercise, inspired by *The Antigone*: that of being buried alive, of lying straight out in a brick tomb (*Y* 122). There are echoes in this of Rachel's dilemmas in *The Voyage Out*, where the young woman's pursuit of safe grounds of knowledge and truth comes up against middle-class culture's civilising project: the state of marriage at once a promise of maturity and knowledge, and a story of entrapment and death.

In Rachel's education in 'the facts of life', overseen by Helen and

Hirst, Moore's common-sense realism is offered as one point of reality orientation, while Gibbon's regimental sentence with its references to European appropriation of African territory is meant to supply another. Helen Ambrose represents the generation that defines itself by the refutation of idealism. Woolf depicts her reading bits of Moore's *Principia Ethica* (1903) as she works on her 'great design': 'a tropical river running through a tropical forest', with 'a troop of naked natives whirl[ing] darts into the air'. Between stitches she reads a sentence about 'the Reality of Matter, or the Nature of Good'.[10] Helen, of course, is just as much caught up in the imperialist economy as everyone else, stitching Moore's *de rigeur* philosophical questioning into the fashionably orientalist design of her embroidery much in the same way as the subsequent up-river expedition to 'see the natives in their camps' serves the Flushings' enterprise of supplying the metropolitan craze for all things 'primitive' and 'Oriental'. The irony of such implication is given a further twist in Mr Dalloway's enthusiastic affirmation of the 'value' of philosophical reasoning as training for politicians and colonial administrators alike – 'just the kind of thing' one used to debate until five in the morning with 'Duffy – now Secretary for India' (*VO* 77–8).

As Bishop Berkeley passes through Woolf's fiction, then, he enters into more than one constellation. In the relation between generations he is the Father as opposed to the sons, the Victorian opposed to the moderns. In narratives of subject formation, education and *Bildung*, he flags questions of knowledge and its limits, of solipsism contra intersubjectivity and the commensurability of perspectives, of 'I' or 'we', of marriage and the union of minds. Returning to *Orlando*'s sentence with the question of what accrues to the bishop at this point – what it could mean to Woolf and her immediate (Bloomsbury) circle of readers in 1928 to kiss a negress in the dark as a relief from reading Berkeley's philosophy – it is evident that the allusion brings with it a broad scope of reference. What is in play, first of all, is the position of the moderns against the nineteenth century: an assertion of the reality of the body and illicit desire over mind, of what goes on in the dark under the father's nose, but equally of a mode of thought and language that overcomes difference and subjective perspectives to establish knowledge of (and as) what we have in common. What is also activated in this reference, as I have argued, is the philosophical and epistemological origins of Woolf's modernist aesthetic: the elaboration over several works of a narrative mode that ventures beyond the individual perceiver's range, a mobility and flexibility of perspective that culminate in the unoccupied perspectives and 'eyeless' vision of *The Waves*. Placing *Orlando* in a relation of continuity with *The Voyage Out*, however, may reveal that this modernist aesthetic has its beginnings less in a refutation of idealism than in the exposure to an other's gaze – more precisely that of the 'negress'.

The negress and Woolf's Amazonian women

In Woolf's first novel, as we have seen, philosophy – Moore's refutation of idealism – figures as one term in a process of female *Bildung*: those negotiations between individual freedom and socio-cultural framework (here specifically marriage and an imperialist economy) that define the *Bildungsroman*. Significantly, however, it is the dissolution rather than formation of character that marks the beginnings of Woolf's modernist aesthetic. As Jed Esty observes, the failure of Rachel's *Bildung* appears as the precondition for the successful artistic development of Virginia Woolf as a writer of modernist fiction.[11] Esty points to the decisive importance of the colonial setting to this innovation in form and style. If *The Voyage Out* shows Woolf place the question of knowledge in a constellation with women's *Bildung*, marriage and a colonial frame, the negress, as much as the Bishop, has a role to play in that constellation and in the remaking of the *Bildungsroman* that ensues from it. Jaime Hovey alerts us to the metonymic chain of racial others in which *Orlando* inserts the negress: the orientalist series of Moors, Turks, Gypsies and Egyptian girls that serves to displace imperialism along an axis of primitivism and exoticism. Extending that chain intertextually to Woolf's first story of the formation of the woman artist, in which the encounter with the gaze of the 'native women' becomes the moment when colonialism decisively disrupts the *Bildungsroman*, allows us to speculate further on some intriguing associative links between *Orlando*'s negress and those women in the Amazonian jungle in Rachel's voyage out. There, in a village among huts like 'strange wooden nests', Woolf imagines women 'squatting on the ground in triangular shapes', 'their long narrow eyes' fixed upon the visitors 'with the motionless inexpressive gaze of those removed from each other far far beyond the plunge of speech'. The stare follows them as they look around the village and peer into huts, 'passing over their legs, their bodies, their heads, curiously not without hostility, like the crawl of a winter fly' (*VO* 332).

In *Orlando*'s sentence, as I have said, the 'negress' facilitates unification: the establishment of an epistemological and hermeneutic position that overcomes difference. The gaze of the 'native women' in *The Voyage Out* also brings about recognition, but of a kind that negates the possibility of union. Where the negress in *Orlando* is appropriated as sign of the modern and the new, the women at the heart of the Amazonian darkness figure as primordial nature, the source or manifestation of some original and eternal truth, as Rachel perceives it: 'So it would go on for ever and ever, she said' (*VO* 270). What is 'it' here? Is it Christine Froula's maternal life world in which to be a woman is always to be inscribed in and circumscribed by natural cycles of birth and death?[12] Or is it perhaps that 'vast and impersonal system, in which sex, gender, labor, and power are socially organized', that Esty and others see?[13] In either case, it comes as a dark reply to the novel's question of knowledge and the push for an individual formation founded on modern rationality, signalling the end to the humanist dream of 'a special developmental destiny' (and the attainment of maturity and knowledge in marriage) that defines the *Bildungsroman*.[14] From now on, as if infected by some dark and foreign virus, the narrative can only head towards paralysis and death.

Given that *Orlando*'s negress and the women in the village are metonymically and associatively connected, it is apposite to ask where Woolf's Amazonian women originate from; from what cultural imaginary they derive. Conrad's ethnographic discourse in *Heart of Darkness* (1899) is one probable source, as suggested by the many intertextual resonances between the two novels. Another would be Leonard Woolf's *The Village in the Jungle* (1913), a novel describing village life in a jungle of Ceylon, which Virginia read in manuscript just after their honeymoon while still revising *The Voyage Out*, and which may have led her to rewrite some crucial scenes in her own work-in-progress. In the transition from *Melymbrosia* to *The Voyage Out*, as Mark Wollaeger has shown, the scene in the village doubles in length, with the striking intensity of the women's stare emerging in considerable more detail.[15] Coming to terms with the 'negress' was part of the Woolfs' courtship and early marriage, involving the reality of Leonard's sexual encounters with Ceylonese women during his years as a colonial administrator in that country, the fictionalisation of those encounters in his *Stories from the East*, along with the eroticised projections of landscape and indigenous women that inhabit his novel.

Faced with the mystery and unknowability of the people in the remote villages of Ceylon, *The Village in the Jungle*, in Leonard's statement, was an attempt 'vicariously to live their lives'.[16] It is an omniscient narrative related almost entirely through the perspective of indigenous characters without the presence of a colonial observer. Like *The Voyage Out*, Leonard's novel has a clear anti-imperialist agenda, which the narrative experiments with perspectives and gazes are attempts at realising. In both cases, the critique of imperialism entails reflections on the nature and limits of knowledge, decentring Eurocentric perspectives, and thinking the racial other as subject rather than object. Leonard strives to imagine a world beyond the colonial field of vision; Virginia imbues the native women with primordial knowledge and an unsettling gaze. Inevitably, both narratives are informed by the discursive frames of ethnography, anthropology and colonial literature, and still they ask to be read as attempts to narratively expand those frames: to imagine what is there when we are not, to overcome but not erase difference.

Orlando's thematic of formation along with its immersion in a repertoire of cultural and literary mediations of the oriental connects it with *The Voyage Out*, making it tempting to read the later novel as a playful take on orientalist and colonial discourse as well as an empowering return to Rachel's failed *Bildung*: to the colony as a site of playful becoming rather than ego-dissolution and deadly disorientation. The paradigmatic Conradian scene of the imperial encounter is one of disorientation and dizziness. In the up-river sequence of *The Voyage Out*, Rachel's story develops a case in point as Woolf lets the South American jungle serve as figure as well as context for a gradual collapse of signification, in which the dizzying strangeness of the surrounding landscape is matched by a disintegration of meaningful utterance evident in an inability of words to carry from one subject to another, and the dominance of non-verbal sound.[17] In the narrative stasis that follows, Rachel remains a site of contradictions, 'poised', as Esty puts it, 'between becoming and unbecoming herself', until she succumbs to the final disorder of illness, hallucination and death.[18]

By comparison, any disorientation that ensues from the colonial encounter is unproblematic in *Orlando*. The Orient is where Orlando becomes herself, or at least where the process of becoming is significantly advanced. The foreign landscape is neither figure nor cause of dissolution: on the contrary, she figures and names it. Where *The Voyage Out* takes the travellers beyond language, to a state of verbal silence and pre-linguistic sound, Orlando remains Elizabethan in her relation to the Orient, responding to the foreignness of the desert landscape not with dizziness and loss of bearings, but with an outbreak of the 'English disease' (*O* 101), as if compensating for Rachel's traumatic voiding of language with linguistic excess in the fashion of the day: anthropocentric word-painting, apostrophe, prosopopoeia and allegory.

Thematically speaking, *Orlando* may also be understood as a return to the former novel in its concern with the connections between marital union and empire. The union of both pairs of lovers alludes to one of the familiar plots of the Victorian novel, where the formation and unfettered expression of character somehow requires the participation, whether by identification or disavowal, of the ethnically or racially other. As Beverly Ann Schlack observes, the deathbed scene in *The Voyage Out* reiterates past literary presentations of love and death in terms of spiritual-mystic attachment, as Hewet transforms his experience of bereavement into a mystic vision of perfect identification in death, feeling that 'he seemed to be Rachel as well as himself' (*VO* 333). The allusion is to one of Rachel's favourite novels, *Wuthering Heights*, in which Catherine proclaims her identification with the dark-skinned 'gipsy' Heathcliff: 'I am Heathcliff'; 'he's more myself than I am'.[19] Similar allusions in the union of Orlando and Shel suggest that what is in play is as much a parodic return to the earlier scene and its allusive background as a proclamation of androgynous subjectivity and writing. Ironically, the union of the modern lovers comes about through a double Brontëan moment deeply immersed in Victorian orientalism, as Orlando moves from declaring herself the bride of 'the moor' in the manner of Catherine Earnshaw (*O* 170) to playing Jane Eyre to Shel's Rochester (*O* 173–4). In the Brontës' novels, union with the 'moor' – whether the dark-skinned alien Heathcliff with his indeterminate colonial origins, or the dark 'gipsy' Rochester with his racially impure marriage – serves to express the white woman's authentic and independent selfhood. By comparison, Woolf's two novels present two versions of the *Bildungsroman*. In the first, Rachel's identification with the 'native' women – the dark knowledge at the heart of civilisation – halts *Bildung* and makes marriage death, a narrative turn that is sublimated by Hewet through the literary plot of romantic union. The second gives the project of *Bildung* and marriage a positive spin by recasting the 'negress' as the figure that triangulates desire, androgynous union, and, ultimately, the proclamation of a fully formed modern self.

The swift marriage

Jaime Hovey asks whether *Orlando*'s reconfigured, domesticated desires serve to resist or consolidate empire, which leads me to another, related question: in the proposed constellation with *The Voyage Out*, does *Orlando* emerge as no more than Woolf's playful, empowering return to the questions her first novel broached so seriously and torturously? In the biographer's assertion, the 'natural desire' affirmed in the union of Orlando and Shel is of a kind to interrupt and confound the 'forging of links' that constitutes an empire (*O* 204). At the level of plot, however, things are more ambiguous. The kiss in the dark of which our sentence speaks is situated between Berkeley and Pascal: Shel, we are told, reads Pascal after having been seduced by a negress. For Woolf, Pascal contained a lesson in imperialist greed – *Ce chien est à moi* – which both she and Leonard invoked in writing against imperialism: Leonard had used it as an epigraph in *Empire and Commerce in Africa* (1920), while Virginia went on to juxtapose the dog and the black woman in her discussion of the imperialist instinct in *A Room of One's Own*.[20] In the plot of *Orlando*, however, Shel fails to pick up on the lesson, deciding to sail for Cape Horn, living the imperialist dream.

For Jaime Hovey the signifying practice their union represents is one of projection, strategic displacement and concealment. With Shel, Orlando achieves a level of linguistic sophistication that enables advanced hermeneutic operations and a further level of verbal mastery. Like Vita Sackville-West, though, she hardly amounts to a great writer; nor does 'The Oak Tree' read as an exemplary androgynous, modernist text. Woolf's sentence, by contrast, performs the signifying practice it thematises, of freakish constellations and capricious displacements. I have argued that in order to appreciate what is at stake in the joke, we need to take into consideration the range of allusive references at play, as well as what is framed in the marriage of signifying chains.

The joke of the bishop and the negress carries the freight of more than one marriage: behind the union of Orlando and Shel are those of Vita and Harold, Virginia and Leonard, Rachel and Hewet. In this perspective, what the 'double-dealing rascal' brings to light is metropolitan modernism's implication in colonialism as lifestyle and aesthetic. Our sentence, though, also brings about another marriage – that of the philosophical project with the related project of the anti-imperialist. It is only if we think of *Orlando*'s negress as intertextually connected with the disturbing gaze of the native women in *The Voyage Out* that we become aware of the resonances among these different epistemological breakthroughs that feed into the development of modernist fiction: analogous if not symmetrical projects of extending knowledge, of thinking beyond available perspectives through imaginative, linguistic and hermeneutic operations. In the last instance, then, what our sentence nudges us to see is that the negress and the bishop each has a role to play in the story of the formation of the woman artist. Ultimately, what is framed in their swift marriage is the colonial sources of a modernist aesthetic.

Notes

1. Virginia Woolf, *Orlando: A Biography* [1928] (London: Penguin Books, 1993), p. 179.
2. Woolf used this phrase to describe the style of *Orlando* (D3 184).

3. Jaime Hovey, '"Kissing a Negress in the Dark": Englishness as a Masquerade in Woolf's *Orlando*', *PMLA*, 112.3 (May 1997), pp. 393–404.
4. Ibid. pp. 401–2.
5. Gillian Beer, *Virginia Woolf: The Common Ground* (Edinburgh: Edinburgh University Press, 1996), pp. 29–47.
6. Virginia Woolf, *The Waves* [1931] (London: Penguin, 1992).
7. See, for instance, Ann Banfield, *The Phantom Table: Woolf, Fry, Russell and the Epistemology of Modernism* (Cambridge: Cambridge University Press, 2000), especially Chapter 3.
8. Beverly Ann Schlack, *Continuing Presences: Virginia Woolf's Use of Literary Allusion* (University Park: Pennslyvania University Press, 1979), p. 161.
9. Virginia Woolf, *The Years* [1937] (London: Granada, 1977), pp. 118–25.
10. Virginia Woolf, *The Voyage Out* [1915] (London: Penguin Books, 1992), p. 30.
11. Jed Esty, 'Virginia Woolf's Colony and the Adolescence of Modernist Fiction', in Richard Begam and Michael Valdez Moses (eds), *Modernism and Colonialism: British and Irish Literature, 1899–1939* (Durham, NC and London: Duke University Press, 2007), pp. 70–90.
12. Christine Froula, *Virginia Woolf and the Bloomsbury Avant-Garde* (New York: Columbia University Press, 2005).
13. Esty, 'Virginia Woolf's Colony', p. 84.
14. Ibid.
15. Mark Wollaeger, 'The Woolfs in the Jungle: Intertextuality, Sexuality, and the Emergence of Female Modernism in *The Voyage Out*, *The Village in the Jungle*, and *Heart of Darkness*', *Modern Language Quarterly*, 64.1 (2003), p. 36.
16. Leonard Woolf, *Beginning Again: An Autobiography of the Years 1911–1918* (London: Hogarth Press, 1963), p. 47.
17. Nick Montgomery, 'Colonial Rhetoric and the Maternal Voice: Deconstruction and Disengagement in Virginia Woolf's *The Voyage Out*', *Twentieth Century Literature*, 26.1 (Spring 2000), pp. 34–55.
18. Esty, 'Virginia Woolf's Colony', pp. 79–80.
19. Schlack, *Continuing Presences*, p. 15.
20. '[The male instinct] murmurs if it sees a fine woman go by, or even a dog, Ce chien est à moi [. . .] It is one of the great advantages of being a woman that one can pass even a very fine negress without wishing to make an Englishwoman of her'. Virginia Woolf, *A Room of One's Own* [1929] (London: Granada, 1977), pp. 49–50.

Chapter 16

Orlando and the Politics of (In)Conclusiveness

Judith Allen

Orlando then came to the conclusion (opening half-a-dozen books) that it was very odd that there was not a single dedication to a nobleman among them; next (turning over a vast pile of memoirs) that several of these writers had family trees half as high as her own; next, that it would be impolitic in the extreme to wrap a ten-pound note round the sugar tongs when Miss Christina Rossetti came to tea; next (here were half-a-dozen invitations to celebrate centenaries by dining) that literature since it ate all these dinners must be growing very corpulent; next (she was invited to a score of lectures upon the Influence of this upon that; the Classical revival; the Romantic survival, and other titles of the same engaging kind) that literature since it listened to all these lectures must be growing very dry; next (here she attended a reception given by a peeress) that literature since it wore all these fur tippets must be growing very respectable; next (here she visited Carlyle's sound-proof room at Chelsea) that genius since it needed all this coddling must be growing very delicate; and so at last she reached her final conclusion, which was of the highest importance but which, as we have already much overpassed our limit of six lines, we must omit.[1]

Readers encounter this lengthy and complex sentence about twenty-five pages from the end of the last chapter of *Orlando*. It depicts Orlando's attempt to come to a final conclusion about nothing less than 'the whole of Victorian literature' (O 189). 'Accustomed to the little literatures of the sixteenth, seventeenth, and eighteenth centuries', Orlando has now crammed her house with 'innumerable volumes' from a nineteenth-century London bookshop, and is 'appalled by the consequences of her order' (O 189–90). In addition to reading these books, she must comply with the binary constraints set out by the narrator:

> there are only two ways of coming to a conclusion upon Victorian literature – one is to write it out in sixty volumes octavo, the other is to squeeze it into six lines of the length of this one. Of the two courses, economy, since time runs short, leads us to choose the second; and so we proceed. (O 189–90)

As readers, we laugh at the narrator's authoritative decision, but we also question the narrative and rhetorical strategies that create it. Questions abound in *Orlando*, and answers are provisional, non-existent or contradictory, hence the difficulties of knowing selves, texts, or the words from which they are constructed. Taking Woolf's comic sentence as a starting point, this chapter will explore the problematics of concluding that pervades so much of *Orlando*, while assessing the political ramifications of the text's rhetorical strategies. These strategies function, quite self-consciously, to expose the hybrid and inconclusive qualities of *Orlando*'s genre, the transformative nature of gender, the plurality of identity, and, importantly, Woolf's interrogation of the referentiality of language.

I begin with the experimental nature of my chosen sentence, its very unusual structure, and the significance of its rhetorical repetitions; along with the specific use of the number six, these repetitions foreground Woolf's frequently ironic emphasis on the exact and the precise. Overemphatic precision is utilised by Woolf's narrators in many of her works – *A Room of One's Own* is a clear example – and functions to distance her readers, while keeping them in touch with the equivocal nature of her writing. Regarding such exaggerated precision, Rachel Bowlby addresses 'the pretense of completeness and objectivity' maintained by the historians and biographers of the Victorian period.[2] Woolf's parodic sentence, with its satirical anthropomorphisms, also validates many clichéd qualities of Victorian literary production: the verbosity and literal weight of these volumes, their dryness and rigidity, their didactic qualities, as well as their sentimentality and the seemingly required focus on class issues. The rigid constraints of Victorian literary conventions, imbued with issues brought about by the censorship and social purity movements of this period, served to shape its politics and aesthetics. In sharp contrast to such constraints, my chosen sentence expresses a politics of inconclusiveness, enacted in a work for which 'satire [was] to be the main note – satire and wildness [. . .] Everything mocked [. . .] And it is to end with three dots . . . so' (D3 131). The satirical aspects of this novel/biography expose the patriarchal conventions of Victorian literature, particularly, as we shall see, those that implore women to 'suffer and be still'.[3] Resistance to these patriarchal norms is expressed and enacted by the 'wildness' that Woolf set as one of her goals for *Orlando*. Wildness was also, for Woolf, a significant goal for women, as shown by her frequent linkage of wildness with women in *A Room of One's Own*,[4] with the movement of the 'essayistic' and its resistance to fixity, and with the freedom of words themselves.

Given the pervasive contradictory nature of Woolf's writing, readers will also perceive the seriousness that underpins *Orlando*'s unusually long and complex chronological trajectory. Against this background, I will also argue that in this hybrid text, there are multiple intertextual connections with one of Woolf's favourite writers: the sixteenth-century creator of the essay, Michel de Montaigne. I will show how the politics of the essayistic mode resonates with a politics of inconclusiveness in the writings of both Montaigne and Woolf. The essayistic mode is defined notably by its movement, openness and resistance to totality and systems; it also has links with being 'other', hybrid and wild, and has frequently been called an 'anti-genre'.[5] Given its many resonances with *Orlando*, Woolf's 1925 essay 'Montaigne' will be an important resource for this study. Montaigne's scepticism about the possibility of knowing people or things with any degree of certainty is encapsulated in his motto 'Que sais-je?' – just as the questioning of identity pervades *Orlando*. I will also allude to Walter Pater's analysis of Montaigne's essayistic mode,[6] Gertrude Stein's use of lists in 'Composition as Explanation',[7] and Laurence Sterne's black, blank, and mosaic pages in *Tristram Shandy*.[8] Lastly, I focus on the spatial elements in *Orlando*, as they offer readers the freedom to fill in the unknown and the inconclusive space; this is achieved with a partially blank page (O 165) – a bow to Sterne that adds to the multitude of ellipses in Woolf's text. With this in mind, I will attend specifically to the word 'vast': a word that has been closely linked with Baudelaire,[9] but which also seems to have a special place in Woolf's lexicon. Although it appears only once in my selected sentence, the word 'vast' is repeated twenty-six times throughout *Orlando*, and this adds another layer to the novel's complex politics of inconclusiveness. As we shall see, these intertexts resonate in differing ways with questions regarding the referentiality of language, connections between the verbal and visual, and, ultimately, the individual freedom to imagine and create – or to resist.

My chosen sentence involves repetitions and a list, and enacts the wildness that Woolf links with satire in her diary entry on *Orlando*. Wildness is evident in the reader's freedom to create within this unusually structured sentence; each iteration of the word 'next' suggests sequentiality, but we quickly grasp the ironic trajectory of these interim conclusions. Although readers know that the narrator has decided on 'six lines the length of this one', they are not counting; they are engaged and awaiting the 'final conclusion', whose sudden omission is clearly mitigated by its comedic aspects. With the elision of her final conclusion Orlando stands 'looking out of the window for a considerable space of time', and we are given an important explanation: 'when anybody comes to a conclusion it is as if they had tossed the ball over the net and must wait for the unseen antagonist to return it to them' (*O* 191). This tennis analogy echoes Montaigne's very modern reader-response theory, which involves the complex relationship between writer and reader, as well as the openness inherent in these dialogic transactions:

> Speech belongs half to the speaker, half to the listener. The latter must prepare to receive it according to the motion it takes. As among tennis players, the receiver moves and makes ready according to the motion of the striker and the nature of the stroke.[10]

Woolf's narrator alludes to 'half the process of reading' as described in 'How Should One Read a Book?' (1932; *E5* 579), which reflects Montaigne's reading process, and, like the theories of Roland Barthes and Mikhail Bakhtin, extols the reader's role in co-creating the text.[11] Returning to my selected sentence, however, we are immediately struck, as readers, by the repetitive presence of the number six. The appearance of this number in Chapter VI, with the word 'next' repeated six times in six clauses, must cause readers to ask: why six? The number six was considered by the Greeks to be one of the rare perfect numbers and has links with biblical and mythological references.[12] Perhaps the perfection of a number was attractive for Woolf's purpose of undermining that kind of certitude. References to precision and exactitude act as red flags in many of Woolf's works, since she privileges openness and freedom – things that cannot be quantified – and resists any semblance of perfection, rigidity or labels. But counting is pervasive in *Orlando*, and includes things as disparate as selves, tedious lists, inventories and age, to name a few.

The repetition within this sentence is accentuated by its embedded list, and resonates with the multitude of lists in *Orlando*. Woolf was writing *Orlando* in 1927, after Gertrude Stein had presented her talk 'Composition as Explanation' at Cambridge and Oxford in 1925. Stein's work, with its references to lists and series, was published by Leonard and Virginia Woolf's Hogarth Press in 1926, and one is not surprised to find many lists reproduced in *Orlando*. The list is structurally significant because it doesn't conclude; it is not hierarchical; it can simply go on forever. As Stein's narrator states in 'Composition as Explanation', 'by lists I mean a series'.[13] This confusing pairing is explored by Rachel Blau DuPlessis: 'Lists and series are really different. With lists the order doesn't matter; with a series it does. Lists are flat; series have shapes'.[14] The repetition in this sentence, like Stein's 'beginning again and again',[15] also serves to draw attention to the materiality of the word, and 'to the condition of its visibility'.[16] Given Woolf's focus on the visual aspects of language, it is revealing to find that so many other lists throughout

Orlando show links to Stein's 'experiments with the signifying capacities of words'.[17] While Woolf's innovative narrative techniques in *Orlando* echo Stein's experimental style, manifest in the playful lists permeating this text,[18] they also enact a resistance to conventional narrative modes, distancing readers as they react to these unusual strategies. In her biography of Roger Fry (1940), Woolf quotes part of a list compiled by Fry's mother. Her list consists of two categories: 'things that were not' and 'things that were'. Significantly, Woolf adds that Lady Fry 'drew no conclusion', 'and it is left for us to infer that there were more denials than delights, more austerities than luxuries in the life of the little Quaker girl' (*RF* 17). As Bowlby observes, 'precisely because [the list] offers "no conclusion", Lady Fry's list is rich in suggestions for ways of thinking about the representation of historical change and the significance of "things" in a biographical story'.[19] Importantly, Woolf's readers decide how the list is to be interpreted, as we determine how to integrate the many lists in *Orlando*.

Along with questions regarding lists, many formidable questions regarding history, identity and class also permeate *Orlando*: 'What is an "age", indeed? What are we?' (*O* 134). It is during the eighteenth century, when Orlando is serving Alexander Pope tea in her role as patron, that she thinks about 'how women in ages to come will envy me' (*O* 139); but the biographer also intrudes to inform the reader that Orlando 'had a positive hatred for tea', and perhaps for Pope's derogatory writings about women. Pope's mention of a famous line from his 'Of the Characters of Women' (1735), specifically repeated in *A Room of One's Own* – 'most women have no character at all'[20] – drives her to 'let the sugar fall with a great plop [. . .] into Mr. Pope's tea' (*O* 140). The tea scenes from Chapter VI are reprised in my sentence, but this time with Christina Rossetti. One reason why 'it would be impolitic in the extreme to wrap a ten-pound note round the sugar tongs' when Rossetti is at tea might be that such a gesture would denigrate a woman poet who reportedly earned that yearly amount. This successful poet from a financially poor family is the subject of Woolf's essay '"I am Christina Rossetti"' (1930); while Woolf's narrator relates her financial, religious and personal difficulties, the essay's title echoes the poet's confidence as she takes centre stage to announce herself. Rossetti's talent is opposed to the 'peeress' depicted in my sentence, for the facade of 'fur tippets' and respectability are surely satirised.

Interposed between the different worlds of these two women – Rossetti and the peeress – the subject of 'influence' arises; intersecting with questions of authority, it also touches on the function of lists, for lists do not dictate to readers. Woolf, who disliked lecturing (or any authoritarian stance), also had a problem with literary and intellectual influence, although her spoof Preface, quite ironically, is filled with many canonical authors who have influenced her writings. It is no surprise, then, to find the idea of influence satirised in my sentence. Invited to 'a score of lectures upon the Influence of this upon that', Orlando reflects that 'literature must be growing very dry', and Woolf's capitalisation of 'Influence' is ironically juxtaposed to some seriously insignificant things – 'this upon that'. This interrogation of the word 'influence' continues in Woolf's manifestos *A Room of One's Own* and *Three Guineas*, both of which foreground the gender politics of cultural and literary influence. I would add that literary genres are categories that establish limits and restrictions, and given their patriarchal legacy, they tamper with the woman writer's freedom to innovate. However, by writing a novel and subtitling it *A Biography*, Woolf hybridises the text, thereby resisting the confines of each genre and providing an inconclusiveness that expands the textual encounter. Indeed, her resistance to labels – which also impede the creative process – pervades her writings.[21]

The last point in the list composing my chosen sentence deals with Orlando's visit to Carlyle's soundproof room at Chelsea, and we know from Woolf's own visits that Carlyle could not work with the noise of the city, and that the room did not function properly.[22] This is contrasted with the fictional writer Nick Greene's problem with silence, and his strong need for ambient noise in order to create. During this transitional Victorian period, artists and writers had to utilise their homes for work, and the home was becoming a more feminised space, a place for women, while 'street noise challenged this territorial concern at its problematic core'.[23] The creative man – like Carlyle – needed to create a masculinised space to write, but this was hindered by Jane Carlyle's household duties that became inside noise. As John M. Picker notes: Victorian men 'were beginning to endorse gendered conceptions of levels of sound. Women were increasingly socialised as the quieter if not the silent sex, while bravura noise-making was an essential masculine identity for much of this era'.[24] Woolf's sentence shows that given these restrictive codes, the desire for the freedom to create and experiment was clearly gendered.

Following the reference to Carlyle, the narrator's arbitrary decision to set up a ridiculous binary for concluding almost echoes the gendered differences restricting the freedom of women's artistic endeavour. One cannot help but think of the famous but less humorous refusal to come to a conclusion in *A Room of One's Own*:

> I should never be able to come to a conclusion. I should never be able to fulfill what is, I understand, the first duty of a lecturer – to hand you after an hour's

discourse a nugget of pure truth to wrap between the pages of your notebook and keep on the mantelpiece forever. (*AROO* 6)

In conjunction with the problematics of gender surrounding this notion of a lecturer's duty, the reader focuses on that 'nugget of pure truth', for we know that it does not exist, and that Woolf would never offer it. Interestingly, the opening of *Orlando*'s second chapter similarly undermines 'truth' with a reference to 'the first duty of a biographer', 'which is to plod, without looking to the right or the left, in the indelible footprints of truth' (*O* 42). As we learn from Woolf's review of Harold Nicolson's *Some People*, 'The New Biography' (1927):

> Truth of fact and truth of fiction are incompatible; yet [the biographer] is now more than ever urged to combine them. For it would seem that the life which is increasingly real to us is the fictitious life; it dwells in personality rather than in the act. (*E4* 478)

Woolf suggests that there must be a balance between fact and fiction: that while the biographer may use 'the novelist's art of arrangement, suggestion, dramatic effect to expound the private life', he risks thereby carrying 'the use of fiction too far, so that he disregards the truth [. . .] he has neither the freedom of fiction not the substance of fact' (*E4* 478). She finds it difficult to name a biographer able 'to present that queer amalgamation of dream and reality [. . .] of granite and rainbow' (ibid.), but stresses that the modern biographer 'chooses; he synthesizes; in short, he had ceased to be a chronicler; he has become an artist' (*E4* 475).

In another essay from 1927, 'Poetry, Fiction and the Future', Woolf asks: 'must the duty of the critic always be to the past, must his gaze always be fixed backward?' (*E4* 429). There is a great desire to speculate,

> for this is an age clearly when we are not fast anchored where we are; things are moving round us; we are moving ourselves. Is it not the critic's duty to tell us, or to guess at least, where we are going? (*E4* 429)

However, at the height of the modernist period, this desire to know and pinpoint the literary directions of the future is thwarted, for as readers, we must deal with much doubt and remain in an unsettled state where 'everything, in fact, was something else' (*O* 94). And so Montaigne's trenchant question – 'Que sais-je?' – seems to be an important subtextual presence for many of Woolf's writings during this period.

As Dudley Marchi points out, 'the fluid contours of Montaigne's *Essays*, as well as those from *Orlando*, are so suggestive that they never produce unequivocal meanings and demand constant interaction on the part of the reader'.[25] Montaigne's essayistic mode of writing is defined by its indefiniteness and its resistance to the constrictions of social institutions. Walter Pater, who is referenced in the novel's Preface, 'identifies Montaigne's essays with the dialectic method of Plato's dialogues' and finds that 'there will always be much of accident in this essentially informal, this unmethodical method'.[26] Considered a true sceptic, Montaigne 'suspects that certain knowledge is unattainable through reason', and 'mocks human pretensions to systematic knowledge'.[27] As Montaigne himself states: 'I do not see the whole of anything': 'Nor do those who promise to show it to us'.[28] *Orlando* is only one of Woolf's many texts that subvert genre – and in this case subversion involves 'the satire of the patriarchal convention of biography, a genre in which she believed one can never fully capture the inexpressible particularities of human experience, as Montaigne would claim, but only pursue them'.[29] As Montaigne asserts:

> The world is but perennial movement. All things in it are in constant motion [. . .] I cannot keep my subject still [. . .] I do not portray his being: I portray passing. Not passing from one age to another [. . .] but from day to day, from minute to minute [. . .] If my mind could gain a firm footing, I would not make essays, I would make decisions; but it is always in apprenticeship and on trial.[30]

Montaigne feels his mind is always in a provisional state, always at risk, and not knowing what it needs to know; therefore, he cannot make a decision, or come to a conclusion.

Woolf's essay 'Montaigne' provides a vivid account of his modern aesthetics and politics, and reveals his significance for her work; there seem to be many important links between the depictions of Orlando and Montaigne's persona in his *Essays*. In 'Montaigne', the narrative voice and Montaigne's words get confused and are easily conflated. One is not always certain who is speaking. Reading and comparing these texts show how Montaigne's *Essays* inform *Orlando*, which is evident in the affinities between their politics and style, and in the essayistic mode characterising Woolf's provocative sentences. Her narrator also enacts what Montaigne's persona states regarding his language: 'my language has no ease or polish; it is harsh and disdainful, with a free and unruly disposition'.[31] 'My conceptions and my judgment', he observes, 'move only by groping, staggering, stumbling, and blundering', and so 'I let my thoughts run on'.[32] Elsewhere Montaigne writes: 'My understanding does not always go forward, it goes backward too' in 'a drunkard's motion, staggering, dizzy, wobbling, or that of reeds that the wind stirs haphazardly as it pleases'.[33] The essayistic mode in *Orlando* produces a similarly 'discontinuous narrative adventure', as Marchi points out,[34] in line with Woolf's early notion of the novel as 'an escapade; the spirit to be satiric, the structure wild [. . .] half laughing, half serious: with great splashes of exaggeration' (D3 167-8). Woolf's 'Montaigne' also echoes her ideas for *Orlando*: 'let us [. . .] fling out the wildest nonsense, and follow the most fantastic fancies without caring what the world does or thinks or says' (E4 75). This passage can be linked with the advice given in Woolf's essay 'How Should One Read a Book?': in speaking about the 'duty of the reader', Woolf encourages us not to defer to authorities, but to 'come to [our] own conclusions' (E5 573).

Among the multiple connections between Montaigne's and Woolf's essayistic adventures, Woolf's 'Montaigne' perhaps expresses some of their most difficult desires and goals: 'Communication is health; communication is truth; communication is happiness' (E4 76). This also brings in the need, so important in writing a life, 'to conceal nothing; to pretend nothing' (E4 77), but 'truth' is, of course, problematic. Readers sometimes contribute to that 'truth', as we note in *Orlando*'s tip of a hat to Laurence Sterne's black, blank, and marbled pages in *Tristram Shandy*. The presence of a blank space, situated in Chapter V and measuring five typed lines, is not unrelated to the subject of inconclusiveness. Here we have a blank canvas, a small space that engages the freedom of Woolf's readers to use their imagination. We recall her observation, in 'The New Biography', that the 'biographer's imagination is always being stimulated to use the novelist's art of arrangement, suggestion, dramatic effect' (E4 478). The rigid, singular path, the straight line that was the duty of the Victorian biographer to navigate, is gone; the modern biographer gives us an artist's rendering of a life. This recalls the claim that for Montaigne, 'rigidity is death, conformity is death': 'let us say what comes into our heads' (E4 75). Woolf's rejection of categories, definitions and certainties leads to the openness that is privileged in *Orlando*. The possibilities are endless, and perhaps that is the point.

The numerous signifying acts of omission, the many ellipses, Sterne's two black marbled pages, the contradictory and equivocal passages inviting the reader to make decisions – even if provisional – and, importantly, the pervasive use of the word 'vast' in so many varied contexts, all play a crucial role in this satirical work. My sentence has one mention of 'vast', and it refers to 'a vast pile on memoirs' delivered with Orlando's book order, meant to include the best of Victorian literature. In other places in the novel, one finds 'the vast congeries of rooms' (O 12); 'the deserts of vast eternity' (O 64); 'this vast, yet ordered building, which could house a thousand men and perhaps 2000 horses, was built, Orlando thought, by workmen whose names are unknown' (O 69); 'the vast cathedral' (O 105); and the 'vast empty hills' (O 114). These few examples lead to thoughts about how all of these references to vastness function in the context of inconclusiveness. In *The Poetics of Space*, Gaston Bachelard speaks of distance, of 'hidden grandeur' and 'images of immensity';[35] he also relates these images to daydreams – at times 'the movement of a motionless man'.[36] In following, the daydreams that the single word 'vast' inspired in Baudelaire, Bachelard suggests that this word marks the 'infinity of intimate space'.[37] Calling 'vast' 'one of the most Baudelairean words', he finds that, as with Woolf's use of this word in *Orlando*, it often has a very ordinary meaning; in my sentence it refers to 'a vast pile of memoirs', but in its other references 'it opens up unlimited space'.[38] The repetitive use of the word 'vast' in *Orlando* offers differing visions of the spatial openness and freedom that this word enacts. Like the other words that reflect inconclusiveness, the word 'vast' – in its spatial openness – is a call for freedom as it provokes the imagination, creativity and risk.

Ultimately, Woolf's use of the essayistic mode, alongside varied lists, provides the necessary suggestiveness to risk new trajectories, new spaces and transformative identities. Her narrative practice in *Orlando* looks back to the richness of her essay 'Montaigne', and to his 'unmethodical method'; it is in this essay that Woolf's narrator resists any 'obligation to others', and expresses the significance of 'our enthralling confusion, our hotchpotch of impulses, our perpetual miracle' (E4 75). This is the 'wildness' that Virginia Woolf imbeds in the narrative of *Orlando*.

Notes

1. Virginia Woolf, *Orlando: A Biography* [1928] (New York: New American Library, 1956), p. 190.
2. Rachel Bowlby, *Feminist Destinations* (London: Basil Blackwell, 1988), p. 133.
3. See Martha Vicinus (ed.), *Suffer and Be Still: Women in the Victorian Age* (Bloomington: Indiana University Press, 1972).
4. See Judith Allen, *Virginia Woolf and the Politics of Language* (Edinburgh: Edinburgh University Press, 2010), pp. 65–84.
5. See Judith Allen, *Virginia Woolf: Walking in the Footsteps of Michel de Montaigne* (London: Cecil Woolf, 2012), p. 11.
6. Walter Pater, *Plato and Platonism* (London: Macmillan, 1912), pp. 185–6.
7. Gertrude Stein, 'Composition as Explanation', in G. Stein, *What are Masterpieces?* (New York: Pitman Publishing, 1940), pp. 23–38.
8. Laurence Sterne, *The Life and Opinions of Tristram Shandy: Gent.* (New York: Oxford University Press, 1983), p. 181.
9. Charles Baudelaire, 'Intimate Immensity', cited in Gaston Bachelard,

The Poetics of Space, trans. Maria Jolas (Boston: Beacon Press, 1969), pp. 183–210.
10. Michel de Montaigne, *The Complete Essays of Montaigne*, trans. Donald M. Frame (Stanford: Stanford University Press, 1965), III: 13, p. 834. The 1965 Frame edition is divided into three books, and all references to the *Essays* are in the following form: book, chapter, and page number.
11. See Roland Barthes, 'From Work to Text', in R. Barthes, *Image, Music, Text*, trans. Stephen Heath (London: Fontana, 1977), pp. 155–64; Mikhail Bakhtin, *The Dialogic Imagination: Four Essays*, trans. Caryl Emerson and Michael Holquist (Austin: University of Texas Press, 1981).
12. A perfect number is a positive integer that is equal to the sum of its proper divisors. The smallest perfect number is six, which is the sum of 1, 2 and 3.
13. Stein, 'Composition', pp. 23–38.
14. Rachel Blau DuPlessis, 'Woolfenstein, the Sequel', in Janet Boyd and Sharon J. Kirsch (eds), *Primary Stein: Returning to the Writing of Gertrude Stein* (Plymouth: Lexington Books, 2014), pp. 37–56.
15. Ibid. p. 47.
16. Jo Anna Isaak, 'The Revolutionary Power of a Woman's Laughter', in Richard Kostelanetz (ed.), *Gertrude Stein Advanced: An Anthology of Criticism* (London: McFarland & Company, 1990), p. 26.
17. Ibid. p. 29. As Isaak observes, Stein's lists in 'How to Write' (1931) resemble Tristan Tzara's techniques for writing a Dadaist poem.
18. Varied lists are found on the following pages of *Orlando*: 35, 70–1, 151, 184, 196, 200, 202–3.
19. Bowlby, *Feminist Destinations*, p. 118.
20. As Susan Gubar notes, Pope's line here comes from one of his *Moral Essays*, 'Of the Characters of Women'. The line appears at the beginning of his poem, and the work ends praising woman as 'a softer Man'. V. Woolf, *A Room of One's Own* [1929], annotated and intro. Susan Gubar (Orlando: Harcourt, 2005), p. 122.
21. In Woolf's *Three Guineas*, the word 'feminist' is burned because it is construed as a label. See Berenice A. Carroll, '"To Crush Him in Our Own Country": The Political Thought of Virginia Woolf', *Feminist Studies*, 4.1 (1978), pp. 99–131.
22. Woolf made four visits to Carlyle's house. See her essay 'Great Men's Houses' (1932), *E5*, pp. 294–300. See also V. Woolf, *Virginia Woolf: Carlyle's House and Other Sketches*, ed. David Bradshaw (London: Hesperus, 2003).
23. Peter Bailey, *Breaking the Sound Barrier* (Cambridge: Cambridge University Press, 1998), quoted in John M. Picker, 'The Soundproof Study', *Victorian Studies*, 42.3 (Spring 1999/2000), p. 435.
24. Ibid. p. 209.
25. Dudley M. Marchi, 'Virginia Woolf Crossing the Borders of History, Culture, and Gender: The Case of Montaigne, Pater, and Gournay', *Comparative Literature Studies*, 34.1 (1997), p. 20.
26. R. Lane Kauffman, 'Essaying as Unmethodical Method', in Alexander J. Butrym (ed.), *Essays on the Essay: Redefining the Genre* (Athens: University of Georgia Press, 1989), pp. 221–40. Kauffmann quotes Pater's *Plato and Platonism*, pp. 185–6.

27. Ibid. p. 224.
28. Montaigne, *Essays*, I: 50, p. 219.
29. Marchi, 'Virginia Woolf', p. 17.
30. Montaigne, *Essays*, III: 2, pp. 610–11.
31. Montaigne, *Essays*, II: 17, p. 483.
32. Ibid. I: 26, p. 107.
33. Ibid. III: 9, p. 736.
34. Marchi, 'Virginia Woolf', p. 17.
35. Bachelard, *The Poetics of Space*, pp. 186, 190.
36. Ibid. p. 184.
37. Ibid. p. 197.
38. Ibid.

Aftersentence

Rachel Bowlby

How many sentences does it take to change Orlando? Or – how many to make *Orlando*? Even in this present age of digital marvels, post-*Orlando* though probably not post-Orlando, those might not be straightforward questions to answer. Word counts are the everyday background of writing (just click on the tool or look at the bottom of the screen). Distracting, depressing, whatever. But sentence counts? Unknown. That might be because a sentence, for all its supposed simplicity of appearance and definition – the upper-case start, the full-stop end; the subject and the indicative verb – is a little more doubtful a being than a word.

Like the one I just wrote.

Or like this!

Or, like Orlando's three-word incantation, on her final-day visit to the London department store, Marshall & Snelgrove's: 'boys' boots, bath salts, sardines'.[1] It's clamped between dashes, a mini-citation in the middle of a proper sentence, and it's evidently not – so we later learn – a complete recitation of the text that she holds in her hands. Later, the one thing she does buy, just because it is there (on the list) and there (where she happens to be in the store), is bed linen: 'And indeed, she was about to descend again, without buying anything, but was saved from that outrage by saying aloud automatically the last item on her list, which happened to be "sheets for a double bed"' (*O* 287).

A list is not a sentence (though 'A list is not a sentence' is). But other than a few gleanings from her (and his) poem 'The Oak Tree', this minimal shopping list is *Orlando*'s only example or sample of Orlando's writing. Boys' boots, bath salts, sardines. Oh, and sheets for a double bed. Canonical, clearly.

But let's look into it a little further. For some reason, Orlando has decided to buy these various things in a grand store in the centre of London. Well, each to his own. Or hers. The sheets, sure, yes, you could understand. Only the best for a stately home. Especially when they haven't been changed for hundreds of years. But sardines? What's wrong with the local shops? Later, she even passes through the town on her car journey home from London. There's talk on the narrator's part of market day and mention, even, of the fishmonger's, can you believe (O 298). Some in-joke, apparently, about Vita and her legs in the fish shop in Sevenoaks. Footnote needed. Legnote.

But I digress. Like Orlando. Wrong turning. Well no, nothing like Orlando. She knows her way, odd as it may be. List or no list. Never puts a foot wrong. Even if she does forget all about the sardines. Assuming she really wanted them in the first place, and the list wasn't just an excuse. Something to do. The writing of it. Then the doing of it. The shopping. The list as staying alive. Keeping on going. Through the day. Through the centuries. That's our Orlando!

So anyway, there we have it. Orlando, complete extant works. Or fragment thereof. Some lines of the poem. Plus boys' boots, bath salts, sardines. And/or sheets for a double bed.

Nothing to speak of. Not even a decent sentence.

But while we're on the subject of shops and such in Virginia Woolf novels. (Which we are.) Quite a few of those, actually – you could make a list. I won't. But for instance. That other novel that happens just down the road from where Orlando's standing. Practically the same time, too, given all of Orlando's years. June 1923. As against October 1928. And bang into shopping, very first sentence. So here's a sentence that's not there but might have been:

The Lady Orlando said she would buy the sheets herself.

Immediately followed by:

For Louise had her work cut out for her.

Louise, you remember? – the servant who's found a hole in the linen after all these ages, not worth darning even, presumably, and so that's the reason for buying replacements. Never mentioned before. Just once after. Compared with whom Mrs D.'s Lucy is virtually a star. Best supporting at least. But Orlando a lot grander than Mrs D. Hundreds of servants, not just the one Lucy or Louise.

But back to the shop. Because why would Orlando be buying this stuff in person? It's not as if she's any kind of expert in the linen department. Let alone the fish. Boots we don't know. At least Mrs D. knows her flowers. Knows the shop. Knows the woman who runs it, even. But Orlando, she just randomly asks a random person for sheets. Just happens to have fetched up in the exactly correct spot in the very big shop. Magic. Pure chance. As for the rest of the stuff on the list – forget it. The bath salts – feminine pleasure, think Mrs D. and the flowers. Ladylike thing to buy is what I mean. The boys' boots – well why would she be buying them without the boy or boys to be fitted. Vita had a couple (of boys), so possibly some joke there. Who cares. Anyway she doesn't (buy them). Just seems to abandon the lot, I mean these other things, the plan of buying them, once she's ticked the sheets off. Metaphorically speaking. Admittedly the most important thing – even though the last. On the list. But even so. Funny way to behave. Not rational. When she's bothered to make a list. Which frankly, not really what you expect from O. Given the performance to date. I mean, household management, management in general, planning stuff. Not really her thing. Not his, either, back in the day.

To be fair though you could have the opposite interpretation of this. The list thing. Because we don't just get the thing quoted – well, bits of it. We also get a whole little theory of lists, the list, the shopping list, whatever. I know, how crazy is that? In a Virginia Woolf novel. But really. I mean it. I'll show you. The actual sentence no couple of sentences if I can find it yes here it is and I quote:

> 'Any napkins, towels, dusters to-day, Ma'am?' the shopman persisted. And it is enormously to the credit of the shopping list, which Orlando now consulted, that she was able to reply with every appearance of composure, that there was only one thing in the world she wanted and that was bath salts; which was in another department. (O 289–90)

Ironic. Of course. Odd passage though for a novel. Especially one of hers. As I've said. Almost a textbook, sensible shopping. Tips for the modern consumer. Late 1920s, not impossible historically. Number one, make a list. Number two, stick to it. Especially with the pushy assistant – comes in handy then.

Lots of wavy green lines under the words I'm typing. Pretty! Means they're not sentences. Haha. That was the idea. Ooops.

Anyway, upwards & onwards, marshall & snelgrove, out of the shop & on to the road. I'll just have a quick coffee if you don't mind. While we're waiting for Orlando to start up her motor car. Not that there's anywhere to get it round here in 1928. Decades and decades to wait. But that's blink of an eye, mere squirt of the foam, in *Orlando* time. 2017, there'll be Addison and Pope on show in a Costa. As per.

Dare say you could do with a break as well. From all this shopping nonsense nonsentences. Don't know quite how we got off on that track.

*

Well so but now let me say something about this actual book. This book that you've just been reading, I mean. The one about the sentences, not the one that the sentences come from.

So there's this one chapter. Starts off like they all do with the one sentence of *Orlando*. The special selected sentence served up for analysis commentary discussion in matters modernistical syntactical and every which way educational – as advertised promised elucidated horizontally vertically consubstantially in the Introduction.

They all, all the writers, go off in different directions after doing that – after sticking their very own sentence down. What Steven Putzel does is he tells us a story of something he did with his sentence once he had chosen it. What he did was he sent it. Sent it, yes, like you might send a parcel or a payment or I don't know, your love. And he didn't just send it, like, hey, here's a Send button, let's press Send. No. He had a purpose. He had recipients. Number unspecified, generic identity very much specified. 'My first step in examining the sentence', he says, 'was to send it to a few grammarians'.

My first step. To send it to a few grammarians. Have you ever knowingly encountered a grammarian? In the flesh? In a suit? In a sentence? In a nutshell? Would you know one if you saw one? Are they wholly respectable? Do you have one in your address book? Or even a few? Obviously, it's not quite like having a GP or a lover or a lawyer – you get to have several at once.

A mailing moment of pure sentential perfection. Only a little less sublime the comedy that follows, perfectly paced by our witty correspondent. Because the grammarians, no doubt following some tribal rule for how to do things with sentences, write back. Says Putzel: 'Reading one of the responses, I realised I had neglected to reveal that Woolf was the author. I was firmly told: "I suggest you rewrite the sentence".'

Now it's true – it cannot be denied – that the sent sentence may not represent Virginia Woolf's finest grammatical hour. Nevertheless, it was chosen. Nevertheless, it was sent to 'a few grammarians'. And nevertheless, he didn't say, he *neglected to reveal* that the sentence happened to have been written by Woolf. What might the grammarians have thought, singly or plurally, alone or a few, when they opened their messages and found that particular sentence (or non-sentence) in it? Just sitting there, lying there, flat or round, Calibri or basic old Times New Roman, however it happened to be dressed that morning. Authorless. We presume. Doing its ungrammatical exercises, or whatever it is that sentences do when they're not being looked at. What did they think they were meant to do with the thing?

Seemingly, it was a sentence unsuited for a grammarian's use. 'I suggest you rewrite the sentence'. Withering! But then again, what a chance for Virginia! Send it all the way back to her! Because while she's about it, why stop at the sentence? Why not rewrite a few more things too? How about History! Biography! Sex! Oh, and Gender, of course! Good old-fashioned gender as they knew it in those *Orlando* days. Proper grammatical gender: 'He (for there could be no doubt of his sex)' . . .

So Steven Putzel's sentence is chosen and set down and sent and returned. But what of the other lucky phrases? There they sit, each one of them, at the top of the page at the start of their own personal chapter, kept apart from each other and patiently hosting their own individual commentaries. But they can't talk back. It's the curious double aspect of their situation. A sentence is a sentence is a sentence: set in type, fixed for all time. And yet a sentence is transposable to any context and any medium, old or new, here or there. It can go from print back to handwritten page, copied out as a quote – for pleasure or for revision. (Yes – *Orlando* has done its time and had its moments, unevenly, as a set text for school exams; it was on an A-level syllabus already by the start of the 1960s.)[2] Or it can pop up on a tiny screen, a smartphone or a laptop. It can be spoken aloud when someone is giving a lecture – or just for the relishing. Copied or reprinted it can shape itself into any typeface, any format, any quality of paper. You can sew it on a tapestry, paint it on a poster, spray it on a cake, why not? But it will always remain the same words in the same order, the sentence, the whole sentence, and nothing but the sentence. Because that's what it is: a published sentence. It changes and changes, everywhere and all the time, it travels from paper to screen to spoken word, from new edition to student essay to random citation and even, in these sixteen special cases, to the volume that you are presently reading. It means what it means, depending on where it's fetched up and who's reading it and when and why. And it is also everywhere and forever the same sentence.

All the *Orlando* sentences chosen for this book have been given a rare status: pulled out and put in a prominent position, honoured with many further sentences that refer to them. But as Elsa Högberg and Amy Bromley point out in their Introduction, *Orlando* has been – as Woolf's novels go – a lot less studied. Many of the contributions demonstrate how much scholarly potential there is in these pages which till now for the most part have mainly been treated as a fast-moving exercise in subversive comedy (with a seriously critical edge). Reading the present book, we come to see an *Orlando* steeped in religion and philosophy and ancient history (even if Orlando isn't): an *Orlando* whose conscious allusions go far beyond the adoring jokes about Vita Sackville-West, her aristocratic history and her domestic and erotic dilections. Several essays intricately unpick many literary intertexts – Eliot, Joyce, Stein; De Quincey or Browne – that are woven into *Orlando* along with Woolf's parody of what she referred to as her own 'lyrical vein'. Many of these new critical sentences, the sentences about Woolf's sentences, are models of precision and elegance in their own right; no grammarian, past or present, could send them back for a rewrite, and many will surely be quoted on other pages, in other textual places, in the future.

Some of the essays – and not only the ones about sex or queens – are written not just for the critical pros but for anyone, all-comers. Just as *Orlando* itself was, an instant bestseller: a fun read even if you know none of the background stuff, whether the gossip or the literary history. And some of the essays are paragons of the scholarly, expertly conducting their readers through remotenesses of the rhetorical landscapes that underlie the surface words of *Orlando*. (Anadiplosis, anyone? It enters naturally into Jane de Gay's piece. And it's not a dinosaur, that much I can tell you.)

Orlando is open to all. But despite the proliferation of writings about its author and her other books, the critical guides to this one have been slower to emerge. This must be partly because of the novel's status or role in Woolf's oeuvre as the book of light relief from weightier projects with longer-lasting ambitions. It was only ever expected to be ephemeral: to glow with the shortlived success of the current bestseller that it did indeed become. It had its day.

But as Bryony Randall suggests, with her focus on the particular, multifaceted day at the end of the book, long in page-length, short in actual time, that indeterminacy is crucial to this novel. This last *Orlando* day in the first part of the twentieth century takes up a wholly disproportionate space in a narrative that's gone through four centuries to get to it. By my rough calculation, it occupies more than ten percent of *Orlando*. But in real time, one day out of just one year is less than a third of one percent; out of 400 it comes out as the unimaginably tiny 0.0007%. If time can slow down to this degree – giving more than a tenth of the space to less than a thousandth of the time – then why would it ever start up again? Why not remain always settled in that poised afternoon of 11 October, 1928? Happily paused between town and country, between youth and middle age: Orlando is thirty-six. No reason to travel further, out of the casual enjoyable day and into the history of the future – and especially not, perhaps, into the world of 2017 and beyond (though Orlando, I think, voted Brexit).

But Orlando need not go anywhere to move, or be moved with, the times. In 1928, arriving back at her country seat, she is already a part of an ongoing English heritage. Her homecoming after all these years – for *Orlando* is also, with so much else, an extended *Odyssey* – takes her into historic rooms with a sentence now pinned to their furniture: 'Please do not touch'; she reflects that her home is no longer completely hers. After the war, the Sackville-Wests' real-life Knole in Sevenoaks would be partly acquired by the National Trust; in Woolf's novel, the place of Orlando's occupation has already been opened up. These days, if you pay the price of admission you can walk around almost as if you owned the place, as long as you stay on the public side of the rope and don't touch anything.

This is the careful treatment allowed for the physical contents and surface décor, the chairs and the pictures and ornaments of Knole. Not so differently do we deal with *Orlando*'s sentences when we look at them and write about them (but never, grammarians take note, dare to mend or improve them) many years after their time. We may carry them over onto some current concern, as self-contained blocks of sense or suggestion to bolster an argument. (At one time, not so long ago, *Orlando*'s sentences about whether the clothes wear us or we them were the go-to quote for an anti-essentialist line; but those days, and that argument, are gone.) We may quote for the sheer enjoyment of their composition: there's plenty of that sort of sentence in *Orlando*. Or – and as most of the essays do here – we may situate them and celebrate them and search and explain their connections to the sentences of all the writers and times in the wealth of Woolf's reading and thinking.

The possibilities for the future, the sentences for the sentences: endless. Like Orlando's life. But unlike Orlando's book. Or this one.

22 March 2017

Notes

1. Virginia Woolf, *Orlando: A Biography* [1928], ed. Rachel Bowlby (Oxford: Oxford University Press, World's Classics, 1992), p. 286.
2. Thanks to Alan Sinfield for this information. He studied *Orlando* for A level with the JMB (Joint Matriculation Board of the Universities of Manchester, Liverpool, Leeds, Sheffield and Birmingham).

Index

abstraction, 45, 73, 76, 81, 88, 90, 99, 104
aestheticism, 62–174
Agamben, Giorgio, definition of 'contemporariness', 113
allegory, 92–103, 194
Alt, Christina, 83
ambition, 106–10, 123, 129
   creative, 25, 94, 107, 121, 215
anachronism, 62–6, 97, 135, 144
analepsis, 57, 60–5
ancestors, 21–9
   ancestral home, 21–9, 33, 39, 44, 64, 84, 130, 132; *see also* Knole
androgyny, 36–7, 42, 65–6, 112, 136, 147, 188, 195, 196
anonymity, 63, 66, 110–11, 124; *see also* Woolf, Virginia, ESSAYS: 'Anon'
Arendt, Hannah, on 'immortal fame', 112
Ariosto, Ludovico, *Orlando Furioso*, 107
Arnold, Matthew, 'The Scholar Gipsy', 96
atheism, 93, 165
Austen, Jane, 58, 71, 182
   and the sentence in *A Room of One's Own*, 58
autobiography, 45, 162, 178–9; *see also* Woolf, Virginia, ESSAYS: 'De Quincey's Autobiography'

Bachelard, Gaston, 207
Bakhtin, Mikhail, 69, 77, 153, 154, 201

ballads, 63
   'The Four Maries', 21
Banfield, Ann, 7, 76
Barthes, Roland, 151–61, 201
   A Lover's Discourse: Fragments, 151–61
   on the sentence, 154
Battershill, Claire, 120
Baudelaire, Charles 200, 207
Bazargan, Susan, 95–6
Beer, Gillian, 21, 116, 189–90
Bell, Vanessa
   illustrations for *Kew Gardens* (1927), 123–4
   as Vanessa Stephen, 80
Benjamin, Walter, 113; *see also* Spiropoulou, Angeliki
Bennett, Arnold, on *Orlando*, 3, 107
Berkeley, George 'Bishop', 186, 189–91, 195
bibliography, 27, 116–27
   bibliographic code, 120–1, 123
Bildung, 190–5
Bildungsroman, 192–3, 195
biographer, 47, 136, 178, 199, 204, 206
   of *Orlando*, 40, 47–8, 111–12, 116, 118, 131, 136, 153, 157, 161n17, 176, 178, 180
biography, 73, 104–5, 112, 129, 136, 154, 214
   Orlando as mock-biography, 18, 27, 44–5, 104, 120, 136, 153, 199, 203, 205

biography (*cont.*)
  Virginia Woolf's theory of, 28, 44, 178–9, 205–6
  see also Woolf, Virginia, ESSAYS: 'The New Biography'
birth, 27, 63, 75–6, 116–27, 130–1, 132, 193
Blyth, Ian, 62
body, 2, 21, 22–3, 32–43, 58–9, 65–6, 74, 133–4, 152, 157–9, 166, 179, 190–1
  embodiment, 16, 49–50, 80, 95, 113
  female, 32–43, 119, 157–9, 190
  gendered, 32–43, 133
  maternal, 125–6, 131
  sexed, 32–43
  sexual, 32–43, 47
  and writing, 32–43, 58, 63, 80, 111, 145, 190
Boiardo, Matteo Matia, *Orlando Inamorato*, 107
Bowlby, Rachel, 107, 199, 202
Breton, Nicholas, 'An Invective Against Treason', 25
Briggs, Julia, 118–19
Brontë, Charlotte, and the sentence in *A Room of One's Own*, 58
Brook, Peter
  'Deadly Theatre' and 'Rough Theatre', 145
  'Holy Theatre', 149
Browne, Thomas, 32, 33, 63, 106, 148, 175–84, 185n18, 215
  Religio Medici, 148, 177
  Urn Burial, 177, 180–1, 182
Burckhardt, Jacob, 105–6

Campbell, Mary, relationship with Vita Sackville-West, 59, 82
canonicity, 1, 50, 53n11, 71–2, 106, 111, 182, 203, 210
Carlyle, Jane, 203
Carlyle, Thomas, 106, 198, 203, 218n22
Caughie, Pamela L., 32
censorship, 16, 57–8, 66, 118, 124, 188, 199; *see also* Hall, Radclyffe
Cervetti, Nancy, 36–7
Chaucer, 63, 99, 181

Cheyfitz, Eric, 183
Cixous, Hélène, on women's writing and pleasure, 58
Colburn, Krystyna, 95
Coleridge, S. T., 165
  and the androgynous mind, 65–6
colonialism, 16, 158–9, 175–6, 183, 186–97
composition, 84, 88–9, 95
  literary, 47, 60, 216
  musical, 54n27
  process for *Orlando*, 6, 7, 8, 13n5, 82, 117–19, 121, 153, 156, 178–9
  visual, 84, 95
  see also Stein, Gertrude: *Composition as Explanation*
Connor, Steven, 129–30
Conrad, Joseph, 182
  Heart of Darkness, 193, 194
Constantinople, 85, 95
Cosgrove, Denis E., on landscape, 92
Cramer, Patricia, 38
Crisp, Quentin, in Sally Potter's adaptation of *Orlando*, 21
Cuddy-Keane, Melba, 41

dailiness, 128–38
  the everyday, 162–5, 168, 172, 190, 210
  one-day narrative, 129–30, 136–7
  see also Opus Dei; temporality: daily
Darwin, Charles, 166–7, 168, 170
De Quincey, Thomas, 44–55, 215
  'Dream-Fugue', 44–52, 54n27: and music, 54n30, 55n33, 55n38
  and 'impassioned prose', 46–7
  and the sentence, 47, 49
death, 48–9, 52, 73–4, 102, 125, 134, 179–84, 190, 193, 194–5, 206
  of Jane Ellen Harrison, 93
  of Virginia Woolf's mother, 121
  warrant *see* Mary Queen of Scots
  see also remains
Detloff, Madelyn, 60
Devil, 24–5, 72, 168; *see also* printer's devil
Dickinson, Violet, 154, 161n13

discourse, 5–6, 8, 72 102n22, 151–60, 187
   ethnographic, 193: 'orientalist and colonial', 194
   of history, 66, 128–9
   homoerotic, 54n30, 58–62
   of love, 151–61, 187
   patriarchal, 60, 66, 72
   religious, 172
   see also law
Doyle, Laura, 35
DuPlessis, Rachel Blau, 87–8, 201

ecstasy, 38, 171–2
Eliot, George, and the sentence in *A Room of One's Own*, 58
Eliot, T. S., 68–79, 117, 215
   on literary tradition, 63, 111
   'The Love Song of J. Alfred Prufrock', 68–9, 73–5
   relationship with Virginia Woolf, 69–70
   The Waste Land, 5, 76, 78n18
Elizabethan era, 16, 17, 38, 62, 64, 105, 106, 109, 144, 184, 194
Elkins, Amy, 124
Englishness, 83–4, 88–9, 100, 101n9, 194, 215–16
epiphany, 100, 102–3n23, 149, 171–2; *see also* dailiness: the everyday
eroticism, 6, 14n20, 15–17, 18, 32–43, 45, 47–8, 50, 61, 107, 188, 193, 215
   autoeroticism, 15, 17, 35, 40, 58
Esty, Jed, 192, 193, 194
ethics, 32–3, 39, 77, 104, 110, 171, 175, 183
evolution, 125, 162–71

Fabian, Johannes, concept of 'allochrony', 99
faith, 24, 162–74
fame, 94–5, 104–15, 116–27
feminism
   feminist theory and criticism, 53n11, 121, 126n6, 126n8, 127n23, 154
   in *Orlando*, 15, 17, 58, 66, 90, 117–18, 127n23
   Woolf's, 16, 90, 121–2, 208n21

Fineman, Joel, 98
Fish, Stanley, 7
Forster, E. M., 70, 71
   Maurice, 70
Freud, Sigmund
   on dream language and jokes, 188
   on the structure of the mind, 110, 133
Froula, Christine, 193

Gass, William H., 7
gender, 21, 68, 71, 104, 110, 124, 133–4, 199, 214
   identity, 16–17, 32–7, 41–2; *see also* body: gendered
   politics, 16–17, 21, 25, 27, 32–7, 39, 40–2, 45, 46, 49, 50, 64, 92, 111, 118, 123, 124, 133, 134, 158–9, 188, 193, 199, 203
   pronouns, 19, 22, 214
   queering, 16–17, 61, 94–6, 123, 134, 163, 188
   and the sentence, 25–6, 33–7, 46, 72
   transgender (Orlando as), 82, 117, 118–19, 101n9: 'trans-sexual', 19; 'gender reassignment', 27
genre, 33–4, 203
   hybridity of *Orlando*, 199, 200, 203
   subversion, 205
   transfers, 69, 72
   see also autobiography; biography; novel
georgic, 62, 94, 96, 120
Gilbert, Sandra, 129
'gipsy', 27, 31n41, 95–6, 102n14, 195
   Vita Sackville-West's use of 'gipsy code', 112n14
   see also Arnold, Matthew, 'The Scholar-Gipsy'
goose, 17, 18–19, 165, 171–2
Graffius, Jan, 24
Greece, 92–103, 105; *see also* Harrison, Jane Ellen; Hellenism

haecceity, 132–3
   Gilles Deleuze and Félix Guattari's definition of, 132
Hafley, James, 128, 130, 136

Hall, Radclyffe, *The Well of Loneliness*, 16
Harrison, Jane Ellen, 83, 92–3, 94, 97, 99
  'Alpha and Omega', 93
  appearance in *A Room of One's Own*, 93
  Hellenism, 92, 93
  Reminiscences of a Student's Life, 97
Harvey, Benjamin, 121
hauntology, 71
Hegel, Georg Wilhelm Friedrich, theory of subjectivity, 108
Hellenism *see* Harrison, Jane Ellen
Helsinger, Elizabeth, on landscape, 99
Heraclitus
  Herakleitean flux, 164
  on 'immortal glory', 108–9
history, 66, 70–1, 77, 104–14, 128–9, 180–4, 214–15
  literary, 1, 63–4, 66, 70–1, 104–14
  see also discourse: of history
Hogarth Press, 25, 87, 97, 107, 117, 121–6
  edition of *Orlando*, 4, 142
Hollander, Rachel, 41
Hovey, Jaime, 188, 189, 192, 195, 196

inconclusion, 198–209
influence, 69, 105–6, 198, 202–3
Ingarden, Roman, 140, 141, 143
  concept of *satzdenken*, 140–1
intertextuality, 4–5, 44–55, 60–5, 68–79, 81, 86, 123, 192–3, 196, 200, 215
  literary allusions, 50, 61–2, 70, 85, 98, 195
Irigaray, Luce, 58–9, 60, 62
  on the patriarchal sentence, 60
  on women's writing and pleasure, 58–9

James, Henry
  The Painter's Eye, 83
  Woolf's reading of, 83
  see also Englishness; nature
joke(s), 60, 64, 187–9
  Orlando as, 5, 13n5, 117

Joyce, James, 70, 71, 129, 130, 215
  in 'Modern Fiction', 164–5
  Ulysses, 15–16, 70, 129
juxtaposition, 176, 186, 187

Kellman, Steven G., 129, 136, 137
Keynes, John Maynard, definition of the 'religious mentality', 163
kleos, 105
Knole, 15, 16, 18, 21–2, 26, 44, 45, 82, 125, 216
  inheritance, 13n14, 27–8, 45, 53n4
  tapestries *see* tapestries: arras
  see also Mary Queen of Scots; Sackville-West, Vita
Knox, John, 17, 22, 29, 30n10
  The First Blast of the Trumpet Against the Monstruous Regiment of Women, 17
Kristeva, Julia
  'poetic paragram', 78n10
  theory of intertextuality, 69

Lackey, Michael, 165, 172
landscape, 16, 76, 92–103, 132, 156, 165, 187, 193, 194, 215
law
  of inheritance, 45: primogeniture, 15, 45, 55n37; *see also* Knole
  lawsuits, 27–8, 33, 44–6
  legal reforms, 129
  legal sentence, 5, 44–5, 55n37, 58, 59, 60
Lawrence, D. H., 70, 78n8
  Lady Chatterley's Lover, 16, 70
lesbian, 16, 38, 59–66
  invisibility, 59; *see also* Rich, Adrienne
Levinson, Marjorie, on 'activist formalism', 6
life, 22, 65, 68–79, 83–6, 100, 116–18, 129, 147, 162–7, 172–3, 180, 182–3
  common, 65
  daily, 40, 89, 173
  imaginary, 94
  'life spirits', 93
  of the mind, 36

Orlando's, 22, 84, 85, 89, 96, 125, 159, 171, 216
Woolf's, 82–3, 95, 117, 120–3
-writing *see* autobiography; biography
lists, 89, 201–2, 208n18, 210–12
Lady Fry's, 202
see also Stein, Gertrude
love, 117–18, 151–62; *see also* discourse: of love
love letter, 16, 18, 151, 154, 160

MacCarthy, Desmond, on *Orlando*, 3
McIntire, Gabrielle, 133, 135, 136
Mansfield, Katherine, 122
Marchi, Dudley, 204, 205–6
Marcus, Laura, 121
marriage, 26, 27–8, 29, 52, 55n37, 59, 172, 186–97
as Victorian institution, 40
of Vita Sackville-West and Harold Nicolson, 26
see also body: maternal; Knole; law; Pepita, Josefa
Marvell, Andrew, 'The Garden', 98
Mary Queen of Scots, 17, 20–6, 163, 168
execution, 21, 23, 25
gifts to Knole, 21–3
and John Knox, 17, 22
as poet, 26
prayer book, 23–4, 25, 26, 163, 168
maternity, 29, 116–27, 136, 193
Meisel, Perry, 101n8, 164
Mepham, John, 86
Merleau-Ponty, Maurice, 34–5, 36, 37
Mildenberg, Ariane, 41
Milton, John, 61, 177
Minow-Pinkney, Makiko, 38
Montaigne, Michel de, 200–7
on dialogic reading, 201
essayistic mode, 200, 204–5
'Moor', 16, 22, 146, 147, 157–9, 172, 176, 182, 192
Moore, G. E., 189
contra Berkeley, 189
influence on the Cambridge 'Apostles' and Bloomsbury, 189
in *The Voyage Out*, 190–1, 192

morphology, 1–2, 6, 7, 12, 19, 24
Mortimer, Raymond, on *Orlando*, 3
Mount Athos, 92, 97, 100

Nagy, Gregor, 105
Nancy, Jean-Luc, on landscape, 100
nature, 63, 73–4, 77, 81, 83–5, 120, 146, 148, 193
human nature, 166
'negress', 186–97
Nicolson, Harold, 26, 48
marriage to Vita Sackville-West, 26, 187, 189
Some People reviewed by Virginia Woolf, 178, 204; *see also* Woolf, Virginia, ESSAYS: 'The New Biography'
novel, the
as genre, 1, 34, 58–9, 154
one-day novel, 136–7
Victorian, 194–5
Virginia Woolf on, 164–5
see also Woolf, Virginia, ESSAYS: 'On Re-Reading Novels'
Nussbaum, Martha, 39

obscurity, 110–12, 181–3
Opus Dei, 173
Orient, the, 95, 96, 187, 194
orientalism, 59, 187, 188–9, 191–5
orgasm, 15–17, 29, 36, 37–8, 48–9, 52
Ovid, *Metamorphoses*, 4, 13n10, 50; *see also* tapestries: motifs from Ovid's *Metamorphoses*

painting, 4, 84, 87, 194
Post-Impressionist, 88, 90; *see also* abstraction
still-life, 84, 96
parody, 2, 4, 54n26, 71, 156, 186, 215
self-parody, 84–6
Pascal, Blaise, 195–6
pastiche, 2, 186
Fredric Jameson's definition of, 71
see also intertextuality
pastoral, 61–2, 92, 94–6, 99–100
Pater, Walter, 94, 164, 166, 168, 178, 200
aestheticism, 166

Pater, Walter (*cont.*)
  Imaginary Portraits, 94
  influence on Virginia Woolf, 101n8, 164
  on Montaigne, 200, 205
  The Renaissance, 164
  see also aestheticism; Meisel, Perry
Pepita, Josefa (Josefa Durán), 27–8
  marriage, 27–8
  in *Orlando* as Rosina Pepita, 27–9, 31n41, 102n14: textual variant (Rosina Lolita), 28–9
  subject of Vita Sackville-West's *Pepita*, 27
  see also Sackville-West, Vita
Pepys, Samuel, 144, 146, 150n16
performance, 139, 143, 146, 160; see also Shakespeare, William; theatre
Pessoa, Fernando, 112–13
Phillips, Kathy J., 183
Picker, John M., 203
Plato, 205
  on ambition and fame, 110
poetics, 14, 16, 83, 104
  poetic prose, 45–7, 50–2, 77
poetry, 21, 24–7, 34, 62, 63, 65, 68–73, 77, 105–10, 152
  Orlando as poet, 56, 92, 94–5, 109–10, 171: 'The Oak Tree', 24, 26, 56, 59, 62–3, 73, 81, 82, 94, 104, 109, 111, 116, 117, 118, 120, 124, 125, 130, 131, 168
Pope Pius X, against modernism, 169–70
Potter, Sally, filmic adaptation of *Orlando*, 3, 21
printing, printer's devil, 25, 28, 29; see also Hogarth Press
Proust, Marcel, 129, 136
  À la recherche du temps perdu, 136

Queen Elizabeth I, 15, 16, 17, 19–20, 21, 37, 148, 171, 184
  Queen Elizabeth II, 20
queens, 15–31
  queer, 18–21
  see also Mary Queen of Scots; Queen Elizabeth I

race, 186–97; see also colonialism; 'Moor'; 'negress'
Raitt, Suzanne, 59, 121
reading, 3, 5–8, 29, 175–85, 57, 60, 65, 86–7, 89, 119, 135–6, 139–40, 143, 186–7, 201
  'the reader's part', 175–7, 183
  re-reading, 56–7, 60
  scenes of, 71, 148, 176–7, 190, 191, 198
  see also Woolf, Virginia, ESSAYS: 'How Should One Read a Book?'; 'On Re-reading Novels'; 'Reading'
religion
  Catholicism, 162, 168–9; see also Mary Queen of Scots; Pope Pius X; Roche, Paul
  Catholic and Protestant struggles, 20; see also Mary Queen of Scots; Queen Elizabeth I
  Christianity, 163, 168–9, 172: Christian monotheism, 24; Manichean theology, 24
  gods and goddesses, 18, 23, 24, 28, 88, 93, 163, 165, 167, 169, 170, 172, 173
  messianism, 20–1
  pagan, 22, 30n26, 172, 184
  religiosity, 163–6, 172
  worship, 97: Marian, 18, 20; Woolfian, 163–4, 167, 170
remains, 175, 176, 178, 180–2
ruins, 175, 180–4
Renaissance, 73, 105–6, 144, 177, 183, 184n2
repetition, 47, 50, 51, 60, 82, 88, 104, 130, 142, 155, 157, 183, 199–202
rhythm, 17, 56–67, 34–6, 37, 39, 41–2, 48–50, 68, 72, 82, 116, 120
Rich, Adrienne, 59
Richardson, Dorothy, *Pilgrimage*, 136
Richter, Harvena, 148
Roche, Paul, 162, 172
  Vessel of Dishonour, 162, 164, 172
Rochester, Earl of, 16
Roessel, David, 95
Romanticism, 63
Rossetti, Christina, 202

Sackville, Thomas (Lord Buckhurst), 15, 21, 22, 25, 53n4
  delivery of death sentence to Mary Queen of Scots, 22, 25
  and Knole, 15, 21, 53n4
Sackville-West, Vita, 6, 15, 44–5, 47, 50, 59, 60, 61, 62, 65, 70, 94, 95, 102n14, 107, 135, 151–6, 196, 211, 212, 214, 215
  ancestry, 22, 27–8; *see also* Knole
  Another World than This, 68
  Knole and the Sackvilles, 4, 15, 21
  The Land, 56, 62, 81, 82, 84, 95, 96, 112, 120, 124: Hawthornden Prize, 62, 82, 112
  marriage to Harold Nicolson, 23; *see also* Nicolson, Harold
  and *Orlando*, 15, 44–5, 50, 59, 65, 78n14, 94, 95, 107, 119, 125, 135, 151–6, 160, 196, 211, 212, 214
  Pepita, 27; *see also* Pepita, Josefa
  relationship with Virginia Woolf, 13, 14n20, 18, 44, 47, 59, 65, 75, 78n14, 80–1, 82, 84, 91n8, 94, 100, 107, 125, 135, 151–6, 211, 212, 214
Sapphism, 15–16, 59, 95
satire, 18–19, 24, 84, 119, 199, 200, 205
scene(s), 19, 21–3, 47–9, 50–2, 61–6, 95–8, 100, 124, 133–4, 151–61, 182, 193–5, 202
  from *Othello*, 139, 145–7, 158
  of parturition, 117–20, 123, 125, 126n3
  scene-making, 84, 158
  wedding scene, 47, 50–2
  see also reading: scenes of
Schlack, Beverly Ann, 195
sex, 15–16, 44, 48, 61–2, 65, 118, 157, 188, 193, 214; *see also* body: gendered; body: sexed
sexuality, 16–17, 18, 19, 22, 32–43, 53, 57
Shakespeare, William, 22, 63, 65, 71, 106, 110, 145, 146, 149, 155, 171, 177
  Othello, 139, 145–7, 153, 158, 171n24

Showalter, Elaine, 120
Silver, Brenda, 147
Sitwell, Edith, 87
Smyth, Ethel, on Ralph H. Brewster, *The 6,000 Beards of Mount Athos*, 97
space, 35, 37, 39, 41, 46, 92, 95–9, 128, 155, 158, 159, 200, 203, 207, 215
  textual, 63, 80, 85–90, 206
  vast, 22, 34, 51, 200, 206–7
  see also temporality: chronotope
Spenser, Edmund, 61
  The Faerie Queene, 20, 61
spirituality, 109, 162–72, 195
Spiropoulou, Angeliki, 128–9, 137
Stanford Friedman, Susan, 117
Stein, Gertrude, 16, 81, 87–9, 90, 200–2, 215
  Composition as Explanation, 81, 87, 88, 200, 201
  connections with Virginia Woolf, 16, 87, 201–2
  How to Write, 89
  Lectures in America, 89
  The Making of Americans, 87
  'My wife has a cow', 16, 17, 18
  and the sentence, 87–90, 200–2
  see also abstraction; DuPlessis, Rachel Blau; lists; repetition
Stephen, Leslie, 190
Sterne, Laurence, 81–3, 86, 87, 200, 206
  A Sentimental Journey, 83
  Tristram Shandy, 82
Stewart, Jim, 29
Strachey, Lytton, definition of religion, 163
subjectivity, 29, 33–9, 40, 75, 104, 108, 112, 129, 155, 191, 195
  'modern subjecthood', 75
  see also Hegel, Georg Wilhelm Friedrich, theory of subjectivity
Swinton, Tilda, 3

tapestries, 4, 21–3, 54n31, 60, 61, 214
  arras, 4, 22, 61, 118
  motifs from Ovid's *Metamorphoses*, 4, 22, 50, 54n31, 61

temporality, 32, 45, 50, 85, 100, 113, 131, 135, 153
  chronotope, 73
  daily temporality, 130, 131, 136–7
  see also time
textual variants, 27–9, 142
theatre, 139–50
  Elizabethan, 144
  Jacobean, 139, 144, 146
  Restoration, 144
  see also Brook, Peter; Shakespeare, William: *Othello*
theology, 24, 97, 162–74
  and modernism, 167–71
time, 64–5, 71, 81–2, 84–90, 92, 99–101, 104, 105, 117, 119–20, 124, 129–33, 135–6, 148, 149, 166, 169, 181, 182, 212, 215
  fluid time, 148
  kinetic time, 148
  see also Woolf, Virginia, ESSAYS: 'Time Passes'
Toner, Anne, 7
tradition, 49, 64, 92, 95, 105, 106, 110–13, 129, 136, 163, 170
  critical, 53n10, 53n11
  literary, 33, 62, 63–5, 87, 106; see also history: literary
transactions
  dialogic, 65, 77, 110, 201
  intertextual, 70–1
transformation, 88, 100–1, 107, 118–20, 124, 125
  of Orlando, 40, 92, 96–7, 166, 169–70
translation, 28, 40, 70, 96, 176–7, 179, 184, 190
transposition, 63, 69, 71, 75, 106, 107, 186, 214
  and writing, 1, 5, 19, 46, 49, 68–9, 75
transgression, 23, 38, 187
transition(s), 38, 46, 49, 81, 118, 125, 133, 193, 203
transvestism, 95
Trefusis, Violet, relationship with Vita Sackville-West, 96, 102n14

vision, 77, 84, 95, 101, 121–2, 168, 171–2, 184, 190–1, 194
  allegorical vision, 99; see also Harrison, Jane Ellen
  moment of vision, 171
  'visionary approach', 83
  visions, 17, 44, 48, 52, 75, 92, 95, 98–9, 100–1, 107, 121, 132, 134–5, 144, 173, 182, 184, 195

Walpole, Horace, 22
Waugh, Patricia, 33, 35
Weninger, Robert, 129
West, Rebecca, on *Orlando*, 3
Westling, Louise, 35
Westman, Karin E., 154
Wilde, Oscar, 19
wildness, 4, 23n11, 17–19, 32, 51, 119, 159, 165, 199–200, 206–7; see also Wilde, Oscar
windows, 23, 73, 128, 130–1, 132, 171, 200
  at Knole, 19, 21, 23
Wollaeger, Mark, 193
women, 97, 99, 117–18, 192–6, 199, 202–3
  and art, 122, 203
  disinheritance of, 52; see also Knole
  education of, 190–2
  labour of, 86, 90, 116–17
  sovereignty of, 27–8
  and tradition, 110–12
  and writing, 33, 58, 60, 64, 66, 72, 93
Woolf, Leonard, 122, 193–4, 196, 201
  Empire and Commerce in Africa, 196
  The Village in the Jungle, 193
Woolf, Virginia
  and the Hogarth Press, 117, 121–6
  on the literary sentence, 1–8, 15, 32, 33–4, 36–7, 46, 58, 72
  as Virginia Stephen, 80, 145
Woolf, Virginia, *writings*
  BIOGRAPHY
  Roger Fry: A Biography, 202
  DIARIES
  on *Orlando*, 15, 18–19, 32, 84, 107, 108, 119–20, 154, 155, 199
  on Vita Sackville-West, 22–3, 44

ESSAYS
'Anon', 66, 111
'Craftsmanship', 5, 83–4, 186
'A Dialogue upon Mount Pentelicus', 64
'De Quincey's Autobiography', 47, 50; *see also* De Quincey, Thomas
'The Elizabethan Lumber Room', 184
'The English Mail Coach', 53n7; *see also* De Quincey, Thomas: 'Dream-Fugue'
'Friendships Gallery', 154; *see also* Dickinson, Violet
'Hours in a Library', 177, 179
'How it Strikes a Contemporary', 113, 182
'How Should One Read a Book?', 7–8, 179, 201, 206
'"I am Christina Rossetti"', 202
'"Impassioned Prose"' 53n7; *see also* De Quincey, Thomas
'The Lives of the Obscure', 115n17, 182
'Modern Fiction', 164–5, 182
'Montaigne', 200, 205–7; *see also* Montaigne, Michel de
'The New Biography', 44, 105, 178–9, 204, 206
'On Not Knowing Greek', 70, 182
'On Re-reading Novels', 7
'The Pastons and Chaucer', 181; *see also* Chaucer
'Phases of Fiction', 8, 82–3, 86

'Poetry, Fiction and the Future', 204
'Professions for Women', 122, 160n12
'Reading', 63–4, 177, 179
A Room of One's Own, 1–2, 4, 7, 16, 26, 30n10, 32, 33–4, 36, 46, 50, 58, 63–4, 66, 93, 109, 111, 188, 196, 199, 202, 203–4
'The Sun and the Fish', 5
Three Guineas, 111, 203
'Time Passes', 81, 84–6, 190
'Waxworks at the Abbey', 20
'Women and Fiction', 72
LETTERS
to Gerald Brenan, 117
about *Orlando*, 28, 59
to Vita Sackville-West, 59, 100
NOVELS
Between the Acts, 5, 111
Jacob's Room, 32, 80, 164, 190
Mrs Dalloway, 3, 32, 46, 54n30, 129–30, 132, 160, 162–4
To the Lighthouse, 3, 8, 28, 32, 35, 39, 66n2, 76, 81–6, 121–2, 189–90
The Voyage Out, 28, 186–7, 190–6
The Waves, 3, 46, 76, 87, 107, 134, 159, 164, 190, 191
The Years, 76, 190
SHORT FICTION
'Kew Gardens', 122–5
'The Mark on the Wall', 118
Monday or Tuesday, 80
Wordsworth, William, 56, 57, 60–2, 65